LAW AND THE CONTRADICTIONS OF THE DISABILITY RIGHTS MOVEMENT

LAW AND THE
CONTRADICTIONS
OF THE DISABILITY
RIGHTS MOVEMENT

Samuel R. Bagenstos

Yale University Press
New Haven & London

Published with assistance from the foundation established in memory of
Philip Hamilton McMillan of the Class of 1894, Yale College.

Set in Electra type by Tseng Information Systems, Inc.
Printed in the United States of America.

Library of Congress Cataloging-in-Publication Data
Bagenstos, Samuel R.
Law and the contradictions of the disability rights movement / Samuel R. Bagenstos.
p. cm.
Includes bibliographical references and index.
ISBN 978-0-300-12449-1 (cloth : alk. paper) 1. People with disabilities—
Legal status, laws, etc.—United States. 2. Discrimination against people with
disabilities—Law and legislation—United States. 3. People with disabilities—
Civil rights—United States. I. Title.
KF480.B345 2009
342.7308′7—dc22
2008046981

A catalogue record for this book is available from the British Library.

This paper meets the requirements of ANSI/NISO Z39.48–1992 (Permanence of Paper).
It contains 30 percent postconsumer waste (PCW) and is certified
by the Forest Stewardship Council (FSC).

10 9 8 7 6 5 4 3 2 1

For Harry and Leila

CONTENTS

Preface and Acknowledgments

When I went to law school in 1990, I was not particularly interested in disability rights. President George H. W. Bush had signed the Americans with Disabilities Act (ADA) into law just weeks before I began law school, and, as a civil-rights-lawyer-in-training, I was certainly aware and generically supportive of the new law. But it was not a major issue for me. I wanted to work on race discrimination and voting rights, and at the same time that President Bush was strongly supporting the ADA, he was threatening to veto what was then called the Civil Rights Act of 1990—a bill that would have overturned a number of restrictive race and sex discrimination decisions of the Supreme Court. In that context, I had some skepticism about whether the ADA could really be a strong civil rights law, if President Bush supported it so strongly.

When I became a practicing lawyer, I went to work at the Civil Rights Division of the United States Department of Justice. As I had hoped in law school, I focused most of my work on voting rights cases. But I eventually began to take more and more disability rights cases. At the beginning, the motivation was the fairly selfish one of getting high-level legal experience: the ADA was still new, so ADA cases gave me an opportunity to argue and make important law in the courts of appeals. As I got into the cases, though, I found something that was very familiar to me from race discrimination cases—the same prejudice and stereotypes—overlaid with a paternalism that made it particularly hard for the defendants to comprehend that they were doing anything wrong. I came to realize something I should have known all along—that disability rights protections were as important as any other civil rights protections.

I remained interested in why so many conservatives could support a broad disability rights statute like the ADA at the same time they were supporting retrenchment on civil rights in the race discrimination area. An uncharitable reading would assert that racism is the explanation, but I saw something else at work: Much of the rhetoric of the American disability rights movement was framed in the quite conservative terms of self-reliance and independence, and the ADA was adopted in a political era in which calls for welfare reform gathered more force with every year. The disability rights movement had radical goals, but it used a rhetoric that seemed to have authentic appeal to conservatives. This odd political juxtaposition made me especially interested in exploring disability rights issues once I became an academic.

While my first article on disability rights was still in the editorial process, my twins were born. Harry and Leila showed from the first that they are wonderful children. Harry was born with a physical disability, and, in dealing with doctors, insurance companies, and schools—not to mention other parents on the playground—I began to see disability rights issues from yet a new perspective. The stigma, stereotypes, and failure to take account of disability came home to me in an especially pointed way. I am sure that this personal experience is a key reason why, despite wide-ranging interests, I continue to devote so much of my writing to disability rights.

I am keenly aware of the complicated relationship between the disability rights movement and the nondisabled parents of children with disabilities. The relationship may be especially complicated in my case: Although I consider myself a strong supporter of the disability rights movement, and I devote much of my "free time" to representing individuals with disabilities and disability rights organizations in litigation, much of my scholarly work focuses on the tensions and conflicts within the disability rights movement. I have always despised party lines, and I find that the best scholarship challenges rather than parrots them. I hope that, at its best, my work challenges significant elements of the party lines of both movement advocates and their opponents; it comes from a position of deep support for disability rights.

My intention is to write for many audiences. For legal and social movement scholars, I hope to show how the development of disability rights law—an important area of legal doctrine—has stemmed from and interacted with the development of the large and contentious disability rights movement. I hope that my work will disabuse scholars of the notion that the disability rights movement has a single set of goals or tactics, and that it will show them how legal controversies have highlighted significant intramural tensions among disability rights advocates. For disability rights advocates themselves, I hope that pointing up some of the tensions within disability rights thinking will highlight key choices that advocates will have to make as they seek to advance their agenda. I hope my work will help to show why some arguments that once worked well for the movement have lost force, and to point the way to new arguments that will achieve central disability rights goals. And for policymakers and courts, I hope to show how our disability rights laws are falling short and how to improve them.

This book represents my current thinking on some key questions relating to the interaction between the disability rights movement and the law. I have been developing many of the ideas in the book for some time, in articles I have published over the past several years. Much of the book draws from those articles, though I have rewritten them (and in some instances changed my mind on key questions) considerably. In particular, chapters 2 and 3 draw on "Subordination, Stigma, and 'Disability,'" 86 *Virginia Law Review* 397 (2000). Chapters 2 and especially 5 draw on "The Americans with Disabilities Act as Risk Regulation," 101 *Columbia Law Review* 1479 (2001). Chapters 3 and 8 draw on "Comparative Disability Employment Law from an American Perspective," 24 *Comparative Labor Law and Policy Journal* 649 (2003). Chapter 4 draws on "'Rational Discrimination,' Accommodation, and the Politics of (Disability) Civil Rights," 89 *Virginia Law Review* 825 (2003). Chapters 2 and 3 draw on "The Americans with Disabilities Act as Welfare Reform," 44 *William & Mary Law Review* 921 (2003). Chapter 5 draws on "The Supreme Court, the Americans with Disabilities Act, and Rational Discrimination," 55 *Alabama Law Review* 923 (2004). Chapters 7 and 8 draw on "Has the Americans with Disabilities Act Reduced Employment for People with Disabilities?" 25 *Berkeley Journal of Employment and Labor Law* 527 (2004). Chapter 3 draws on "Justice Ginsburg and the Judicial Role in Expanding 'We the People': The Disability Rights Cases," 104 *Columbia Law Review* 49 (2004). Chapters 2, 4, 7, and 8 draw on "The Future of Disability Law," 114 *Yale Law Journal* 1 (2004). Chapters 2 and 6 draw on "Disability, Life, Death, and Choice," 29 *Harvard Journal of Law and Gender* 425 (2006). Chapters 7 and 8 draw on "The Perversity of Limited Civil Rights Remedies: The Case of 'Abusive' ADA Litigation," 54 *UCLA Law Review* 1 (2006). I thank the law reviews for permission to reprint those articles, in revised form, here. I also thank Amanda Norris for outstanding research assistance, and participants in faculty workshops at the Emory Law School, the Ohio State Law School, and the University of Michigan Law School and in panel sessions at annual meetings of the Society for Disability Studies and the Law and Society Association.

I would also like to thank a number of people who assisted me in thinking about and writing this book. The first set of thanks goes to a number of people who schooled me in the disability rights movement and disability rights law, including Ira Burnim, Ruth Colker, Chai Feldblum, Joan Magagna, Jennifer Mathis, Arlene Mayerson, Paul Miller, Becky Ogle, Michael Stein, John Wodatch, and—most of all—Liz Savage. I met Liz the day I interviewed with Deval Patrick for a job in the Civil Rights Division. I was lucky enough to get the job, and I had the pleasure to work with Liz for three years. Every day I worked with her I learned a ton, and I will always value her friendship and counsel.

I would also like to thank the deans who have been so supportive of my work at Harvard and at Washington University. Bob Clark was my first dean, and he was always unflinching in his support; my early years in the academy were tremendously generative for me, and Bob was a major reason. Joel Seligman's enthusiasm rubbed off on everyone who worked with him at Washington University, and he inspired me to be ever more ambitious. And Kent Syverud has been an incredible dean; his commitment to vigorous intellectual debate—and the environment that fosters it—is amazing. I could not have done this without my faculty assistants at Harvard and at Washington University, either. Thanks to Sandy Mays, Nancy Cummings, and Becky Musso for all their help with this project and its progenitors. And incredible thanks to Becky and to Shelly Henderson for their amazing efforts to pull the manuscript together at the end of the process.

My most important thanks, though, go to my family. My mother's hunger for lifelong learning and passion for justice have carried me forward since childhood. My wife, Margo Schlanger, has been a colleague and collaborator since we met. She read every word of this book in draft, and I know I could not have written it (or achieved much of anything in my academic career) without her advice, criticism, and commentary. My children are the most wonderful and fascinating people. I know I do not deserve the pride they have in me. Over the past year or so, Leila would periodically ask, with real interest, "Dad, how's the book going?" Her concern for and interest in others are among the many reasons I love her. Harry, too, was always happy to talk about my book, even though it had little to do with his major loves (baseball and Bruce Springsteen). His enthusiasm and curiosity are among the many reasons I love him. During the long slog of working on this book, I have always looked forward to picking Harry and Leila up from school and spending our evenings together. The book is dedicated to them.

INTRODUCTION

When President George Herbert Walker Bush signed the Americans with Disabilities Act (ADA) into law in 1990, disability rights advocates thought they had won a major victory. For the first time, American law firmly declared that people with disabilities are, and of right ought to be, equal citizens. Comprehensive in its sweep, the ADA broadly prohibits disability-based discrimination by employers, state and local governments, and private good and service providers. Importantly, the statute takes the concept of forbidden discrimination beyond intentional and overt exclusion; it also treats as discrimination the failure to provide "reasonable accommodations" to people with disabilities. In a single legislative act, Congress recognized that society's institutions and structures have been designed without people with disabilities in mind, and that justice requires society to make changes today to include them fully in the life of the community. Senator Tom Harkin's label for the statute—the Emancipation Proclamation for people with disabilities—seemed entirely apt.[1]

Almost twenty years later, matters have not worked out as disability rights advocates had hoped. In a series of decisions, the Supreme Court has read the statute's provisions very narrowly. In all federal courts, ADA plaintiffs lose their cases at astounding rates—the only litigants less successful than ADA employment plaintiffs are prisoner plaintiffs, who are rarely even represented by counsel. The statutory provisions that require businesses to be accessible are wildly underenforced. And the employment rate for people with disabilities has remained stagnant at best.[2]

As the bleak picture of the post-ADA world has become clearer, a conventional wisdom has emerged among many disability rights supporters. The ADA was a statute with great promise, they argue, but it has been betrayed—by judges who do not understand the principles of the disability rights movement, and by a society that has engaged in a backlash against that movement. In that conventional wisdom, there is nothing wrong with the ADA—or at least nothing wrong that a more enlightened judiciary and populace cannot cure.[3] The conventional wisdom has led many disability rights activists to focus their energies on lobbying for measures like the recent ADA Amendments Act, which explicitly urges the courts to return to the supposed original intent of the ADA.

There is truth in the backlash story, but the argument is vastly overstated. Although measures like the ADA Amendments Act are worthy, they are no magic solution. The general public has been resistant to the ADA, and judges have read the statute more narrowly than they might have. But it is tendentious to call those results a betrayal of the principles of the disability rights movement. Rather, to a large extent they reflect contradictions and tensions within the ideas of the disability rights movement itself. In the years before the enactment of the ADA, many disability rights advocates articulated ideas that are consistent with many (though not all) of the restrictive readings the Supreme Court later put on the statute. Rather than betraying "the" principles of the disability rights movement in these cases, the Court has simply chosen one of a set of competing principles articulated by movement participants. One purpose of this book is to draw out the complexities and pluralism of the disability rights movement, and to show how a richer picture of the movement requires a modification of the standard backlash narrative.

The backlash story is overstated in another respect as well. Although the ADA has had little if any positive effect on the employment rates of people with disabilities, that result simply cannot be attributed to the Court's decisions that have read the statute narrowly. As I show in chapter 3, the restrictive decisions essentially confined the statute's coverage to those people with disabilities who need reasonable accommodations to enter or stay in the workforce—precisely the group one would want to target if one were seeking to use the ADA as a tool to improve employment rates for people with disabilities. The statute's failure to improve those employment rates, I contend, stems from something more fundamental—the inherent limitations of antidiscrimination laws in eliminating deep-rooted structural barriers to work. Even the ADA's requirement of reasonable accommodation, which seems so revolutionary, is far more like traditional antidiscrimination requirements than is commonly recognized. In this book, I hope to highlight the continuities between the ADA and earlier antidiscrimination statutes, and to show why the statute, even if broadly construed, cannot be expected to achieve integration and empowerment for people with disabilities on its own.

The backlash narrative has also had a harmful effect on the focus of disability rights supporters, particularly those in the academy. Instead of grappling with the difficult questions of how best to achieve integration and empowerment for people with disabilities in a world where antidiscrimination statutes have only limited effect, too many academics have been satisfied simply to bemoan the limiting interpretations the Supreme Court has placed on the ADA and seek a restoration of its original meaning. As I make clear in the chapters that follow, I disagree with a number of the Court's key ADA decisions as well. (In one key case discussed in chapter 5, *Chevron v. Echazabal*,[4] I was the lawyer who argued and lost in the Supreme Court.) But a too-ready assertion of backlash or betrayal distracts attention from the important work that the disability rights movement itself still needs to accomplish: the work of mediating, if not resolving, the tensions among the goals articulated within the movement's own ranks, and the work of coming up with policy proposals to go beyond the ADA in achieving those goals. In this book, I seek to contribute to that crucial discussion.

Three major themes run throughout the book: the pluralism of the disability rights movement; the contestable nature of what is "disability" and how society should respond to it; and the surprising narrowness of the accommodation requirement. In the remainder of this introduction, I elaborate a bit on each of these themes.

THE PLURALISM OF THE DISABILITY RIGHTS MOVEMENT

It is common to speak of "the" disability rights movement. But the social movement for disability equality that formed in the United States in the 1970s, and that agitated for passage of the ADA, was incredibly pluralistic. The disability rights movement is a fluid entity that includes people with a range of different disabilities (and even people with no disability at all), different life experiences, different material needs, and different ideological perspectives. The movement includes the wheelchair users who mobilized in Berkeley, California, in the 1970s to seek accessibility and freedom from the paternalistic restrictions imposed by rehabilitation professionals. It includes the "independent blind" who, since at least the 1940s, have sought what one of their greatest leaders (and scholars) termed "the right to live in the world." It includes the culturally Deaf, who use the capital *D* to indicate their view that they are a linguistic minority, and who embrace a somewhat separatist ideology. It includes self-described "psychiatric survivors," who seek deinstitutionalization and an end to the control medical doctors have over their lives. It includes people with intellectual disabilities, who have formed organizations called People First and engaged in self-advocacy against institutionalization and paternalistic treatment. It includes people with diseases such as epilepsy, diabetes, and more recently HIV, who seek appropriate medical treatment and an end to stereotypical assumptions that they pose a threat to themselves and others. It includes people with such "hidden disabilities" as chronic fatigue syndrome and multiple chemical sensitivity, who want others to acknowledge the reality of their conditions and accommodate them. And it includes parents of people in each of these groups, and some professionals who interact with them—though the strongly antipaternalistic sentiments of many movement adherents make the participation of parents and professionals especially fraught.

With such diversity among its adherents, the disability rights movement has inevitably embraced an array of different, and potentially conflicting, goals. Probably the most widely endorsed goal among movement participants has been a negative one: opposition to the paternalism of parents, professionals, and bureaucrats telling people with disabilities what they can and cannot do. But even this goal has been instantiated in a variety of ways. Some activists come close to seeking an end to the disability welfare state that is the locus of much paternalism, while others seek expanded disability welfare benefits under a system that gives people with disabilities more choice and control. Some activists favor a ban on physician-assisted suicide, because they fear that medical professionals and family members will paternalistically pressure people with disabilities to take their own lives; others believe that such a ban is itself paternalistic, because it denies all people with disabilities a choice, through fear that some will misuse it. The presence of supportive parents and professionals, who have at times played an important role in helping to obtain victories for disability equality, has also highlighted the incompleteness of the antipaternalist position.

Integration, too, is a goal that is widely endorsed within the disability rights movement. But many in the organized blind and Deaf communities reject integration as a goal. And even movement adherents who endorse it disagree about what integration should mean in particular settings.

In chapter 2, I discuss a number of the goals articulated by participants in the disability rights movement and the tensions among them. Those tensions go a long way toward explaining the unusual politics of disability rights issues. The ADA's prime sponsors in Congress were liberal Democrats (plus one liberal Republican who has since left the party). But the bill also received strong support from the first President Bush and his conservative attorney general, Dick Thornburgh. The ADA passed overwhelmingly in Congress (377–28 in the House, 91–6 in the Senate)—a surprisingly easy route to passage for a law that seems to intrude radically on traditional business prerogatives. But where liberals saw the expansive next step in the civil rights revolution, conservatives saw something different: a tool to get people with disabilities off the public dole (as I discuss in chapter 3), and perhaps a weapon to be wielded in the ongoing proxy wars relating to abortion (as I discuss in chapter 6).

Both liberal and conservative supporters of the ADA tapped into authentic aspects of disability rights thinking. Those aspects converged in support for the statute as it proceeded through Congress. But as courts have been forced to give concrete meaning to the ADA's abstractions, the disability rights goals supported by liberals and conservatives have diverged. Although some of the Supreme Court's restrictive interpretations of the ADA are inconsistent with virtually any understanding of the goals and principles of the disability rights movement (see especially chapter 5), others are better understood as reflecting a (perhaps controversial) choice among a set of principles, each of which has a solid disability rights pedigree.

For example, most commentators who support disability rights have been harshly critical of the Supreme Court decisions that have narrowly read the ADA's definition of "disability." Those decisions excluded a large number of people from the statute's protections, though the recent ADA Amendments Act overturns them to some extent. As I show in chapter 3, however, the Court's decisions are consistent with one goal that many disability rights advocates have expressed through the years: the goal of moving people with disabilities off the benefits rolls and into the workforce. To a far greater degree than is commonly acknowledged, the decisions also are consistent with the view expressed by many activists that disability is a minority group status. That is not to say that the Supreme Court's decisions are correct as a legal or normative matter, but appreciation of the tension in disability rights thinking does complicate the claim that the Court has engaged in a backlash against the disability rights movement.

Similarly, as I discuss in chapter 4, courts have narrowly read the ADA's requirement of "reasonable accommodation" for individuals with disabilities. In so doing, they have drained the statute of much potential for addressing the deep-rooted structural barriers that keep people with disabilities out of the workforce. But the restrictions courts have placed on the accommodation requirement can be readily understood as reflecting the position of many disability rights activists that antidiscrimination law, and not charity or social welfare, is the proper response to disability. As I indicate in chapter 4, many activists hold that charity and welfare impede equality by infantilizing people with disabilities and sending the message that they are proper objects of pity. By limiting the accommodation

requirement as they have, courts have reduced the ADA's transformative potential, but they have at the same time reduced the risk that the statute will require
actions that are too readily understood as charity or welfare instead of antidiscrimination.

There is an inherent tension here: the disability rights activists who oppose
charity and welfare make a powerful case that fully equal citizenship requires
"independence" from those sorts of interventions. But many of the same activists
make an equally powerful case that fully equal citizenship requires opportunities to work and live in integrated settings. If work and community integration
require interventions that many people regard as charity or welfare, disability
rights activists are left on the horns of a dilemma. While many disability rights
supporters have attributed the ADA's limited success to a backlash against the
statute and the disability rights movement, I hope to show that it instead stems
in large part from the inevitably difficult efforts to negotiate that dilemma.

THE CONTESTABLE NATURE OF "DISABILITY"

To most disability rights advocates, "disability" is not an inherent trait of the
"disabled" person. Rather, it is a condition that results from the interaction between some physical or mental characteristic labeled an "impairment" and the
contingent societal decisions that have made physical and social structures inaccessible to people with that condition. The proper remedy for disability-based
disadvantage, in this view, is civil rights legislation to eliminate the attitudes and
practices that exclude people with actual, past, or perceived impairments from
opportunities to participate in public and private life.

Beginning in force in the 1970s, the disability rights movement mobilized
against this country's then-prevalent policy response to disability, which focused
on medical treatment, physical rehabilitation, charity, and public assistance. According to most activists, the dominant approach treated disability as an inherent
personal characteristic that ideally should be fixed, rather than as a characteristic
that draws its meaning from social context. That view individualized disability
by treating it as a personal tragedy. It encouraged dependence on doctors, rehabilitation professionals, and charity. And it stigmatized people with disabilities
by defining them as something less than normal. Perhaps most significant, the
view of disability as a personal tragedy obscured the social practices that exclude
"the disabled" from the opportunity to participate fully in society.

For these reasons, disability rights activists have argued that disability should
not be considered to be the unmediated product of limitations imposed by a

physical or mental impairment. Such a view, they contend, erroneously regards existing social arrangements as a neutral baseline. Instead, disability rights activists argue that we should understand disability as the interaction between societal barriers (both physical and otherwise) and a medical impairment.

Consider, for example, a person with paralysis that prevents her from walking. If workplace entrances are accessible only by stairs, or they are too narrow to accommodate a wheelchair, then she cannot work. If the bus route that runs by her apartment does not employ buses equipped with wheelchair lifts, then she may not be able to shop, worship communally, or engage in recreational activities. And if the sidewalk around her building does not have curb cuts, then she may not even be able to leave her block. Such a person's paralysis is very real. But in each of these examples, disability rights activists have urged, it is not her physical impairment that has disabled her: what has disabled her is the set of social choices that has created a built environment that confines wheelchair users to their homes. As I discuss in chapter 3, the same point can be made about a whole array of "disabling" impairments.

Once one thinks of disability as arising primarily from the human environment, rather than from anything inherent in an individual's physical or mental condition, one's thoughts about proper responses tend to turn toward social change instead of individual cure. Rather than providing charity or public assistance—an approach that both stigmatizes its recipients and leaves the disabling aspects of the environment in place—most disability rights activists insist that society as a whole has a responsibility to eliminate the social and physical structures that create "disability" by denying opportunities to people with some impairments. The activists thus seek to remake society to eliminate "disability" as a disadvantaged group status. They seek this result not through the medical means of eliminating impairments, or through the eugenic means of eliminating people with impairments, but through the means of civil rights law—by changing the social structures and practices that make particular conditions disabling.

But the widespread agreement among disability rights advocates on this broad orientation toward disability obscures some very significant divisions. If disability is a social creation and not an inherent fact about an individual, does it ever make sense to treat people with disabilities as a distinct class uniquely entitled to certain legal rights? One school of thought holds that the answer is no: all of us have greater abilities in some areas than others, and all of these abilities are distributed on a spectrum. There is no sharp line between having a disability and not having one. If the law defines a category of "disability," in this view, it merely highlights the salience of that category and entrenches the erroneous social view that there is a fundamental difference between people who have disabilities and people who do not. Rather, this view holds, the law should treat disability as a universal trait, one we all possess in one way or another.

Much of the criticism of the Supreme Court's definition-of-disability decisions stems from that universal-disability view. The Court has, to be sure, interpreted the ADA's "disability" definition as embracing only a discrete class of individuals. It has emphatically rejected interpretations of that definition that would sweep in a large number of people.[5] (One key case, *Sutton v. United Air Lines*, involved the question whether wearing eyeglasses is a disability; in a perhaps surprisingly controversial decision, the Court said no.) But critics overlook the degree to which the Court's categorical approach to defining disability has roots in the thinking of disability rights activists. Many activists reject the notion that disability is a universal condition. Even if disability is a social rather than a medical phenomenon, these activists argue, it makes little sense to deny that society has created a category of "people with disabilities." People in that category face systematic exclusion through prejudice, stereotypes, and physical structures and social institutions that have been designed without them in mind. They thus have an acute need for the antidiscrimination protections and accommodation mandates that the ADA imposes. People who have impairments that do not trigger such systematic disadvantage—like eyeglass wearers—have no such need. Moreover, lumping people with widely stigmatized impairments together with people whose impairments are considered to be relatively "minor" may trivialize and distract attention from the exclusion directed at the stigmatized group. As I show in chapter 3, consideration of the disability rights pedigree of the categorical minority-group approach puts some of the Supreme Court's much-criticized decisions in a better light (though I, too, have quarrels with those decisions).

THE NARROWNESS OF THE
ACCOMMODATION REQUIREMENT

The most significant legal innovation of the disability rights movement has been the expansion of the concept of discrimination. Disability rights advocates have urged that discrimination consists not merely in treating similarly situated people differently but also in failing to accommodate differences between people. It is not equal treatment, they have urged, to say that a job is open to everyone who can make it up the stairs to the employment office; equality requires providing some way for people who cannot climb stairs to get there as well. To a large extent, those advocates have been successful in incorporating that expanded understanding of discrimination into statutory law, most notably in the "reasonable accommodation" requirement of the ADA.

Both supporters and opponents of the ADA's accommodation requirement have urged that it is a potentially far-reaching tool for social transformation — particularly in the employment context. Supporters have highlighted the requirement's challenge to managerial prerogatives: the accommodation requirement demands that employers alter the way jobs and work tasks are structured so that they take account of people with disabilities. Some have gone so far as to argue that the ADA's accommodation requirement offers a model for rethinking and expanding civil rights protections in the "traditional" race and gender contexts. Opponents agree that the accommodation requirement represents an innovation in civil rights law, but they believe it to be an extremely problematic one. In particular, they argue that the requirement imposes costly mandates on employers: unlike race and gender antidiscrimination laws, which demand that employers desist from conduct that is irrational to begin with, the ADA is said to require employers to desist from entirely rational conduct.[6]

But both supporters and opponents of the ADA's accommodation mandate have overstated the differences between it and the requirements of earlier civil rights laws. For one thing, accommodation is often far more rational than people commonly think. Prejudice, stereotypes, and bounded rationality lead employers to ignore the many accommodations they provide to nondisabled employees while exaggerating the cost of accommodations demanded by individuals with disabilities.

For another thing, rational discrimination is not a new problem in civil rights law. Since the earliest days of employment discrimination jurisprudence, it has been clear that even intentional race and sex discrimination will often be rational from an employer's bottom-line perspective: customer preferences, co-worker prejudice, and the unavailability of more fine-grained statistical proxies for performance might all, at times, make an employer better off financially by discriminating. But courts have consistently held that even such rational discrimination is generally illegal. While it may be rational for any individual employer to discriminate on the basis of race or sex in many circumstances, that discrimination nonetheless causes a grave harm to society by entrenching the subordinated status of minorities and women. As I show in chapter 4, the requirement that employees with disabilities receive accommodations looks very much like the prohibition on rational intentional discrimination against women and racial minorities. In both circumstances, the law calls upon employers to pay some cost to avoid contributing to a subordinating system.

Moreover, although it would certainly be possible as a formal matter to interpret the ADA's accommodation requirement as imposing on individual defendants the obligation to make "reasonable" contributions to undoing broad structural employment barriers, courts have employed a number of doctrines to relieve individual businesses of that burden. Through those doctrines, which I also discuss in chapter 4, courts have removed entire classes of possible accommodations from the requirement's scope. And they have done so even if the requested accommodations could be provided at "reasonable" cost.

These limitations on the scope of the accommodation requirement are not obvious from the text of the ADA, and their application to particular cases is indeterminate in substantial respects. But their agenda seems clear. The limitations confine the accommodation requirement so that, like a classic antidiscrimination requirement, it simply demands that defendants provide redress for their own wrongful conduct that uniquely disadvantages a protected class. Even if disability rights activists can overcome their more general resistance to a social welfare approach and urge an expansive interpretation that would eliminate those structural barriers, it seems very unlikely that courts will read the ADA's broadly phrased accommodation requirement in a way that would force individual employers to bear the burden of bringing people with disabilities into the workforce.

The requirement of accommodation thus represents nothing more than a special case of civil rights law's more general prohibition of rational discrimination, and courts have consistently assimilated that requirement very closely to traditional antidiscrimination rules. Those who believe that the ADA represents a profound innovation on previous antidiscrimination law—both those who support it and those who oppose it—exaggerate the nature of the innovation the statute has effected.

That fact should bolster the ADA's legitimacy, but it has a downside that disability rights activists should confront. The accommodation mandate, far from being a profound innovation, is merely an incremental addition to the "traditional" antidiscrimination laws. To effect the kind of social change that will achieve employment and integration for people with disabilities, measures going well beyond the ADA are necessary. I discuss some of these measures in chapter 8.

THE PLAN OF THIS BOOK

I hope this introduction gives a sense of the range of issues treated in this book. But it may be useful to lay out more directly the book's organization. I begin, in chapter 2, with an introduction to the history of the American disability rights movement and its many, sometimes conflicting, projects. Chapters 3 through 6 then engage questions of legal doctrine—questions that I hope will illuminate the tensions among the disability rights movement's projects. Chapter 3 discusses the definition of disability under the ADA. Chapter 4 discusses the requirement of reasonable accommodation. Chapter 5 discusses disability discrimination motivated by fear of safety risks—an important area of disability rights litigation, and one that highlights questions of paternalism and the role of professionals. And chapter 6 discusses an array of life-and-death issues, including selective nontreatment of newborns with disabilities, assisted suicide, and prenatal testing; these issues highlight tensions among various ways the antipaternalist project of the disability rights movement can be cashed out. Chapters 7 and 8 then turn to policy questions. Chapter 7 reviews the evidence regarding the effects of the ADA, and chapter 8 discusses future directions disability policy might take to respond to the limitations of the ADA.

In many respects, the disability rights movement has been a remarkably successful social movement. People with disabilities are much more visible and integrated into the broader community than they were forty years ago, and the efforts of movement activists are largely responsible for that happy result. The ADA, for all of its limitations, has made our society more accessible, so much so that the United States is the envy of disability rights activists around the world. But people with disabilities in America still live, on average, in circumstances of great disadvantage. The ADA has proved unable even to begin to overcome the deep-rooted structural obstacles to disability equality. To attack those obstacles will require doing more than simply criticizing the judicial decisions that have read the statute narrowly. Rather, it will require confronting the tensions within disability rights thinking and coming to terms with the limits inherent in the antidiscrimination and accommodation paradigm. Disability rights activists must not abandon the ADA model. They must build on it and, indeed, go beyond it. But doing so requires, first of all, an honest assessment of the ADA's successes, failures, limitations, and ambiguities. I hope this book will be one step in that direction.

THE PROJECTS OF THE AMERICAN DISABILITY RIGHTS MOVEMENT

The disability rights movement has been a remarkably successful social movement in the United States. Barely visible in 1970, by 1990 the movement had secured achievement of its greatest legislative priority—the adoption of the ADA. Along the way, it picked up support from the left and the right, Democrats and Republicans, civil rights advocates and those with no particular interest in civil rights generally. Although courts have narrowed the application of the ADA (as I discuss in the next few chapters), disability rights ideals retain substantial political currency.

But in many respects it is fallacious to speak of "the" disability rights movement, as if there were a single organization with unified goals and tactics. No social movement is a unitary actor. Social movements are collections of people who feel various affiliations and have a variety of motivations. The goals, strategies, and ideas of a social movement are always evolving and are always contested within the movement.[1] The disability rights movement is no exception. It embraces people with a range of different disabilities, different life experiences, and different ideological perspectives. Thus, it is an oversimplification to speak of the "goals of the disability rights movement" as if the term referred to some stable and uncontroversially defined category. It makes more sense, I think, to speak of the disability rights movement as having various *projects*—projects that are interconnected, though sometimes in tension, and that are emphasized in different ways and to different degrees by different movement participants at different times.

In this chapter, I offer an introduction to those various projects. I begin with a brief tour of the major components of the disability rights movement, with a particular focus on the movement's development in the two decades leading up to the passage of the ADA in 1990. I then discuss the one position that approaches consensus within the movement (and is to some extent key to how I define the movement)—the endorsement of a social rather than a medical model of disability. I turn then to discuss the intramovement tensions that the broad agreement on a social model obscures. I give particularly extensive treatment to the tensions within the notion of "independence" that has been a fulcrum of disability rights thinking in the United States. Those tensions have come to the fore, in interesting and underappreciated ways, as courts have made decisions interpreting the ADA and advocates have considered further legislation. My discussion of intramovement tensions in this chapter therefore lays the groundwork for my discussion of those court decisions and legislative initiatives in subsequent chapters.

A BRIEF TOUR OF THE DISABILITY RIGHTS MOVEMENT

The American disability rights movement had its origins in the depths of the Great Depression, when a group of job-seekers with disabilities in New York City mobilized as the League of the Physically Handicapped to protest discrimination by state and federal relief agencies.[2] New Deal programs—like other programs of poor relief in Anglo-American history—treated disability as a condition that exempts an individual from the ordinary obligation to work and entitles him to relief.[3] But members of the league, and other new associations of people with disabilities, argued that the seemingly "charitable" exemption from work requirements was not so charitable. Instead, by labeling people with disabilities as "unemployable," poor relief programs "simultaneously stigmatized and segregated them, codifying job market discrimination into law."[4] League members wanted work opportunities, not charity.

The League of the Physically Handicapped petered out, but new organizations of people with disabilities arose. The National Federation of the Blind, founded in 1940, was a notable example. Federationists favored "independence" for blind people. They successfully urged states to adopt "white cane laws" (which gave blind pedestrians carrying white canes the right of way when crossing the street) and "guide dog laws" (which eliminated restrictions on the use of service animals by blind people). Those laws, and other similar legal developments, were crucial to giving blind people the same freedom of movement enjoyed by the nondisabled.[5]

But a pan-disability movement did not really arise in the United States until the early 1970s. A key contributor was the independent living movement, which was led largely by wheelchair users with physical disabilities.[6] The first independent living center, the Center for Independent Living in Berkeley, California, began as an organization of students with disabilities at the University of California.[7] The first of those students, Ed Roberts, was admitted to the university in 1962. As a result of polio, contracted when he was fourteen, Roberts used a wheelchair and spent substantial amounts of time in an iron lung. Although the university initially sought to revoke its acceptance of Roberts when it learned of his disability, the institution relented after a doctor at Cowell Hospital, located on campus, proposed to house him on a floor of that facility. Several other college-age people with disabilities who used wheelchairs learned of Roberts's arrangement and, in the next few years, obtained admission to the university as well. Like Roberts, these students were housed in Cowell Hospital.

Perhaps owing to the political consciousness of the times, particularly on the Berkeley campus, the students who resided at Cowell Hospital began to see their situation in largely political terms.[8] They organized a political group called the Rolling Quads and urged the university to eliminate the architectural barriers that prevented wheelchair users from moving freely about the campus. They also organized a student-run class entitled "Strategies of Independent Living." With a grant from the federal Office of Education, the Cowell residents launched the Physically Disabled Students' Program (PDSP) in 1970. That organization, run by and for students with disabilities, aimed to provide such students with the services they would need to lead independent lives that were integrated into the broader community. Services included attendants to assist in dressing, personal hygiene, and other activities of daily living, as well as prompt and reliable wheelchair repair services—a necessity for wheelchair users who sought to live in the community.

From the beginning, people with disabilities from both the student body and the Berkeley community sought to participate in the PDSP's services. The organizers of the program soon decided to create a new organization that was designed to serve the community at large. That organization, the Center for Independent Living (CIL), was incorporated in 1972. The founders of Berkeley's CIL sought to create an organization controlled by and serving people with diverse disabilities, which would provide "services that [people with disabilities could] control on their own terms, and [would be] dedicated to independence and the transcendence of other institutions."[9] Instead of providing care and maintenance to people with disabilities, those services would promote independence from medical and rehabilitation institutions. Above all, the center dedicated itself to the principle of consumer control—the principle that people with disabilities should control the services they receive.

At roughly the same time, independent living centers began to spring up throughout the country. In 1972, the same year that Berkeley's CIL was incorporated, disability activists in Houston started a cooperative living project that was dedicated to the same basic principles.[10] Other disability activists founded the Boston Center for Independent Living in 1974.[11] Today, there are hundreds of independent living centers throughout the United States. Although each center is different, as befits "a profoundly local movement, bred of the specific needs of individual communities as divergent as Berkeley and Columbus,"[12] most independent living organizations subscribe to several fundamental premises. "These premises include the notion that each individual is different and unique; that people with disabilities are the most knowledgeable experts about our own needs and issues; and that programs serving disabled people should be designed to serve all disability groups."[13] As analyzed by Gerben DeJong, one of the movement's most important chroniclers, the independent living movement drew heavily on the civil rights, consumerism, self-help, demedicalization, and deinstitutionalization movements of the 1970s for several basic ideas: that discrimination is what prevents people with disabilities from achieving full integration into the community, that people with disabilities rather than medical and rehabilitation professionals should decide what services they receive and how they receive them, and that people with disabilities should have the opportunity to make their own decisions about their lives, bearing whatever risks those decisions entail.[14]

For a variety of reasons, the independent living movement became a major driving force behind the broader disability rights movement of the 1970s and 1980s, and "most of the early disability rights leaders were identified with CILs."[15] The Berkeley Center for Independent Living, in particular, self-consciously positioned itself to groom disability rights leaders. For example, activists at the Berkeley CIL encouraged Judy Heumann, then a young disability rights activist in New York, to move to Berkeley to attend graduate school and become involved in the disability community there.[16] The Berkeley CIL also organized the most significant protest of the early disability rights movement—a twenty-eight-day sit-in in the San Francisco office of the U.S. Department of Health, Education, and Welfare to protest Secretary Joe Califano's refusal to sign the regulations implementing Section 504 of the Rehabilitation Act.[17] Even after these early days, the independent living movement continued to play a major role in the disability rights movement by providing staging areas for disability activists in communities throughout the country, a network through which those activists could share information, and, perhaps most important, organizations with paid staff who could support disability rights activities.[18] Given the significant institutional role of the independent living movement in broader disability rights struggles, it should hardly be surprising that "the philosophy of independent living formed much of the basic philosophical underpinnings of the larger [disability rights movement]."[19]

At the same time the independent living movement was growing, other disability-related movements were arising around the country. The deinstitutionalization movement, which had clear ideological connections to the independent living movement, had great success during the early 1970s. Cases involving institutions like Willowbrook in New York and Pennhurst in Pennsylvania called public attention to the horrific conditions in which states confined individuals who were believed to have mental retardation. Cases like *Wyatt v. Stickney* in Alabama similarly called attention to the horrific conditions in which states confined people who were believed to be mentally ill. Lawyers who brought these cases saw institutionalization as a massive and gratuitous deprivation of liberty. Pointing to the origins of institutionalization in the United States in the eugenics period of the early twentieth century—and to similar treatment of individuals with disabilities in Nazi Germany—they also argued that institutionalization rested on and instantiated prejudices against people with disabilities. Some went so far as to adopt Thomas Szasz's view that mental disability is a "myth" or a label attached to certain societally deviant people. That view seemed particularly powerful when considered in the light of the evidence that many institutionalized persons were neither mentally ill nor mentally retarded under accepted definitions at the time they were admitted, and that the institutional environment *itself* seemed to cause mental illness and intellectual and adaptive regression.[20]

At the beginning, the deinstitutionalization movement was largely led by nondisabled lawyers, journalists, and psychologists with a civil libertarian or civil rights bent. But as it moved forward, and more and more people were deinstitutionalized, individuals with mental retardation and mental illness began to organize their own advocacy groups.[21] People with mental retardation founded People First, a nationwide self-advocacy organization that brings lawsuits seeking deinstitutionalization and lobbies Congress and state legislatures for programs that support people with mental retardation who live in the community. People with mental illness formed a "psychiatric survivors" movement that similarly sought community treatment, as well as freedom from involuntary medication.

The organization known as ADAPT (originally American Disabled for Accessible Public Transportation, now American Disabled for Attendant Programs Today) brought together aspects of both the independent living and the deinstitutionalization movements, with a more radical edge. ADAPT is an organization of people with disabilities who challenge institutionalization both in large state congregate institutions and in nursing homes and who seek support for people with disabilities to live in the community. Challenging "the social and economic elitism of the mainstream disability movement," ADAPT founder Wade Blank explained how his organization (which is now nationwide) was distinctive: "The Ed Robertses and the Judy Heumanns don't deal with nursing homes. They've never been in one. They don't understand them. . . . You go to the independent living centers, and you'll see a lot of post-polios and a lot of spinal cord injuries. But you won't see a lot of people who slobber and can't speak clearly like you do here."[22] ADAPT has used the techniques of civil disobedience, protest, and street theater, as well as litigation, to pursue its goals.

Another strand of the movement that developed in the early 1970s sought access to elementary and secondary education. At the time, public schools were free to deem individual children with disabilities "uneducable" and refuse to provide them any education. In 1975, Congress found that more than a million children with disabilities nationwide were entirely excluded from public education, and millions of others were excluded in significant respects. Civil rights attorneys like Marian Wright Edelman joined with parents and special-education teachers to challenge that massive exclusion. A series of largely successful lawsuits throughout the country was followed by Congress's enactment in 1975 of the Education for All Handicapped Children Act (later renamed the Individuals with Disabilities Education Act), which guaranteed all children with disabilities a "free appropriate public education" in the "least restrictive environment."[23]

In the 1980s, the AIDS crisis expanded the constituencies of the disability rights movement. Although HIV initially prompted responses from people concerned with either public health or gay civil rights (or both), legal advocates began to see the potential in characterizing the disease as a "handicap" under the then-existing disability discrimination laws. In time, people with HIV came to be understood as an essential part of the disability rights movement—even to the point that disability rights activists successfully opposed efforts to amend the proposed ADA to exclude that condition from the statute's definition of "disability."[24]

The 1980s also saw the integration into the broader disability rights movement of the culturally Deaf. Although the emphasis Deaf activists placed on cultural separatism stood in tension with the integrationist demands of independent living and deinstitutionalization advocates, these activists helped catalyze the efforts to pass the ADA with their "Deaf President Now" protest at Gallaudet University in 1988. Gallaudet, "the world's premier school for the deaf,"[25] had never had a deaf president in the 124 years since it was chartered. When the school's Board of Trustees passed over deaf candidates and installed a hearing woman, Elizabeth Zinser, to replace the departing president, students and alumni waged a weeklong protest. They framed the issue as one of discrimination, and members of Congress and Vice President Bush issued statements of support. Zinser ultimately resigned and was replaced by I. King Jordan, who became Gallaudet's first deaf president. That high-profile recognition of discrimination against deaf people was a key moment in the efforts to obtain comprehensive antidiscrimination legislation.

FROM A MEDICAL TO A SOCIAL MODEL

Given its variety of constituent groups, there should be no surprise that the movement has embraced a variety of different ideas and goals. But at least one broad point of overlapping consensus exists: that the movement should seek to change society's understanding of disability from a "medical" to a "social" model. To most disability rights advocates, "disability" is not an inherent trait of the "disabled" person. Rather, it is a condition that results from the interaction between some physical or mental characteristic labeled an "impairment" and the contingent decisions that have made physical and social structures inaccessible to people with that condition. The proper remedy for disability-based disadvantage, in this view, is civil rights legislation to eliminate the attitudes and practices that exclude people with actual, past, or perceived impairments from opportunities to participate in public and private life. Disability rights activists often call this view the "social model" of disability.[26]

At the time the disability rights movement began to form in the 1970s, America's prevalent approach to disability focused on medical treatment, physical rehabilitation, charity, and public assistance. The social model is best seen as a reaction to that "medical/pathological paradigm" of disability.[27] Activists with disabilities believed the dominant approach inappropriate because it treated disability as an inherent personal characteristic that should ideally be fixed, rather than as a characteristic that draws its meaning from social context. Where disability is treated as a medical condition or functional deficit, it is readily seen as a "personal tragedy"—"some terrible chance event which occurs at random to unfortunate individuals."[28] Such a view, activists believed, encourages dependence on doctors, rehabilitation professionals, and charity.[29] It also stigmatizes people with disabilities, by defining them as something less than normal, and it directs them into confining social roles in which they can enter society only "on the terms of the ablebodied majority."[30] Perhaps most significant to disability rights activists, the view of disability as a personal tragedy obscures the social practices that exclude "the disabled" from the opportunity to participate fully in society.[31]

Most American disability rights activists have therefore recoiled against approaches that (in the words of the British scholar-activist Michael Oliver) "locate[] the 'problem' of disability within the [disabled] individual."[32] In their place, they have embraced significant parts of what Martha Minow calls the "social-relations approach" to difference. That approach treats human differences as constructed by, and residing in, social relationships.[33] British scholar-activists were the first to elaborate this approach, and their thinking soon spread across the Atlantic to the United States.[34] Adherents to the social model argue that disability should not be considered to be the unmediated product of limitations imposed by a physical or mental impairment. To them, such a view erroneously regards existing social arrangements as a neutral baseline. The social model instead treats disability as the interaction between societal barriers (both physical and otherwise) and the impairment. As Harlan Hahn put it, "From this perspective, disability is attributed primarily to a disabling environment instead of bodily defects or deficiencies."[35]

Crucially, disability rights advocates have characterized the environmental barriers that attach disadvantage to impairments as a form of discrimination—as at least reflecting, in the terms used by constitutional scholars, "selective sympathy and indifference."[36] This phenomenon is most obvious in the built environment. Architects design structures with a model of the "normal" user in mind, and that model has typically been a person without any discernible impairments.[37] This "assumption of able-bodiedness as the norm"[38] can be seen in buildings with unnecessary stairs, doorways that are too narrow to accommodate wheelchairs, and entrances that fail to provide any detectable warning for people with visual impairments. But the phenomenon of selective indifference extends beyond the decisions that have constructed our physical architecture. It affects our patterns of social organization as well. Among other things, it affects the structure of jobs and the means by which businesses and governments deliver services.[39]

Why have those who construct our social and physical environment failed to consider people with disabilities as among the "normal" users? One explanation might look to the history of prejudice against and stereotypes about people with disabilities. For much of our history, people with a variety of physical and mental disabilities were "shunted aside, hidden, and ignored."[40] People with impairments ranging from epilepsy to blindness to mental retardation were segregated from the community in a collection of congregate institutions.[41] Such segregation "perpetuate[d] unwarranted assumptions that persons so isolated are incapable or unworthy of participating in community life."[42] Even among those who were not institutionalized, people with disabilities frequently did not work, patronize businesses, or use government services outside the home.[43] A person designing a particular building, production process, or job description thus had no ready image of people with disabilities as potential customers or workers. The designer might have had no particular negative attitudes toward "the disabled." Indeed, it might never have entered her mind that people with disabilities might wish to use her building or work in her business; she might simply have had no ability to imagine people with disabilities as ordinary people with ordinary needs and tastes.[44]

The social model had a clear policy payoff for disability rights activists, one that pointed away from medical treatment and charity and toward civil rights. Once one thinks of disability as arising primarily from the human environment, rather than from anything inherent in an individual's physical or mental condition, it becomes (in Martha Minow's words) "a problem of social choice and meaning, a problem for which all onlookers are responsible."[45] Rather than providing charity or public assistance—an approach that both stigmatizes its recipients and leaves the disabling aspects of the environment in place—most disability rights activists insist that society as a whole has a responsibility to eliminate the social and physical structures that deny people with "disabilities" access to opportunities—the structures that, in a significant way, create "disability."

CONTINUING TENSIONS

THE UNIVERSAL VERSUS THE MINORITY GROUP MODEL

The general agreement among disability rights activists on choosing the social over the medical model has at times masked some significant tensions that remain within the movement. One major tension relates to the coverage of disability civil rights laws. The social model recognizes that all people's abilities lie on a spectrum, and there is no *a priori* line that divides the level of ability we call "normal" from the level we call "disability." Instead, it is society that explicitly and implicitly draws that line. But that diagnosis hardly dictates the proper prescription for disability policy.[46] To the contrary, it could call for one of two diametrically opposed policy responses. One possible response would be to take society's construction of disability and go with it: through prejudice, stereotypes, and neglect, one might say, society has created a distinct (though not *naturally* distinct) minority group of people with disabilities. By analogy to the affirmative action remedies that were adopted in the race context, one might then argue that the proper policy response is to direct resources and accommodations at that group. The work of the scholar-activist Harlan Hahn articulates that "minority group" model of disability, and many disability rights activists have operated on the basis of that model.[47]

The opposite policy prescription, equally consistent with the social model of disability, would be to declare that the disability label is arbitrary and useless, and to pursue (in the words of Irving Zola, another prominent scholar-activist) "universal policies that recognize that the entire population is 'at risk' for the concomitants of chronic illness and disability."[48] To continue with the affirmative action analogy, this universalist position might be akin to William van Alstyne's call to "get[] beyond racism by getting beyond it *now*."[49] It might see people with socially identified disabilities as canaries in the coal mine, whose incompatibility with existing physical or social structures calls our attention to problems that all individuals can face in dealing with a world that often fails to take individualized needs into account. But the proper response would not be disability specific — it would be the universal design of the built environment to embrace the largest variety of potential users, as well as a general rule of flexibility to recognize that all people are different.

In subsequent chapters, I discuss a number of implications of the tension between the minority group and the universal understanding of disability. For now, however, what is crucial to note is that *both* understandings are firmly rooted in the social model.

THE CRITIQUE OF, AND RELIANCE ON, PROFESSIONALS

Another significant, though often unacknowledged, tension within disability rights thinking relates to the role of professionals. During the 1970s and 1980s, disability rights activists of many stripes developed a critique of professionalism. These activists criticized the (nondisabled) professionals who worked on disability issues — doctors, psychiatrists, physical therapists, rehabilitation counselors, welfare caseworkers, and so forth — as paternalistic, arbitrary, and oppressive. They argued that society gives too much deference to the views of professionals, and they sought a regime under which people with disabilities could make their own choices, without being required to seek outside validation.

Many of these advocates saw their critique of professionalism as flowing directly from the social model.[50] The professional's preferred response to disability, these advocates contended, is one of domination and dependence: the professional dominates, the person with a disability remains dependent. Professionals' responses to disability, in this view, principally serve the interests of the professionals themselves, by creating a class of disabled people who must turn to the professionals for help.[51]

In the context of disability benefits programs, this critique took the form of a challenge to the paternalistic, arbitrary, and oppressive aspects of welfare administration. Receipt of benefits depended on compliance with the dictates of rehabilitation counselors and welfare caseworkers. Influenced by an ideology that led them to believe that they, rather than the clients themselves, knew what was best for their clients, caseworkers' dictates extended to core life decisions.[52] As the great blind scholar-activist Jacobus tenBroek put it in a classic article he wrote with Floyd Matson, "It is the agency of welfare, not the recipient, who decides what life goals are to be followed, what ambitions may be entertained, what services are appropriate, what wants are to be recognized, what needs may be budgeted, and what funds allocated to each. In short, the recipient is told *what* he wants as well as *how much* he is wanting."[53] To Professors tenBroek and Matson, the alternatives for people with disabilities who receive welfare were stark: "obedience or starvation."[54] Other disability rights activists echoed this attack on the administration of disability welfare benefits.[55]

But the critique of professionalism stood in tension with the actual practices of disability rights movement activists, who often relied on the assistance and endorsement of professionals who shared their views. The movement relied on lawyers, often ones who had no disabilities themselves, to bring disability rights cases; it relied on the assistance of psychologists who opposed institutionalization and forced medication; it relied on the nondisabled parents of disabled children, especially in efforts to secure educational rights; and it relied on special-education teachers. Given the deference professionals often receive in our culture, that reliance has clearly been useful—perhaps essential—in achieving many of the movement's goals. But it has probably had the ironic effect of even further enhancing the stature of professionals and entrenching the deference they receive. This tension has manifested itself in disability rights law on a number of occasions, as I show in subsequent chapters.

INDEPENDENCE AND WELFARE

Perhaps the most important tension in disability rights thinking, and one that deserves extensive discussion, relates to the ideal of "independence." Disability rights activists seized on that ideal as a basic frame for describing their goals. The activists argued that people with disabilities do not want charity, pity, or government handouts; instead, they simply want the opportunity to live in the community and work for a living. The independence frame was useful in gaining external support for the disability rights movement, particularly from conservatives. But it was also useful in uniting the diverse strands of disability rights activism. All factions of the movement—even those who disagreed on very significant issues—could agree on a program of independence instead of pity. At the same time, however, in their efforts to secure passage of the ADA disability rights activists necessarily relied on the charitable attitudes held by people without disabilities, and the law does impose significant requirements that can readily be understood as a form of government-mandated largesse. Movement activists have given too little thought to the ways in which the tools they seek to obtain independence merely entrench the charitable ideal those activists oppose. As I show in subsequent chapters, that tension has arisen again and again in disability rights law and policy.

WARINESS ABOUT WELFARE

As I have already noted, one of the key points of agreement among disability rights activists centered on the need to move away from welfare programs as a response to disability—to move, in the title of Richard Scotch's important book, "from good will to civil rights."[56] Opposition to welfare within the movement came from a number of different political perspectives, however.

From the left, many activists contended that disability welfare programs promoted political quiescence among people with disabilities. They argued that disability welfare programs are essentially symbolic government acts that, in the words of one activist, merely "buy off" a potentially troublesome group.[57] Instead of making fundamental changes to social relations or the built environment that would allow people with disabilities to achieve actual integration and equality in society, the nondisabled majority uses relatively small cash benefits as a means of dulling any urge among people with disabilities to protest existing power arrangements.[58]

From the right, many disability rights activists argued that welfare programs promoted a culture of dependence among people with disabilities. Professors tenBroek and Matson themselves had argued that the existing scheme of administering disability benefits "perpetuate[d] dependency and discourage[d] initiative."[59] But they remained sanguine that a welfare scheme could be structured in a way that avoided these problems.[60] Other disability rights activists did not appear so confident, however. To the contrary, they spoke in terms that would resonate quite strongly with later critiques of the welfare system articulated by such conservative commentators as Charles Murray.[61] Ed Roberts, for example, urged that people with disabilities should move away from a dependent "welfare mentality."[62] And a group of activists that included Justin Dart, who played the central role in lobbying for the passage of the ADA,[63] wrote that disability welfare programs "support[ed] large segments of the population in relatively idle dependency."[64] These activists criticized the position they characterized as the "'give me' socialist" view "that 'society' should and can provide certain benefits to each human with no corresponding obligation on the part of the individuals."[65]

Each of these fundamental challenges to disability welfare was broadly compatible with another critique asserted by disability rights activists, one that rested on the double-edged nature of categorical welfare programs in a market society. Many nondisabled people believe that disability benefits programs make disability a favored status in society by exempting people with disabilities from the ordinary obligation to work for a living. In that common view, disability welfare is an act of beneficence, one that demonstrates society's intense concern for people with disabilities. They are the paradigm case of the "deserving" rather than the "undeserving" poor.[66]

But activists sought to challenge the notion that society's "beneficence" toward people with disabilities was really beneficial. Disability rights advocates have long contended that (in Harlan Hahn's words) "superficial indications of sympathy, and even pity, for the plight of disabled persons frequently conceal a deeper sense of discomfort and resistance that has perpetuated the segregation and inequality" of people with disabilities.[67] Those advocates believed that the welfare system, which treats disability as an excuse for not working, was a prime example of that phenomenon. To be excused from the social obligations of citizenship, they contended, is also to be excused from the social rights of citizenship.[68] When persons cannot make their own way—even for fully understandable reasons—then a society that undertakes to care for them will necessarily also undertake to make their decisions for them.[69] Many of the more theoretically inclined disability rights thinkers characterized the role of disability welfare recipients as an extended version of the "sick role" described by the sociologist Talcott Parsons.[70] The sick person is excused from ordinary social responsibilities for the duration of the illness, but only so long as the sick person submits to the control and direction of professionals who "treat" the condition.[71] For people with disabilities, who often cannot expect to be "cured," the submission to the control of others—and attendant denial of full citizenship—is lifelong.[72] Activists' opposition to welfare benefits was thus tied directly to their critique of professional paternalism.

Some British disability rights activists in the 1970s turned the same sorts of critiques of disability welfare into a thoroughgoing attack on cash benefits programs.[73] American disability rights activists did not go so far. Many recognized that welfare programs would remain important for a large number of people with disabilities, if only to provide the health insurance benefits they needed to participate in the world.[74] And grassroots disability protests preponderantly focused on demands for benefits rather than civil rights.[75] But a number of important grassroots disability protests did focus on civil rights.[76] And activists (particularly, although not exclusively, elite activists) did urge a fundamental reorientation of disability policy toward a civil-rights-focused approach. Essential to that campaign was an effort to redefine the nature of "independence."

REDEFINING THE NATURE OF "INDEPENDENCE"

At the heart of the independent living movement, and therefore central to the broader disability rights movement, was the sometimes ill-defined concept of "independence." Although the term might in our society generally connote physical independence—the ability to move about and perform tasks of daily life without assistance—movement activists sought to define "independence" in terms of agency, freedom from paternalistic institutions, and the ability to live a full life in the community. Independent living activists thus defined "independence" as the ability of people with disabilities to make their own choices concerning how to live their lives, what services to receive, and how and where to receive them.[77] Even if people with disabilities require assistance in personal hygiene, transportation, or other activities in order to live in the community and effect these choices, that need not compromise their independence. Rather, independent living advocates believe that such assistance actually promotes independence, so long as those who provide the assistance are subject to the control and direction of the individuals with disabilities who receive it. As one analyst put it, the movement treats independence as consisting in "decisional" rather than "executional" autonomy.[78] In DeJong's words, "A person who can get dressed in fifteen minutes with human assistance and then be off for a day of work is more independent than the person who takes two hours to dress and then remains homebound."[79]

Such a position is not inherently antagonistic to the provision of cash and in-kind benefits to people with disabilities. To the contrary, so long as benefits are distributed in a way that leaves the individual recipients with maximum control over their own lives and gives them the greatest chance to live and work in the community, such benefits can be seen as promoting, rather than hindering, independence as the independent living movement defines it. Independent living advocates have often viewed disability benefits in precisely those terms.[80]

As the rhetoric of "independence" suggests, however, many adherents to the independent living movement continually and insistently urged an ethic of self-help and individual responsibility.[81] Individuals with disabilities, these adherents argued, must take responsibility for their own lives and actions.[82] As Justin Dart and his fellow activists put it, "The essence of independence—of human fulfillment—and the foundation of equality is not the granting of rights and benefits by others, but the establishment of self-discipline and self-reliance."[83]

For individuals with disabilities to assume personal responsibility for their lives, on this view, they must make choices and bear the consequences of those choices. To DeJong, this "dignity of risk" is of central importance: "The dignity of risk is the heart of the IL movement. Without the possibility of failure, the disabled person lacks true independence and the ultimate mark of humanity, the right to choose for good or evil."[84] Independent living activists urged that the empowerment and flourishing of people with disabilities would be best advanced by a regime in which people with disabilities had the opportunity to develop their skills, test them in the world, and succeed or fail according to their talents.

Emphasis on personal responsibility and the "dignity of risk" could, of course, accord with the continued receipt of some forms of public and personal assistance. Those kinds of assistance that enable people with disabilities to leave segregated institutions and their homes and enter the workforce are quite consistent with such an emphasis. There is, however, an enormous tension between the major disability benefits programs—which excuse people with disabilities from the obligation to work and pay them a steady cash benefit simply because they have a disability—and the notion that individuals with disabilities should test their skills in the world and experience the "dignity of risk." DeJong, for example, has described activists' views in a way that leaves very little room for traditional benefits programs: "The IL movement rejects the behavioral expectations created by both the sick role and its derivative, the impaired role, asserting that the disabled do not want to be relieved of their familial, occupational, and civic responsibilities in exchange for childlike dependency. In fact, the movement considers any such 'relief' tantamount to denying the disabled both their right to participate in the life of the community and their right to full personhood."[85] In this context, it is hardly surprising to hear leaders of the independent living movement speak approvingly of such things as moving "from a welfare mentality to one that has seen [people with disabilities] become contributing, productive members of society."[86] It could not be accidental that independent living activists, who challenged the existing disability welfare state as creating dependency, adopted the same rhetoric of personal responsibility as have the advocates of trimming back the welfare state more generally.[87]

THE POLITICAL SUCCESS OF THE
INDEPENDENCE FRAME

In examining the ideas of the disability rights movement, I have found it useful to think in terms of the "frame analysis" branch of social movement theory. A number of recent theorists have applied to the study of social movements Erving Goffman's conception of "frames" as the schemata of interpretation that people use to make sense of their experiences—and that are often intentionally manipulated and changed by social actors.[88] These theorists have argued that one significant aspect of social movement activity is the creation and dissemination of "collective action frames"—ways of interpreting the world that encourage support for a movement's program among potential adherents and other relevant audiences.[89] Although these theorists have been regrettably imprecise in defining what kind of collection of ideas would constitute such a "frame,"[90] their analysis provides important insight into the mobilizing role of ideas—shaped by the movements themselves—in social movement activity. As these scholars emphasize, collective action frames are consciously created by social movement actors, but they do not arise spontaneously from the minds of those actors. Rather, framing is an "act[] of cultural appropriation."[91] Successful collective action frames draw on the existing political culture at the same time they seek to transform it.[92] And importantly, a social movement will rarely have any single, uncontroverted collective action frame. Rather, the framing process is itself a locus of intramovement contest.[93]

"Independence," I contend, has operated as a collective action frame for the disability rights movement. And the frame analysis literature helps to shed light on the uses of that frame for the movement. One key use of the independence frame for disability rights activists was to obtain support from mainstream political leaders and the broader public—a use that social movement scholars have observed in other collective action frames.[94]

In one of the leading articles on social movement framing processes, David Snow and his colleagues argue that social movements often follow a strategy of "frame extension"—an effort to bring new constituents and grievances within an established and successful collective action frame. One might have expected disability rights leaders to follow that strategy and rely on a simple extension of the civil rights frame that had been so successful in supporting the expansion of the rights of racial minorities in the 1960s and of women in the 1970s. They certainly did to some extent. Sharon Groch, for example, argues that the disability consciousness of early disability rights/independent living leaders drew directly on the "oppositional consciousness created by African Americans and brought to the public's attention during the Black civil rights movement of the 1950s and 1960s."[95] Sharon Barnartt and Richard Scotch make a similar argument.[96] Those scholars are clearly correct in saying that disability rights leaders were influenced by and drew from the civil rights frame. But the picture is more complicated than that. The civil rights frame played an important role in the disability rights movement. But the deliberate decision by many disability rights leaders to move beyond the civil rights frame and toward a focus on independence—and concomitant discomfort with welfare—is particularly important to understanding the trajectory of that movement.

As the 1970s gave way to the 1980s, the civil rights frame presented difficulties for the disability rights movement. A series of developments during the 1970s— the implementation of school busing in the North, the rise of disparate-impact theories of discrimination, and the widening adoption of affirmative action programs, to name the most obvious ones—all combined with a tight economy to make civil rights policies increasingly controversial in the public at large.[97] Increasing opposition to the extension of civil rights policies was a major factor in the election of Ronald Reagan in 1980.[98]

The agenda of disability rights leaders would extend the civil rights frame even further in the same controversial direction. Instead of simply seeking the elimination of invidious, intentional discrimination, disability rights leaders demanded that individuals with disabilities receive reasonable accommodations on the job—accommodations to which nondisabled employees would not necessarily be entitled.[99] Disability rights leaders also demanded elimination of architectural and transportation barriers to the full integration of people with disabilities into the community. As the extensive, hard-fought battle for accessible public transportation that began in the 1970s made clear, removal of such barriers could be costly and would arouse the opposition of well-organized, well-funded interests.[100]

At a time when deregulatory ideas were ascendant, and much of the public was impatient with minority groups' claims for ever-expanded entitlements in the name of civil rights, a simple extension of the civil rights frame did not hold out substantial prospects of success.[101] Disability rights leaders self-consciously aimed to solve these problems by couching their demands in terms of the elimination of dependency and the promotion of independence.[102] Such a frame enabled the movement to harness a related aspect of the conservative politics of the early 1980s. When President Reagan took office, he rode (and fed) a wave of resentment of public spending—particularly spending on welfare programs.[103]

As Reagan's large tax cut and defense buildup left the federal budget in a seemingly perpetual state of deficit, the pressure on domestic spending rose even more. In part due to the president's continuing attacks on the subsidization of idleness and dependency, the pressure on welfare spending was particularly intense. The Social Security disability system did not escape these pressures. In keeping with its welfare reform agenda, the Reagan administration sought very early to tighten eligibility for the Social Security disability programs, though its efforts were ultimately thwarted by Congress and the courts.[104]

In this context, the value of the independence frame to disability rights advocates should be obvious. To achieve their goals, disability rights leaders could almost endorse the wave of fiscal conservatism and opposition to welfare programs. They could say that people with disabilities do not want to be dependent on disability benefits; they "simply want to work." Unlike a presentation of disability rights laws as the logical next step in the increasingly fragile expansion of civil rights protections, the presentation of disability rights laws as a means of achieving independence resonated strongly with the ascendant conservative ethic of individualism, self-reliance, and fiscal restraint.

Indeed, presenting disability rights as fostering independence paid immediate dividends for the movement. When the Reagan administration took office in 1981, it quickly embarked on a program of regulatory reform spearheaded by Vice President Bush. One of the first targets of that program was the set of regulations adopted to implement Section 504 of the Rehabilitation Act of 1973. The still-emergent disability rights community responded fiercely to the threat to what was, at that time, the most important law prohibiting disability-based discrimination.[105]

Evan Kemp was a major "point person" for the disability community in its efforts to defend the Section 504 regulations. Kemp, a Republican who was then serving as the director of the Nader-affiliated Disability Rights Center, made a national name for himself in 1981 by attacking Jerry Lewis's Labor Day telethon for its role in propagating patronizing stereotypes of pity for and fear of people with disabilities.[106] Making his case to Bush and his counsel, C. Boyden Gray, against the rollback of Section 504's regulations, "Kemp used a conservative argument. Disabled people wanted independence, Kemp told Bush. They wanted to get out of the welfare system and into jobs."[107] Bush found this argument (backed by significant political mobilization in the disability community) persuasive, and his Task Force on Regulatory Relief ultimately decided to make no changes to the Section 504 regulations.[108] (When Bush became president, he appointed Kemp to chair the Equal Employment Opportunity Commission.)

THE SUCCESS OF THE INDEPENDENCE
FRAME IN THE MOVEMENT

But the independence frame was not useful merely as a way of obtaining external political support in a conservative era. It was useful also as a way of mobilizing support for the disability rights movement among people with disabilities themselves. This is an extremely important point, for it demonstrates that the adoption of the independent living frame was not simply a strategic decision of a monolithic preexisting community, which could be judged on its net utility in achieving the community's external goals. Rather, adoption of that frame by disability rights leaders represented a very important step in creating the disability community itself.

Students of the disability movement in America have consistently noted a major obstacle to widespread mobilization of people with disabilities: historically, social institutions have divided people with disabilities into separate categories and groups based on the particular impairments they have. People with blindness, deafness, mobility impairments, mental illness, and mental retardation (and, in more recent times, HIV) have each dealt with separate, impairment-specific government programs, charitable institutions, and lobbying organizations. This division into separate institutions had an effect on the consciousness of individuals with disabilities, who often did not perceive or acknowledge that they had anything in common with people who had different impairments. The resulting fragmentation of the disability community diluted its political strength and led to counterproductive struggles for resources among different impairment-specific groups.[109]

When the modern American disability rights movement began in the early 1970s, movement leaders believed that a significant part of their task was to forge a collective identity of "people with disabilities" from that disparate collection of impairment-specific identities.[110] In this, the disability rights movement was hardly unique. Many scholars in recent years have emphasized the role of the formation of collective identity in the activity of social movements. Writing specifically of "movements for the liberation or integration of negatively privileged status groups," David Snow and his colleagues have argued that "the success of their mobilization efforts . . . rests in part on effecting changes in the way their potential constituents view not only their life situation, but also themselves."[111]

The frame of independence offered a means of aiding the effort to forge a collective identity of people with disabilities, for the frame promised to resonate with a broad group of people with a wide range of conditions. For one thing, the independent living frame seemed to accord with the experiences of a large number of people with diverse impairments.[112] The wheelchair users who left Cowell Hospital were not the only ones who sought independence from medical and other professionals who attempted to run their lives. Blind activists in organizations like the National Federation of the Blind and the American Council of the Blind also sought to escape dependence on rehabilitation professionals and charities that controlled and limited their opportunities.[113] People with mental retardation who participated in People First sought freedom from institutionalization and the constant control of institution staff.[114] Many people with psychiatric disabilities too sought deinstitutionalization and also the establishment of consumer-controlled alternatives to the physician-dominated mental health system.[115] Even the culturally Deaf, whose embrace of separatism sat uneasily with the movement's general aim of integration, could get behind a program of "independence."[116] For they too sought to escape the control of professionals who thought they knew what was best (in this case, professionals who forced individuals with hearing impairments to struggle to speak orally and read lips, rather than permitting them to speak sign language).[117]

Although there were many differences among these groups, all sought to make their own decisions concerning their lives, with all the risks that would entail. All sought freedom from professionals and welfare bureaucracies that paternalistically made decisions for them. All sought what they understood as self-reliance rather than dependence on the state or charity.[118]

Moreover, people with disabilities remain members of the broader society. Ideas like independence and self-reliance have deep cultural resonance in America.[119] People with a wide range of impairments were likely to be moved by appeals to such resonant cultural concepts.[120] And the self-help and demedicalization movements extended throughout the culture, to people with no impairments at all as well as those with both minor and major impairments.[121] Any constituent of these movements thus became a potential constituent of the welfare reform/independent living frame, regardless of whether she had an impairment that was theretofore considered a "disability."

Finally, it is worth noting that not all people with disabilities—even politically active people with disabilities—are liberal Democrats or supporters of civil rights generally.[122] The focus on independence and self-reliance provided a way of appealing to the more conservative people with disabilities without alienating those who held more liberal orientations.

In short, the independence frame served a very useful *internal* purpose for the disability rights movement: it helped to create the collective identity of "people with disabilities." Not all people with disabilities experienced people cringing or recoiling from them in public. Nor did all people with disabilities experience

discrimination in employment or transportation. Nor did they all seek full integration into the broader community. But people in all of these groups sought
"independence" from the control of professionals, welfare bureaucracies, and
charity. And people in all of these groups sought the opportunity to succeed or
fail according to their own choices.

INDEPENDENCE'S TENSIONS

Although the independence frame has proved exceptionally useful for the
disability rights movement, it contains an inherent tension. Movement adherents claim to seek "independence," "self-reliance," and "self-help." But to obtain
the "independence" they seek, they rely significantly on assistance from third
parties. This is true even if the demands of the disability rights movement are
characterized in the narrowest possible terms—as a demand for protection from
intentional discrimination against people with disabilities in employment, public accommodations, and government services. Even in that narrow formulation, people with disabilities must depend on others to achieve "independence,"
for they rely on courts (and perhaps government enforcement agencies) to guarantee their right to participate in community activities. Of course, independent
living and disability rights advocates have not sought merely a traditional guarantee of "nondiscrimination." Rather, they have sought, and obtained, a guarantee
that employers, public accommodations, and government services afford people
with disabilities reasonable accommodations—a guarantee I discuss extensively
in chapter 4. Implementation of a reasonable accommodation regime adds an
additional layer of "dependence." People with disabilities depend on employers
and others to make (perhaps costly) changes in workplace routines to facilitate
their employment, and they depend on the courts to ensure that employers
make such changes.

And the demands of the disability rights movement do not stop there. Many
disability rights activists demand publicly funded personal assistance services,
to enable individuals with disabilities to live full lives in the community.[123] They
also demand publicly financed health care for people with disabilities, to eliminate the fear that going to work means losing health care benefits.[124] As Barnartt
and Scotch's extensive empirical research demonstrates, the plurality of disability protests in the past three decades has asserted demands for state-provided
services like these, rather than demands for civil rights—and the proportion of
service-related demands increased in the 1990s.[125] Many of these protests involved specific demands for state money.[126]

Programs such as personal assistance services and health care are, in fact,
essential if people with disabilities are to enter the workforce in substantially

larger numbers and live full lives in the community—as I discuss extensively in chapter 8. But they are also expensive, potentially lifetime entitlements. The program of the disability rights movement thus requires dependence not only on courts and employers but also on an expanded welfare state. And charitable feelings by the nondisabled are often a central component of the political support for such programs. To achieve the political goal of securing passage of programs that promote "independence," disability rights activists may therefore ironically feed the view that charity and welfare are the appropriate responses to disability.

CONCLUSION

The disability rights movement is often referred to as if it were a unified actor, but I hope I have shown that matters are far more complicated than that. The disability rights movement has embraced a wide variety of people and views. Though there is broad agreement within the movement on the social model of disability, that general consensus conceals a number of tensions that remain in the movement—tensions over whether disability is universal or demarcates a minority group, over the role of professionals, and over the notion of "independence." As I hope to show in the rest of the book, those tensions are not of mere abstract interest; to the contrary, they help to illuminate some of the major concrete controversies in disability rights law.

3

Defining Disability

In this chapter, I examine the controversy over the definition of "disability" in the Americans with Disabilities Act. American civil rights laws generally have no protected classes. A law that prohibits race discrimination protects blacks, whites, and everyone else; a law that prohibits gender discrimination protects men and women; and a law that prohibits religious discrimination protects believers of all faiths as well as nonbelievers. But disability discrimination law is different. The ADA, for example, protects individuals against discrimination only if they have a "disability" as defined by the statute. Federal courts, including the Supreme Court, have read the ADA's disability definition quite narrowly. Accordingly, an enormous portion of ADA litigation has focused on the threshold question of whether the plaintiff is a member of the protected class rather than on whether the defendant engaged in improper discrimination.

Disability rights advocates have criticized the Supreme Court's definition-of-disability decisions as betraying the promises of the ADA. I share many of the criticisms, but I hope to show that they shed as much light on the limitations of the ADA itself, and the arguments deployed in its favor during the statute's run to passage, as on the limitations of the Court's vision. There is a reason the ADA was constructed and sold the way it was, however. The limitations highlighted by the definition-of-disability cases will not be easy to overcome. Even Congress's recent effort to overcome these limitations, the ADA Amendments Act, raises as many questions as it answers.

THE CRITIQUE OF THE SUPREME COURT'S "DISABILITY" CASES

Following the model of the Rehabilitation Act[1] before it, the ADA protects only those individuals who have a "disability." The statute defines the term to include three conditions: (1) present disability—"a physical or mental impairment that substantially limits one or more . . . major life activities"; (2) past disability—"a record of such an impairment"; and (3) perceived disability—"being regarded as having such an impairment."[2] The ADA's protection against discrimination and its requirement of reasonable accommodation extend only to individuals who have one of these forms of "disability."

The Supreme Court has decided five cases that raised the question of how to interpret the ADA's disability definition. In the first, *Bragdon v. Abbott*,[3] the Court seemed to embrace a broad reading of that definition. Holding that HIV disease is an impairment "from the moment of infection," the Court further concluded that, even in its asymptomatic phase, the disease substantially limited the plaintiff, Sidney Abbott, in her major life activity of reproduction. Although HIV disease does not prevent a woman from bearing children, the risk of transmission to one's child is enough to keep many people (including Abbott) from wanting to have children; that risk was therefore enough to constitute a substantial limitation. In dissent, Chief Justice Rehnquist argued that the Court's decision created an unduly broad disability category, one that would embrace all individuals with genetic markers for harmful diseases.[4]

But in its next four cases—*Sutton v. United Air Lines*,[5] *Murphy v. United Parcel Service*,[6] *Albertson's, Inc. v. Kirkingburg*,[7] and *Toyota Motor Manufacturing v. Williams*[8]—the Court seemed to reverse course and emphasize that it regards the threshold "disability" determination as an important device for cabining the reach of the ADA.[9] The Court made the point explicit in its unanimous decision in *Toyota*. Ruling against an individual with carpal tunnel syndrome, the Court held that a plaintiff can establish a substantial limitation in the major life activity of "performing manual tasks" only by showing that her impairment "prevents or severely restricts [her] from doing activities that are of central importance to most people's daily lives."[10] The Court reversed a lower court decision that held that the inability to perform manual tasks associated with a single job was sufficient. In so doing, the Court emphasized that the terms "substantially limits" and "major life activities" are terms that "need to be interpreted strictly to create a demanding standard for qualifying as disabled."[11]

The significant effects of the Court's narrow reading of the disability definition are particularly evident in the 1999 trilogy of definition-of-disability cases:

Sutton, Murphy, and *Albertson's*. In *Sutton*, the Court addressed the so-called mitigating measures issue. Many people with disabilities use various measures to mitigate the limiting effects of their impairments. A person with epilepsy, diabetes, or schizophrenia might take medication; a person with an amputation might use a prosthetic; and so forth. *Sutton* presented the question whether "disability" determination should look to the limitations the plaintiff's condition imposes in its unmitigated state or whether, instead, that determination should take account of the effects of whatever mitigating measures the plaintiff uses.

If the "disability" determination looked to the condition in its unmitigated state, the statute would likely have broader coverage. The whole point of using mitigating measures, after all, is to mitigate the limitations imposed by a disability.

The Court in *Sutton* ultimately ruled against that broad position. In determining whether a plaintiff satisfies the ADA's present-disability prong, the Court ruled, the proper inquiry is whether—even after the application of mitigating measures—the plaintiff's condition substantially limits major life activities.[12] Accordingly, to the extent that the plaintiff was taking a medication or using a device that removed any substantial limitation imposed by her impairment (without imposing a substantial limitation of its own), she would not be covered under the ADA's present-disability prong.[13]

The Court applied this principle in *Sutton* to reject the claims of twin sisters who had uncorrected vision of 20/200 in one eye and 20/400 in the other, because their vision improved to 20/20 in both eyes when they used corrective lenses.[14] Although the Sutton sisters' visual limitations might, before mitigating measures were used, have substantially limited the major life activity of seeing, their impairments imposed no substantial limitation once they put on glasses. In *Murphy*, the Court applied the same principle to hold that an individual with severe hypertension was not substantially limited in any major life activity, because his condition was currently controlled by medication.[15] And in *Albertson's*, the Court stated that the lower court was "too quick"[16] to find that the plaintiff's monocular vision substantially limited the major life activity of seeing, because the lower court did not take account of the way in which the plaintiff's brain adapted to the condition.[17]

In all of these cases, the employers denied opportunities to the plaintiffs based on their physical impairments notwithstanding the fact that the plaintiffs were able to control the effects of their impairments through corrective measures.[18] Yet in all of these cases, the Court said that the plaintiffs' use of such corrective measures could remove them from the protection of the ADA. Although the corrective measures did not protect the plaintiffs from discrimination, those measures did deprive them of the right to show that they were in fact qualified for the positions at issue and that their employers had acted on the basis of prejudice or stereotypes.

Many advocates and academics with a disability rights bent have sharply criticized the *Sutton* Court's holding that the present-disability inquiry must take account of mitigating measures. They have argued that the Court's ruling (which rejected specific statements in the legislative history and in the interpretive guidance issued by the Equal Employment Opportunity Commission)[19] would leave unprotected a large number of people with conditions that Congress clearly intended to cover: epilepsy, diabetes, amputated limbs, and severe hearing impairments, for example.[20] As I discuss below, Congress reversed the *Sutton/Murphy* mitigating measures ruling in the ADAAA.

But the critics have responded even more sharply to a different aspect of *Sutton* and *Murphy*—the Court's restrictive interpretation of the perceived-disability prong of the statute's "disability" definition. In both cases, the employers plainly believed that the plaintiffs' physical conditions disqualified them from performing the jobs at issue. But because the employers did not perceive those conditions as substantially limiting the plaintiffs' ability to work generally, the Court held that the perceived-disability prong was not satisfied.[21] Thus, the *Sutton* Court stated, "When the major life activity under consideration is that of working, the statutory phrase 'substantially limits' requires, at a minimum, that plaintiffs allege they are unable to work in a broad class of jobs."[22] "If jobs utilizing an individual's skills (but perhaps not his or her unique talents) are available," the Court continued, "one is not precluded from a substantial class of jobs."[23] Applying that standard, the Court held that the plaintiffs (airline pilots excluded from flying global jets for United) were not substantially limited in the major life activity of working, because "there [we]re a number of other positions utilizing [their] skills" available in the workforce generally; and they were not "regarded as" substantially limited in working, because there was no reason to believe United doubted that they could perform those other jobs.[24] And in *Murphy*, the Court held that the employer's perception that the plaintiff's hypertension disqualified him under federal law from driving a commercial motor vehicle was insufficient to show a perceived substantial limitation in working. Although disqualification from driving such a vehicle would have excluded the plaintiff from literally millions of jobs,[25] the Court found it more significant that the plaintiff (a mechanic) was still eligible to work in mechanic's jobs that did not require commercial motor vehicle certification.[26]

Critics have seen this aspect of *Sutton* and *Murphy* as confirming and endorsing the trend in the lower courts to limit ADA protection to a relatively small group of severely disadvantaged people, a group the courts occasionally call "the truly disabled."[27] Since the Supreme Court's 1999 trilogy, lower courts have often referred to the ADA's supposed purpose "to protect the truly disabled, but genuinely capable."[28] Building on the influential pre-*Sutton* critiques of the "truly disabled" idea by Robert Burgdorf and Arlene Mayerson (both of whom played major roles in drafting and lobbying for the ADA),[29] commentators have urged that the Court's narrow reading of the "disability" definition "seriously undermine[s] the purposes and goals of the ADA."[30] Or, more colorfully, "the Supreme Court has taken many people with disabilities back to the dark ages, by permitting employers and program administrators to discriminate against such individuals at will based on irrational stereotypes and prejudice."[31]

These commentators decry the Court's implication that an employer could defend an irrational refusal to hire an individual with a disability "by indicating that the individual would be capable of working at other jobs at other companies or in other fields."[32] If that implication is correct, they contend, the Court is betraying the core principles of the disability rights movement. It is treating the ADA as a disability benefits program like Social Security Disability Insurance that provides redistributive largesse to a disadvantaged class rather than as a civil rights law.[33] As Matthew Diller puts it, the implicit message "that rather than demanding accommodations, the plaintiff should simply find a job where no alteration of the workplace would be necessary" in the end "defeats the goal of establishing equal access to the job market."[34] Encapsulating the views of these advocates, Linda Krieger argues that the fundamental disconnect between the disability benefits orientation of decisions like *Sutton* and *Murphy* and the purported civil rights focus of the ADA arises from the fact that judges and members of the public "completely fail to understand the ADA's anti-disparate treatment agenda. They do not understand that the ADA, even with its redistributive reasonable accommodation provisions, is an anti-discrimination statute, not a social welfare benefits program like social security disability, which seeks to provide a safety net for the non-working disabled."[35] As I discuss below, the ADAAA attempts to reverse this aspect of *Sutton* and *Murphy* as well, though it remains to be seen how effective the new law will be in that effort.

PROBLEMS WITH THE CRITIQUE

As I explain later in this chapter, I have significant criticisms of the Supreme Court's definition-of-disability decisions myself. But the story of betrayal is far too pat. In fact, many of the decisions of the Supreme Court are consistent with a number of important strands of the thinking of disability rights activists in the 1970s and 1980s. Understanding the degree to which the Court's decisions comport with those disability rights principles not only highlights the tensions within disability rights thinking; it also demonstrates the limits of some prominent conceptions of disability rights.

"INDEPENDENCE" AND THE
DEFINITION-OF-DISABILITY DECISIONS

The Supreme Court's definition-of-disability decisions are in many ways quite consistent with the "independence" frame many disability rights advocates employed in arguing for the ADA in the late 1980s. As I showed in chapter 2, a key aspect of that frame—though hardly the only aspect—was the argument that disability rights laws would save people with disabilities (and society) from wasteful dependency on disability benefits programs.[36] If the ADA is understood, in accordance with this view, as a means of saving society money by moving people off disability benefits rolls and into the workforce, on whom should the statute bestow its protections? One obvious answer is that the statute should focus on protecting those people who would be unable to work—and thus dependent on public assistance—without antidiscrimination and accommodation protection. On such a view, the statute would not protect people who otherwise have a good chance of finding employment, even if discrimination and denial of accommodation deprives them of some opportunities they find very desirable. *Bragdon*, *Sutton*, *Murphy*, *Toyota*, and the lower court cases that limit ADA coverage to "the truly disabled" can be read as drawing a very similar line between those who could find work without the ADA and those who need ADA protection to avoid dependency on disability benefits programs. Indeed, some of the most objectionable aspects of these cases seem to rely on this very distinction.

An example is *Sutton's* statement that "[i]f jobs utilizing an individual's skills (but perhaps not his or her unique talents) are available, one is not precluded from a substantial class of jobs"[37] and hence has no "disability" embraced by the ADA.[38] The Court further stated that an individual cannot satisfy the "regarded as" portion of the disability definition simply by "say[ing] that if the physical criteria of a single employer were imputed to all similar employers one would be regarded as substantially limited in the major life activity of working only as a result of this imputation."[39] These statements make no sense if the goal of the ADA is to provide protection against prejudice and stereotypes. If taken seriously, they would shield the employer who harbors the most extreme prejudices or acts on the most idiosyncratic stereotypes. And indeed, critics of *Sutton* have made precisely that point.

If, however, the ADA is seen as an effort to move people from disability benefits rolls into the workforce, then these statements in *Sutton* seem less incongruous. "If jobs utilizing an individual's skills (but perhaps not his or her unique talents) are available,"[40] then the ADA is not necessary for the plaintiff to avoid dependency. She can stay off the disability benefits rolls by taking one of the available jobs. The ADA's protection of such a plaintiff, therefore, does nothing to reduce the cost of disability benefits programs to public budgets. Similarly, there is no reason to impute one employer's exclusion to other employers, because an individual will not be forced to the dependency rolls on the basis of a single employer's misperceptions.

Linda Krieger and Matthew Diller have criticized decisions like *Sutton* for assuming that the ADA is simply another disability benefits program.[41] When the ADA is viewed as a disability benefits program, Diller has written, "the case law has a certain coherence, although not the coherence intended by the framers of the law."[42] But my discussion should suggest that Krieger and Diller's point is misplaced. If courts took seriously the "independence" argument articulated by the statute's framers and supporters in the campaign to enact the ADA, decisions like *Sutton* would not be justified simply on the ground that the ADA is "just another benefits program" that had to be limited to sufficiently needy and morally worthy recipients. Instead, such decisions would be justified on the ground that the ADA is a regime enacted in significant part as a cost-saving *alternative* to existing benefits programs. An "independence" approach would treat the ADA as a way of getting people out of benefits programs and into the workforce, not as a way of getting job accommodations for people who would be in the workplace anyway. Such an approach would adopt a narrow interpretation of "disability," but not simply because of a general societal view that disability benefits programs should be kept within tightly cabined bounds. It would adopt a narrow interpretation of disability to focus the statute on its target population. Much of the case law fits this model very well.

To be sure, the Supreme Court's definition-of-disability cases are not explicit on this point.[43] Indeed, at least two aspects of the Court's jurisprudence suggest that the Court has not had the "independence" argument in mind in reaching its outcomes. First, the Court has been quite reticent to hold that working is a "major life activity" under the statute.[44] Second, in the *Toyota* case the Court rejected the Sixth Circuit's attempt to tie the major life activity of "performing manual tasks" to tasks performed at the workplace.[45] The Court explained that the ADA's definition of disability applies not only in employment discrimination cases but also in cases involving public transportation and places of public accommodation.[46] This broad application, the Court believed, "demonstrates that the definition is intended to cover individuals with disabling impairments regardless of whether the individuals have any connection to a workplace."[47] In its words, at least, the Court thus has seemed to reject the notion that statutory coverage should be tied to an individual's need for accommodation to remain in the workforce.

But my point is not about the intentions of the justices who joined these opinions. It is about what the Court's holdings tell us about the notion of "independence" proffered by disability rights activists. If the Supreme Court decisions that have been so strongly criticized by activists and academics are in fact broadly consistent with that notion — and I think they are — this suggests the problem is not that the Supreme Court has betrayed the promises made in the ADA. Instead, the problem is one that lies within the disability rights notion of "independence" — and the emphasis on avoiding welfare and public benefits — itself.

THE MINORITY GROUP MODEL AND THE DEFINITION-OF-DISABILITY DECISIONS

The overall pattern of the Supreme Court's definition-of-disability decisions is also consistent with an understanding of disability as defining a discrete, stigmatized minority group.[48] Indeed, it would be hard to come up with a pattern of decisions that fit that understanding better than the bottom lines the Court has actually reached. The Court's five definition-of-disability cases have involved plaintiffs with five different conditions: asymptomatic HIV (*Bragdon*); vision of 20/200 and 20/400, correctable to 20/20 (*Sutton*); high blood pressure (*Murphy*); monocular vision (*Albertson's*); and carpal tunnel syndrome (*Toyota*). HIV disease is highly stigmatized, and the Court held that it was a disability. Correctable poor vision — in other words, the need to wear glasses — and treatable high blood pressure are not, and the Court held that they were not disabilities. As Justice Ginsburg explained, "[P]ersons whose uncorrected eyesight is poor, or who rely on daily medication for their well-being, can be found in every social and economic class; they do not cluster among the politically powerless, nor do they coalesce as historical victims of discrimination."[49] Monocular vision and carpal tunnel syndrome are somewhere in between those two poles, and the Court issued in-between rulings: The Court said in *Albertson's* that most cases of monocular vision will probably count as disabilities, but that the lower court was "too quick to find a disability" in the case before it; and the Court held in *Toyota* that the court of appeals had engaged in the wrong analysis in concluding that the plaintiff's carpal tunnel syndrome was a disability, but it remanded for further proceedings on the question.[50]

A minority-group model also supports the much-maligned mitigating measures ruling of *Sutton* and *Murphy*. The ability to use mitigating measures will often make an enormous difference in the way society responds to an impairment; a view of disability as defining a discrete, stigmatized minority group could hardly ignore those measures. The facts of *Sutton* illustrate the point. Uncorrected, the *Sutton* plaintiffs had vision that fell below the threshold of "legal blindness." A person with uncorrectable "legal blindness" would surely be regarded by a broad swath of society as abnormal and "disabled." But if she could improve her vision to 20/20 by wearing eyeglasses, as the *Sutton* plaintiffs could, she would instantly become "normal" and have no need for any special remedy to protect her against systematic disadvantage. Corrective lenses are a readily available, easy to use mechanism that eliminate the limiting effect of the impairment at no appreciable cost. The mitigating measures, in that case, make all the difference regarding whether individuals are in or out of a discrete and stigmatized minority group.

That is not to say that every person who successfully mitigates the immediate effects of an impairment is no longer stigmatized as "disabled." People with epilepsy, diabetes, or schizophrenia may take medications that control their symptoms, but they are still considered disabled by many people in society at large. People who use prosthetic legs for mobility or hearing aids to enhance their auditory sense are also considered disabled by many, even if they can perform any activity.

Although much of the commentary criticizing *Sutton* treats that decision as excluding people with these correctable but stigmatized conditions from ADA coverage—and many lower courts have read *Sutton* that way—nothing in the Court's decisions required such a result. Indeed, the Court left open two clear pathways for coverage of conditions like these. The first pathway would rely on the present-disability prong of the ADA's definition. As the *Sutton* Court explained, the "use of a corrective device does not, by itself, relieve one's disability. Rather, one has a disability . . . if, notwithstanding the use of a corrective device, that individual is substantially limited in a major life activity."[51] And the measures taken to mitigate the effects of an impairment may themselves impose substantial limitations.[52] *Bragdon* demonstrates that a "substantial limitation" in an activity need not be a complete inability to perform that activity: although HIV places no physical obstacle in the path of reproduction, it imposes a condition on reproduction that most people would not want to assume—and the Court found that condition sufficient to constitute a substantial limitation.[53]

Applying the *Bragdon* analysis to medicated epilepsy, diabetes, and schizophrenia—as well as the use of prosthetic limbs, hearing aids, and the like— should be straightforward. People with medicated epilepsy and schizophrenia often cannot perform any major life activities—including, especially, the major life activity of caring for one's self—without taking medication that itself imposes substantial physical consequences most people would not want to accept.

Sutton itself cited a study that "catalog[ed] serious negative side effects of new antiepileptic drugs."[54] The side effects of antipsychotic medications are even more notorious.[55] As for people with diabetes, many will be unable to perform any meaningful activity if they do not monitor their blood sugar levels, follow strict diets, and take insulin on a regular basis. These are conditions that intrude frequently on the diabetic individual's day; they frequently clash with work schedules and other obligations designed without people with diabetes in mind, and they can themselves be quite stigmatizing.[56]

If one takes full account of the notion of stigma, the substantial-limitation element of the disability definition could have been read capaciously even under the Court's jurisprudence. One might say that Bill Demby, the Vietnam veteran from the DuPont television commercial of a few decades ago, is "substantially limited" in the major life activity of walking, even though his two prosthetic legs permit him to "play[] a spirited game of basketball on an urban blacktop."[57] He can walk only on the condition that he wears prosthetic legs—a stigmatizing condition that most people need not experience and that those who have designed our social institutions and physical structures are likely not to have considered.[58] A person who wears a hearing aid ought to have been considered substantially limited in the major life activity of hearing for the same reason: she can hear, but only on the condition that she adorn herself with one of the classic "stigma symbols."[59] In each case, mitigating measures may reduce the physical symptoms, but they do not eliminate the stigma that can lead to systematic exclusion. They may even feed that stigma.

The second pathway left open by *Sutton* would rely on the past- and perceived-disability prongs of the ADA's definition. Here, stigma again takes on particular importance. The ADA protects individuals who are "regarded as having" a substantially limiting impairment.[60] Although courts and commentators typically treat this provision as covering individuals who are regarded *by the defendant* as having a substantially limiting impairment, there is nothing in the statutory text that limits the provision in that way. To the contrary, the statute on its face appears to embrace anyone who is "regarded"—by significant segments of society at large if not by the defendant—as having a substantially limiting impairment. Under that analysis, stigmatized conditions like schizophrenia and epilepsy ought clearly to have been covered. Nothing in *Sutton*—which, after all, involved a basically nonstigmatized impairment—contradicts that point.

Perhaps more important, the *Sutton* and *Murphy* decisions did not at all address the past-disability prong of the ADA's "disability" definition, which protects people from discrimination based on a "record of" a substantially limiting impairment.[61] *Sutton* and *Murphy* would have been particularly poor cases for invocation of the "record" prong: there appears to have been no suggestion in either case that the plaintiffs spent a substantial amount of time with their impairments before they began to use the mitigating measures at issue. The plaintiffs therefore could have had no "record" of a substantially limiting impairment, because their impairments were essentially always "controlled" and hence never (under the Court's assumption) in fact substantially limiting.

Many people with now-controlled medical conditions at some point experienced substantial limitations, however. A person may have been hospitalized for tuberculosis but have fully recovered.[62] Another might have recovered after a yearlong battle with cancer.[63] Still others might have experienced significant, limiting effects from diabetes or seizure disorders before their physicians discovered the appropriate treatment. If an employer denies a job to one of these individuals because of her prior diagnoses—whether by disqualifying her for all time or by disqualifying her until she has shown no symptoms for an arbitrarily fixed period—it seems clearly to have discriminated based on the individual's "record of" a substantially limiting impairment.[64] The past-disability prong provides protection to people who face prejudice and stereotyping based on the lingering stigma of a once-active condition. It does so, however, without ignoring the effects of all corrective measures. Although lower courts did not always appreciate it, the Supreme Court's definition-of-disability decisions left open these ways of protecting individuals whose "controlled" disabilities remain stigmatized.

SUMMARY

I hope I have shown that the wholesale criticism of the Supreme Court's definition-of-disability decisions is misplaced. In both their broad outlines and many of their details, those decisions were consistent with two principles strongly urged by many disability rights advocates: (1) that disability rights law should seek "independence" for a group of people who would otherwise be dependent on welfare and charity; and (2) that people with disabilities constitute a stigmatized minority that needs protection against class- or caste-based prejudice, stereotyping, and neglect. The decisions were clearly inconsistent with another principle urged by many disability rights advocates—that "disability" is universal, because we all have a variety of abilities that exist on a spectrum[65]—but disability rights advocates subordinated that universalist notion to the independence and minority-group arguments in the campaign to enact the ADA.

Indeed, one can pinpoint the moment at which disability rights supporters made the strategic decision to subordinate the universalist view. The original ADA bill introduced in 1988 omitted the "substantially limits" language and defined "handicap" (later changed to "disability") to mean an actual, past, or perceived impairment—full stop.[66] That original proposal represented a conscious departure from the protected-class approach of the Rehabilitation Act, which defined handicap as a present, past, or perceived substantially limiting impairment. The National Council on the Handicapped, which drafted the language that formed the basis for the bills as originally introduced, expressly argued for such a departure in many of the same terms advocates of universalism use today.[67] But the Reagan administration objected to the breadth of the proposed "disability" definition.[68] When Democratic legislators and the disability rights community prepared the bill for reintroduction in the new Congress in 1989, they acceded to the prior administration's objections and reverted to the Rehabilitation Act model, complete with its "substantially limits" language.[69]

In broad outline, then, it is not fair to say that the Supreme Court's definition-of-disability decisions disregarded the principles of the disability rights movement. It is more accurate to say that those decisions took sides in a dispute within that movement. Those decisions, in my view, did fail to promote disability equality in a variety of ways. (I'll discuss those ways below.) But their failures must be attributed in significant part to the limitations of the independence frame and the minority group model of disability themselves.

Therein lies a cautionary lesson: there were good reasons at the time for movement activists to fasten on the independence frame and the minority group model when they were seeking enactment of the ADA. The independence frame, as I showed in chapter 2, had a great deal of appeal for political and fiscal conservatives. And the minority group model helped to align the ADA with the canonical civil rights laws of the 1960s and therefore appealed to moderates and liberals. Had the ADA been framed and defended differently—as a universal requirement of antidiscrimination and accommodation for any physical or mental difference—it almost certainly would not have passed. Indeed, disability rights advocates could not pass a universalist ADA Restoration Act; they ultimately had to settle for the more modest ADAAA. But the independence and minority-group framings may also have limited the effectiveness of the statute whose passage they secured. Passing judgment on the Supreme Court's definition-of-disability decisions therefore entails passing judgment on the strategies and ideals of disability rights movement activists themselves.

THE FAILURES OF THE SUPREME COURT'S DECISIONS—
AND THE INDEPENDENCE AND MINORITY-GROUP MODELS

This is not to defend the Supreme Court's decisions. They do fail in significant ways to promote disability equality. But their failure should be understood as a commentary on the independence frame and the minority-group model of disability. As the cases show, each of these orientations draws the focus of equality protection too narrowly.

THE NARROWNESS OF THE INDEPENDENCE FRAME

The cases clearly demonstrate the narrowness of the independence frame. Many individuals, like the plaintiffs in the cases the Supreme Court has decided, have physical and mental conditions that employers and others use as the basis for arbitrarily limiting opportunities. Such individuals may be "independent"—they can hold jobs and live in the community without receiving welfare checks—but they face unfair restrictions on their opportunities. In particular cases, those limitations will result in individuals not receiving jobs and other benefits they would receive if they had no physical or mental impairments. In the aggregate, those limitations can substantially drag down the opportunity range of a broad class of people with their conditions. If the goal of disability rights law is to promote equal opportunity to participate in the economic and civic life of the community, the law must strike at those limitations, even if they do not compromise individual "independence." Mere "independence," without equality, is not what disability rights activists *really* seek, and a statute constrained by a focus on independence is unduly limited.

THE MINORITY-GROUP MODEL AND
THE PERILS OF TARGETING

The minority-group model in some ways appears more promising. The model's goal, after all, is to target for protection those individuals who are likely to experience the arbitrary limitations on opportunities that create a disadvantaged class of people with disabilities. If one cares about equal opportunity, the minority-group model appears a better fit than the goal of "independence." Yet the minority-group model is also too narrow as a basis for disability rights law, for a number of reasons.

First, even if one thinks that the *goal* of disability rights law is to provide protection to a particular class of people, achieving that goal through the *means* of limiting legal protection to that class has substantial costs. As the history of American social policy shows, programs that provide benefits to a particular class are far more politically vulnerable than are universal programs. People concerned about redistribution are therefore well advised to embed redistributive rules within broad universal programs wherever possible. (I return to this point in chapter 8.) A protected-class understanding of disability rights law makes the law more vulnerable to political attack, stigmatizes its supposed beneficiaries (just as disability welfare does), and encourages judges to see their job as vigorously policing the line between those who are in and those who are out of the protected class.

And vigorously police the line is exactly what the courts have done. The

Toyota Court's assertion that the ADA's protected-class definition "need[s] to be interpreted strictly to create a demanding standard for qualifying as disabled"[70] is the most overt example. The unanimous Court never explained why the definition "need[s]" to be read in a "strict[]" and "demanding" way. To the justices, it was just too obvious that when a law provides special protections to a particular class, judges must guard the boundaries of that class to assure that those who are undeserving do not partake of those benefits. The lower court cases limiting protection to "the truly disabled" express a similar view. Indeed, many of those cases are explicit in explaining that if the coverage of the ADA is extended too broadly, that will only harm the people who are "truly" in need.

Even if one thinks that disability defines a discrete, subordinated group, then, it does not make sense to target disability law's protections to that group alone: the very act of targeting triggers political and judicial pressures to shrink the size of the protected class and to reduce the protections accorded to that class. A targeted disability law may ironically have exactly the opposite effect from the one the lower courts predict: it may reduce the chances that full protection will be provided to the full intended protected class.

THE MINORITY-GROUP MODEL AND THE NATURE OF DISABILITY INEQUALITY

But there is yet a deeper problem: the minority-group model misstates the very nature of disability inequality. Disability inequality does sometimes consist in society's identifying a discrete class of people with disabilities and discriminating against them. The eugenics movement provides the most salient historical example, and the various stigmatized disability groups discussed above still experience that kind of discrimination. But disability inequality also consists in the neglect of people who differ, physically or mentally, from the norms taken as a given by those who design institutions, and by those institutions' inflexibility in responding to difference. It will be impossible to identify in advance any class of people who are treated unequally in this way. Many will have conditions that are hidden, perhaps from themselves but certainly from others.

Consider the example of learning disability. Mark Kelman and Gillian Lester, the leading skeptics of accommodations for people with learning disabilities, find it "quite contestable" that "there is a great deal of group-based irrational devaluation of people with learning disabilities."[71] They note that "the supposedly 'bigoted' administrator judging the potential of a student with an LD may not even know he is dealing with such a student. He does not misperceive potential because he undervalues people with disabilities; on the contrary he does so for the very reason that he does *not* see that he is dealing with a disability."[72] To a large extent, I agree with that characterization.[73] But that hardly means that people with learning disabilities face no problem of disability inequality. In educational and professional licensing settings in particular, many tests are timed, even though (as Kelman and Lester themselves acknowledge) they purport to test for skills that have relatively little to do with speedy responsiveness.[74] Many people who have the skills for which these examinations purport to test will be unable to demonstrate those skills because their learning disabilities make it impossible to do so within the time allotted. A time limitation imposed for largely administrative purposes therefore ends up excluding people from the educational and professional opportunities to which standardized examinations serve as a gateway—even though they have all of the relevant skills for which the examinations purport to test. People with learning disabilities thus do not experience uniform group-based exclusion; they are excluded from opportunities when those opportunities are controlled by testing institutions that are inflexible to their inability to demonstrate their skills by conventional, timed, means.

Even among people whose conditions are overt neither they nor society at large may characterize their conditions as "disabilities." The inequality inheres not in the targeting or ignorance of a group but in an accumulation of incompatibilities between individuals' abilities and institutional structures. That, it seems to me, is a crucial lesson of the social model of disability.[75]

The Supreme Court's case law, so strongly influenced by the minority-group model, has had a hard time including these individual incompatibilities in its conception of "disability." An example appears in the Court's explanation for why it is "hesitant" to conclude that "working" is a "major life activity."[76] According to the majority in *Sutton*, there is "some conceptual difficulty in defining 'major life activities' to include work, for it seems 'to argue in a circle to say that if one is excluded, for instance, by reason of [an impairment, from working with others] . . . then that exclusion constitutes an impairment, when the question you're asking is, whether the exclusion itself is by reason of handicap.'"[77] To avoid that assumed circularity, the Court held that a person cannot be substantially limited in working unless she is "unable to work in a broad class of jobs."[78] Indeed, as I have shown, the Court went on to say that the "broad class" standard cannot be met "[i]f jobs utilizing an individual's skills (but perhaps not his or her unique talents) are available."[79] These rulings excluded from the ADA's coverage many people who were denied opportunities because their conditions were incompatible with the contingent structure of an employer's workplace and work rules. (The ADAAA makes clear that working is a major life activity.)

The Court's analysis of the perceived-disability prong of the ADA's disability definition shows the refusal to embrace individual incompatibilities even more clearly. In *Sutton*, United Air Lines had refused to hire the plaintiffs for global airline pilot positions, because their *uncorrected* vision was worse than 20/100.

The plaintiffs had argued that United "regarded" them as substantially limited in working, because they would in fact have been substantially limited in working if all global airlines had used United's criteria. The Court, however, found it improper to speculate whether United's vision requirements, if imposed by all global airlines, would make the plaintiffs "substantially limited" in the ability to work. The Court explained that "[a]n otherwise valid job requirement, such as a height requirement, does not become invalid simply because it would limit a person's employment opportunities in a substantial way if it were adopted by a substantial number of employers."[80] A contrary ruling, the court suggested, would call into question employers' ability "to prefer some physical attributes over others and to establish physical criteria" for their employees; such a ruling would therefore override Congress's decision to allow employers "to decide that some limiting, but not substantially limiting, impairments make individuals less than ideally suited for a job."[81]

But that analysis is flawed. For one thing, the well-documented "spread effect"—in which people often assume, for example, that a person with quadriplegia also has cognitive limitations—suggests that an employer who believes a person with a disability to be limited in one way will also believe that person to be limited in others.[82] More fundamentally, the Court's analysis in *Sutton* was improperly driven by a strong desire to exclude from coverage individuals whose physical conditions were incompatible with explicit or implicit physical standards set up by particular employers. Despite the Court's concerns, a decision to allow unsuccessful applicants to satisfy the "regarded as" prong by demonstrating that they failed the employer's physical standards would not necessarily render those standards "invalid." It would merely subject them to scrutiny under the ADA's substantive provisions. By the plain text of those provisions, if the selection criteria at issue were "job related for the position in question" and "consistent with business necessity,"[83] and if the plaintiffs who failed those criteria were unable, "with or without reasonable accommodation, [to] perform the essential functions of the employment position,"[84] then the employer would be free to maintain them. The "regarded as" finding has only a limited effect: it requires the employer to justify general physical criteria that disqualify people with impairments without regard for their individual abilities.[85] Such a result directly advances the cause of disability equality. But the Court, focused on a group-based harm, failed to appreciate that point.

THE MINORITY-GROUP MODEL AND ESSENTIALIZING DISABILITY IDENTITY

The effort to identify a class of people who have "disabilities" and separate them from the nondisabled does not just misunderstand the nature of disability *inequality*. It also misunderstands the nature of disability *identity*. As I showed in chapter 2, the creation of a pan-disability identity served an important political purpose for disability rights activists. It expanded the power base of the movement, helped people with divergent impairments find a sense of common cause, and helped avoid the internecine struggles between impairment-specific groups that had hampered earlier disability advocacy.

But in crucial ways the notion of a single disability identity fails to track the phenomenology of people who have conditions often identified as disabilities. People with some "disabilities" may not consider themselves "disabled" at all. The culturally Deaf, who believe themselves to be a linguistic minority persecuted because they use sign language, are an example. Others may see their problems as diseases rather than disabilities. Still others may understand their conditions as a type of disability but not want their conditions lumped with others in a single pan-disability identity. Here, members of the National Federation of the Blind (whose support for the ADA was at best lukewarm) are the best example. By contrast, some (such as those with "hidden" conditions like chronic fatigue syndrome or learning disabilities) may seek out a disability label as validation of their experience and struggles.[86] Some will prefer civil rights to cure, others vice versa, still others in between. For some people in each of these categories, their affiliation with other people with (the same or different) impairments may be the dominant influence in their lives, for others it may be nonexistent, and for still others it may be one of a set of overlapping and even conflicting affiliations.

In an article published several years ago, I argued that even if there was no natural disability identity, society had created an identifiable class of people with disabilities by its prejudice, stereotypes, and neglect.[87] I still believe that the ADA, given its most attractive reading, is premised on such a view of disability. But I no longer believe that such a view is the correct one. Disability identity is too multifarious, society's responses to conditions identified as disabilities too diverse, for the notion of a societally created disability category to offer much traction.

The "disability" category in the ADA is obviously an administrative proxy designed to target the statute's protections to the intended beneficiaries. I have tried in the past few sections to show that it is not a good proxy—that it keeps disability discrimination law from reaching a great deal of conduct about which we ought to be concerned if we care about disability inequality. But even if the ADA's disability category were a perfect proxy for the people we wanted to protect, the statute's view of disabled identity would still lead to serious problems.

As a number of critics of identity politics have recently argued, legal protections for particular identity groups can at the same time operate to regulate the individual members of those groups. Such laws effectively force group members to conform with the identity script that is dominant within their group at the pain of being denied protection.[88] The ADA's minority-group model, by forcing people with disabilities who want protection to cast themselves as part of a discrete and insular group of outsiders, has done just that. The more integrated a person with an impairment is in the community, and the less she conforms with a stereotypical disabled role, the less likely is she to obtain the ADA's protections. That is a clear lesson of the line of cases from *Bragdon* to *Toyota*, and it is one that sheds negative light on the effort to treat disability as a discrete minority-group status.

POSSIBLE SOLUTIONS?

For those who are critical of the Supreme Court's definition-of-disability decisions, the standard move at this point is to argue that the disability community erred in 1989 when it accepted the "substantial limitation" formula, and that the error should be corrected by going back to the language of the original 1988 ADA bill (which defined "disability" as a present, past, or perceived "impairment").[89] That is essentially the tack disability rights supporters in Congress took in the proposed ADA Restoration Act.[90] Political exigencies, however, forced disability rights supporters to retreat to a much more minimal ADA Amendments Act that would overturn *Sutton*'s mitigating measures ruling, expand protection under the "regarded as" prong in disparate treatment cases, and affirm (contrary to *Toyota*) that the disability definition should be broadly construed. I believe the ADA Amendments Act, which was enacted into law in the waning days of the George Walker Bush administration, is a worthy effort that is likely to make things somewhat better—though its retention of a protected class obviously puts it quite far from what I would prefer. But even if the original ADA Restoration Act were to be adopted, it would be wise not to get one's hopes up too high.

For one thing, I doubt that a mere change in language would overcome the powerful momentum of the minority-group model and the independence frame. One might expect judges who feel the "need[]" to interpret the ADA "strictly" to feel the same way under a differently worded statute. Under a statute with the 1988 definition of disability, "impairment" would be the ticket to ADA coverage. Judges who now read "substantially limits" and "major life activities" narrowly would most likely shift their narrowing constructions to the "impairment" term under such a statute. And indeed, even existing ADA jurisprudence gives judges tools to read "impairment" parsimoniously. Prior to the Supreme Court's decision in *Bragdon*, for example, some courts held that asymptomatic HIV was not even an "impairment."[91] *Bragdon* rejected those holdings, but it did so by emphasizing the serious harm HIV disease does to the body "from the moment of infection."[92] Judges could easily ratchet up the harm required for an impairment finding and thereby reintroduce much of the limiting jurisprudence that a return to the 1988 formulation would be intended to overturn.

To avoid this problem, one might follow the model of Australia's Disability Discrimination Act (DDA) and write a broad disability definition in such detail that judges would have a very hard time narrowing it. The Australian DDA covers anyone who has, once had, "may . . . in the future" have, or is believed to have any of the following: "total or partial loss of the person's bodily or mental functions," "total or partial loss of a part of the body," "the presence in the body of organisms causing disease or illness," "the presence in the body of organisms capable of causing disease or illness," "the malfunction, malformation or disfigurement of a part of the person's body," "a disorder or malfunction that results in the person learning differently from a person without the disorder or malfunction," or "a disorder, illness or disease that affects a person's thought processes, perception of reality, emotions or judgment or that results in disturbed behaviour."[93]

The Australian definition thus goes beyond the ADA's in several respects. First, like the original ADA bill, it imposes no substantial limitation requirement. Second, it includes not only present, past, or perceived impairments, as does the ADA; it includes possible future impairments as well. Third, unlike the ADA, it does not require that the impairment (or "disorder," or "malfunction," or "disfigurement," or "illness," and so forth, or organisms that cause or might cause these things) have any immediately harmful effect on an individual's body.[94]

Australian advocates certainly believe that the broader definition of disability in their DDA "is empowering, because individuals do not need to prove their outsider status in order to use the act."[95] These advocates argue that a narrower definition, which had been used in a number of pre-DDA state antidiscrimination laws, "creates unnecessary confusion and limits the effectiveness of the legislation."[96] The broader definition, by contrast, "affirms the individual's experience of impairment" and avoids the "anomaly" that an individual whom an employer rejects as too disabled for a job may be deemed not disabled enough to challenge the employer's action.[97]

But the Australian Productivity Commission's recent review of the DDA casts somewhat sobering light on this issue. While the statute's broad disability definition plainly does remove a barrier to the success of discrimination claims, it does not appear to have had as significant an empowering effect as its advocates might have wanted. Victims of disability discrimination remain extremely reluctant to file complaints under the Australian DDA. The tangible costs of pursuing a claim, the time it takes to do so, and the stress of participating in the complaints process are all likely reasons.[98]

Even if an Australian-style law would be more successful than the current ADA, one might doubt that such a law could actually be adopted in the United States anytime soon. The quick retreat from the broad ADA Restoration Act seems to confirm that doubt. There is a reason (in addition to their sincere agreement with these positions) why many American disability rights activists accepted an ADA that implemented a minority-group model of disability and why they sold that statute using an independence frame. A minority-group model of disability emphasizes the continuity between the ADA and earlier civil rights laws; it makes the ADA appear as the natural next step in the expansion of "We the People" marked by the civil rights movement.[99] For those who are not persuaded by that suggestion, the independence frame gives disability rights law a role that is different from (and more conservative than) other civil rights laws—the role of moving people off welfare and into work.

A universalist approach to disability rights is much more challenging to the status quo than are the minority-group model and the independence frame. Despite substantial assaults in recent decades, the background principle of American employment law remains the principle of employment at will. Unless they act on the basis of an individual's membership in an identifiable race, gender, or religious group, employers generally may refuse to hire people for whatever reason they prefer—rational or irrational. A universalist version of the ADA would impose a requirement of rationality on employers whenever they refuse to hire someone because of any present, past, or perceived physical characteristic. That would go far beyond existing intrusions into managerial prerogatives, and it is exactly what the Supreme Court seemed determined to resist in *Sutton*. Indeed, a universalist version of the ADA would go even farther than that; its accommodation requirement would demand that employers design physical and institutional structures (including work schedules and work tasks) in a way that reasonably takes account of the largest possible range of physical and mental abilities, and that they provide reasonable flexibility to all potential employees whose physical or mental abilities still are not taken into account.

That would be a truly radical change in American law. Despite the evident costs of not following the universalist course, it is easy to understand the choice of disability rights advocates to tie their cause to the mainstream liberalism of the civil rights movement and the neoliberalism and neoconservatism of the welfare reform movement. A case for a universalist disability rights law would be well worth making, but its prospects are very doubtful politically.

CONCLUSION

It is understandable that the Supreme Court's definition-of-disability decisions have generated controversy, yet much of that controversy is misplaced. Those decisions are deeply flawed, but the flaws do not belong to the Supreme Court alone. Instead, they flow directly from the minority-group model and the independence frame that disability rights activists themselves formulated and promoted. The definition-of-disability decisions highlight the limitations of these core disability rights concepts, but they also create a dilemma for disability rights activists. It is easy in theory to envision a more universalist ADA, but it is likely to be difficult to achieve it in the near term. To achieve it will require extensive *political* work, both within and outside of the disability rights movement. A mere statutory change, while welcome, is unlikely to solve the problem.

4

THE ROLE OF ACCOMMODATION IN
DISABILITY DISCRIMINATION LAW

In this chapter, I discuss the major legal innovation of the disability rights movement—the expansion of the concept of discrimination to include the denial of reasonable accommodation. As the previous chapters have shown, disability rights advocates urge that discrimination consists not just in overt unequal treatment but also in the failure to take account of people with disabilities in the design of the physical environment, social structures, and work routines. A requirement that employers and other entities provide reasonable accommodations to individuals with disabilities counteracts that kind of discrimination. Accordingly, accommodation mandates are the centerpiece of disability discrimination laws such as the ADA.

Most commentators have treated the ADA's accommodation requirement as something fundamentally different from and more intrusive than traditional antidiscrimination requirements. An antidiscrimination requirement, in its prototypical form, prohibits employers and others from taking protected-class status into account in their decisionmaking. But an accommodation requirement seems to demand the opposite—that protected-class status be taken into account.

As a result, many commentators have sought to draw a strong normative distinction between the ADA's accommodation mandate and the antidiscrimination requirements of the civil rights laws that emerged in the 1960s and 1970s. This move has been most obvious among those who are skeptical of the ADA. The following passage, from the economist Sherwin Rosen, is typical: "Fundamentally the ADA is not an antidiscrimination law. By forcing employers to pay for work site and other job accommodations that might allow workers with impairing conditions defined by the law to compete on equal terms, it would require firms to treat unequal people equally, thus discriminating in favor of the disabled."[1] Those who take this view believe that the ADA is essentially a redistributive scheme[2]—one that "distorts a civil rights measure into what is essentially a mandated benefits program for the disabled."[3] But it is not just critics who would draw a sharp contrast between accommodation and antidiscrimination requirements. Even supporters of the ADA argue that, unlike Title VII of the Civil Rights Act of 1964[4]—the canonical employment discrimination statute— the ADA allows protected-class members to "insist upon discrimination in their favor."[5]

Despite the obvious operational difference between antidiscrimination and accommodation requirements, I will argue that—*under the minority-group model that has had such a powerful influence on the interpretation of the ADA*—antidiscrimination and accommodation are very closely aligned normatively. But as was the case with the definition of disability, the normative support the minority-group model provides to the ADA comes at a price. Courts, seeking to assimilate the ADA's accommodation requirement closely to traditional antidiscrimination rules, have read the requirement so narrowly as to deprive the statute of much power to address the structural barriers that keep many people with disabilities out of the workforce. As applied to the definition of disability, the minority-group model kept the ADA from addressing the ways in which disability inequalities affect those who are not labeled "disabled." Here, the minority-group model keeps the statute from fully addressing the inequalities that affect people with conditions we would all consider "disabilities."

THE EQUIVALENCE OF ANTIDISCRIMINATION AND ACCOMMODATION UNDER A MINORITY-GROUP MODEL

In a narrow operational sense, antidiscrimination requirements are obviously different from the ADA's accommodation requirement. An antidiscrimination requirement demands that an entity treat similarly situated persons the same; the accommodation requirement demands that the entity give one class of persons something that it need not provide to others. But the two types of mandate are more similar than is immediately apparent. For one thing, the accommodation requirement often serves to counter hidden conduct that all would recognize as discrimination if it were conducted out in the open. Disability rights advocates commonly charge that employers accommodate the needs of workers without disabilities all the time; in many cases, it is only when a disabled worker asks for accommodation that the employer balks. In such cases, the ADA's accommodation requirement operates as a straightforward antidiscrimination rule.

In many other cases, the ADA's accommodation requirement does not operate so straightforwardly to eliminate what has traditionally been understood as discrimination. But even in those cases, the similarities between antidiscrimination and accommodation requirements are important under a minority-group model. Both types of requirement seek to counteract subordination and social stigma, and both types of requirement target conduct that violates the duty to avoid contributing to a subordinating system, at least where that can be accomplished at reasonable cost. Antidiscrimination laws commonly prohibit discrimination even when discriminating is bottom-line rational for the defendant. When interpreted according to a minority-group model, the ADA's accommodation requirement is at base just an example of that general prohibition on rational discrimination.

EQUIVALENT PURPOSES

Recall that the minority-group model posits people with disabilities as a subordinated class. It posits accommodation as a means to combat that subordination by promoting inclusion in workplaces and other important arenas of economic and civic life. Traditional antidiscrimination laws aim at the same goal. They, too, seek to dismantle a system of group-based subordination and the patterns of occupational segregation that support that system.

The point may be a surprising one. Most people tend to think of antidiscrimination law as targeting the paradigm case of racist animus (and animus against groups analogous to racial minorities). Such affirmative animus is irrational, and most people believe it to be "intrinsically immoral."[6] But we do not prohibit all irrational animus-based discrimination, and our failure to do so indicates that it is not animus but subordination that the law seeks to eliminate. Nor do we limit antidiscrimination protections to *irrational* discrimination; we prohibit rational discrimination as well, where it entrenches and instantiates racial subordination. Those key aspects of antidiscrimination doctrine demonstrate that antidiscrimination law aims at a wholesale, not a retail, injustice; it aims at dismantling subordination and occupational segregation.

THE FORBIDDEN CLASSIFICATIONS

A theory that sees civil rights law as targeting individual animus proves far too much. An employer can act on the basis of animus toward any number of characteristics or traits that are entirely unrelated to the protected-class status of an employee. An employer may have an irrational animus against people who are six feet tall, who are from St. Louis, or who root for the Blue Devils. If the moral problem addressed by antidiscrimination law is treating another as less morally worthy, then antidiscrimination law should extend to all of these arbitrary actions by employers. But it does not. Instead, it extends only to employer actions taken to harm individuals on the basis of one of the enumerated forbidden classifications (race, sex, religion, disability, and so on). Antidiscrimination law extends only to the forbidden classifications because it aims not at attacking individual breaches of the norm of ethical conduct so much as at attacking practices that entrench the systemic subordination of particular groups.[7]

One might argue that the limitation of antidiscrimination law to specific protected classes is less telling than that. Antidiscrimination law focuses on the protected classes, one could say, not because the moral principle it enforces is limited to discrimination based on protected-class membership but rather because legal interventions in private morality should be limited to serious social problems. Discrimination against St. Louisians may be just as immoral as discrimination against African Americans, but because it is not a significant social problem there is no justification for prohibiting it by law—with all the costs and inefficiencies that legal regulation entails.[8] Under this view, the essential immorality of race discrimination remains the animus-based devaluing of another human being. Although plenty of unregulated conduct violates the same moral principle, no moral principle can be legally enforced in every circumstance in which it might be violated. To say that we prohibit action that violates the anti-animus principle only when it leads to significant social harms, like class-based subordination, is not to say that we prohibit all action that leads to such significant social harms, regardless of whether it violates that moral principle. We could instead recognize two distinct conditions on legal intervention in private choices like discrimination: (1) the private choice must contribute to a significant social problem (to justify legal intervention at all), *and* (2) the private choice must be an immoral one (to justify placing the burden of regulation on this defendant).

It is far from clear that such a theory accurately captures what is wrong with discrimination on the basis of forbidden classifications, however. There seems to be widespread agreement that it is normatively worse to treat someone disadvantageously because of his race (and perhaps the other forbidden classifications) than it is to treat someone disadvantageously based on an arbitrary and idiosyncratic animus toward some other characteristic of that person.[9] The reason, I suggest, derives from the history that attends racial (and the other forbidden) classifications in our society and the resulting social harm that such classifications continue to cause. We prohibit racial discrimination not because it is a specific instance of a general moral problem of arbitrariness but because it is worse than the usual arbitrariness. What makes it worse are the societal effects it causes. As Professor David Strauss writes, "[I]t seems reasonably clear that the person-on-the-street basis for disapproving taste-based discrimination is that it is unfair to subject minority groups to the consequences of that form of animus."[10]

THE PROHIBITION OF RATIONAL DISCRIMINATION

That antidiscrimination law is generally limited to discrimination based on certain forbidden classifications certainly provides evidence that the animus-based theory does not account for the shape of antidiscrimination law. But there is more: the law pervasively prohibits protected-class-based discrimination even when it is rational and not rooted in animus. That prohibition of rational discrimination is a central component of antidiscrimination doctrine. The wide degree to which the law prohibits such discrimination reveals the law's strong premise that contributing to a system of subordination is itself immoral, at least insofar as an employer can avoid doing so at reasonable cost.

As David Charny and Mitu Gulati have observed, many of the "types of discrimination-based problems that we face now are different" from what economists call "taste-based animus."[11] One important present-day problem involves rational statistical discrimination, in which employers rationally use protected-class status as a proxy for lower productivity.[12] Such discrimination may then perpetuate itself by leading members of disadvantaged groups to make counter-productive human capital decisions.[13] Discrimination may also be motivated by the costs employers believe they will incur in the course of integrating a firm or in managing the conflicts that inevitably arise in a diverse workforce.[14] Although some of these costs might result from the need to respond to the discriminatory tastes of coworkers, others might result simply from the relative ease of enforcing informal workplace norms in a homogeneous workforce.[15]

Moreover, much disparate treatment "results not from discriminatory motivation, but from a variety of categorization-related judgment errors characterizing normal human cognitive functioning."[16] Recent empirical psychological research demonstrates that people in our society constantly make implicit, unconscious, group-based judgments about members of subordinated groups, and that those judgments persist even when explicit attitudes change.[17] Given those psychological findings, ceasing disparate treatment may require something more than simply abandoning an illegitimate preference; it may also require adopting some noncostless technique for cleansing one's decisionmaking of cognitive bias.[18]

None of these forms of discrimination involves animus or active prejudice on the part of the employer. In each of these cases, the harmful effect on minorities can readily be described as just an unfortunate consequence of the employer's pursuit of the surely permissible end of maximizing profit. The employer has no interest in harming minorities per se; if profits could be maximized without excluding minorities at the same time, the employer would happily do so. But under current law applying Title VII, the basic federal employment discrimination statute, all of these practices would constitute unlawful intentional discrimination. That result follows from *City of Los Angeles Department of Water & Power v. Manhart*[19] and *International Union v. Johnson Controls, Inc.*,[20] which hold that cost is not a valid defense to claims of disparate treatment under Title VII.[21] Pursuant to these holdings, it is clear that the law prohibits statistical discrimination even in cases where it is efficient for an employer to engage in that conduct (in the sense that race or sex is at least somewhat correlated with productivity, and a more individualized inquiry into a potential employee's productivity would be sufficiently costly to outweigh the benefit the employer would obtain from identifying productive workers more precisely).[22]

It seems apparent that the animus-based theory cannot justify the prohibition on rational discrimination. That prohibition is a well-entrenched and central aspect of our antidiscrimination laws in operation.[23] A theory that cannot account for such a significant aspect of our current doctrine can hardly be credited with providing the basic justification for antidiscrimination law.

"Rational" Discrimination as Hidden Animus? — Perhaps, though, one can rehabilitate the animus-based theory. Perhaps one can conclude that even if rational discrimination *need not* rest on judgments of differential moral worth, as an empirical matter it typically *does* rest on such judgments. That, essentially, is the argument that Paul Brest and Owen Fiss offered in their classic articles focusing on race discrimination. Fiss argued that truly rational discrimination is rare, so that purportedly rational discrimination will often be a mere pretext for animus.[24] Brest elaborated that "race-dependent decisions that are rational and purport to be based solely on legitimate considerations are likely in fact to rest on assumptions of the differential worth of racial groups or on the related phenomenon of racially selective sympathy and indifference."[25] Rational discrimination reflects "racially selective sympathy and indifference," in particular, when the decisionmaker would not engage in the same action, however rational, were the racial identity of the disadvantaged class different. This holds true whether or not the decisionmaker knows that he is being racially selective.[26] To Brest, racially selective sympathy and indifference is morally the same as affirmative animus, for unequal treatment that results from selective sympathy and indifference "could be justified only if one group were in fact more worthy than the other. This justification failing, such treatment violates the cardinal rule of fairness — the Golden Rule."[27]

But the analysis that Brest and Fiss offer rests entirely on an undefended empirical premise. Their argument is not that, as a logical matter, rational discrimination *necessarily* reflects an implicit judgment of moral worth. The argument instead is that rational discrimination *often* reflects such a judgment in practice. But neither Fiss nor Brest tries to establish how often rational discrimination reflects a judgment of differential moral worth. It is doubtful that they could do so, for the clear rational profit-maximizing explanation for such discrimination would confound efforts to uncover the employer's "true" motive. And indeed, Fiss concedes that "[s]erious questions can be raised" about the accuracy of the assumption that purportedly rational discrimination is typically just a pretext for racial animus.[28] Given the compelling evidence that discrimination is often (though far from always) rational, the assertion that profit-maximizing employers would not engage in it but for animus seems implausible.

Applied to unconscious discrimination, Brest's theory of "selective sympathy and indifference" takes us well beyond the typical animus/moral-worth theory of antidiscrimination law. A person who discriminates against another because of an unconscious bias is not making an affirmative decision that that individual is less morally worthy than another. Indeed, such a discriminator might honestly believe that the "victim" of discrimination is, and deserves to be treated as, an equal. That is the import of the recent literature in empirical psychology that demonstrates the persistence of implicit or unconscious biases even in individuals who believe that they value equality and the embrace of difference.[29] If the wrong of discrimination is the intentional devaluing of another's interests, discrimination based on (unconscious) selective sympathy and indifference hardly fits the mold.

Rational Discrimination as Impermissible Stereotyping? — There is another possible defense of the prohibition on rational discrimination and the related theory that selective sympathy and indifference is wrong: an antistereotyping principle. Such an argument would, like the animus-based theory, purport to identify conduct that is wrongful irrespective of its effects, but it would focus on a distinct moral flaw in discrimination. The argument would run like this: When an employer intentionally discriminates on the basis of a protected characteristic (race, gender, disability, and so on), he is making a judgment about all members of the disfavored class. He is thus acting on the basis of a stereotype about the group. Such a stereotype is no less a stereotype for being, on average, accurate, nor is it any less a stereotype for being applied unconsciously. A member of the disfavored race, sex, or disability group can legitimately claim that the employer did not treat him as an individual; the employer treated him as being defined by his race, sex, or disability without stopping to consider whether he was any different from the average member of that group. The employer has thus essentialized members of the disfavored group.[30]

But any effort to ground the prohibition on rational discrimination in an ethical objection to stereotyping is unpersuasive. Employers (like everyone else) treat individuals as members of groups all the time; we could not manage all of the information in the world if we did not act on the basis of proxies.[31] Unless we are going to say that we violate an ethical norm every time we treat a person as effectively defined by some seemingly salient characteristic, we cannot hold to a general principle against stereotyping. To justify the prohibition on rational discrimination, then, we must have a theory that explains why stereotyping on the basis of race, gender, disability, and so forth is different from all other stereotyping. One theory that plainly cannot justify the distinction, however, is the notion that racial, gender, or disability stereotyping somehow treats a person as less of an individual than does stereotyping on other bases. All stereotyping treats a person as a member of a group defined by some specific characteristics that do not capture the full range of that person's individuality.[32]

Thus, a more plausible theory for what makes stereotyping based on the forbidden classifications of race, gender, and disability worse than other types of stereotyping is that stereotyping based on those classifications causes greater harm to the groups that are persistently on the "wrong" side of society's stereotypical judgments. As Cass Sunstein writes, "[T]he most elementary antidiscrimination principle singles out one kind of economically rational stereotyping and condemns it, on the theory that such stereotyping has the harmful long-term consequence of perpetuating group-based inequalities."[33] Race, gender, and disability stereotypes are not likely to be idiosyncratic to a particular employer, nor are they likely to be limited to the employment context. When a person loses out on a job because of such a stereotype, that loss is likely to be only the tip of the iceberg. Similar stereotypes are likely to foreclose other jobs and opportunities in society. A person subject to such a stereotype is therefore likely to face stigmatic and cumulative disadvantage.[34]

Indeed, Fiss himself seems to rely on this point. Aside from the empirical assumption that purportedly "rational" discrimination is frequently a cover for animus, Fiss gives three reasons for prohibiting rational discrimination. First, the racial differences that make discrimination rational are themselves the product of earlier irrational discrimination (which, for example, denied opportunities and diminished incentives to develop human capital).[35] Second, "to the victim of the employment decision the appearance of the conduct is identical, whether the use of race is efficiency-related or not."[36] And third, an employer who has the power to work against the underlying problem of cumulative disadvantage, even if it involves "sacrifice," bears "some degree of responsibility" — especially where "[h]olding him legally responsible is not likely to impose crippling costs on any single businessman ('make him go broke,' as opposed to being unable to obtain that marginal dollar)."[37]

These arguments move us well beyond the moralistic focus on animus or the individualistic focus on stereotypes. Rather, they appear to rest on a notion that the primary justification of employment discrimination laws is to protect identifiable groups against practices that cause them cumulative disadvantage—a point Fiss more or less admits.[38] Thus, in Fiss's view, employers have an obligation to absorb the costs of refraining from rational statistical discrimination against African Americans because statistical discrimination merely perpetuates and entrenches the group-based inequalities that have resulted from prior discrimination (discrimination that has denied access to education and discouraged development of human capital) and imposes the same stigmatic group-based harm that irrational discrimination imposes. The law imposes sanctions on the discriminating employer because he would rather retain some personal benefit (be it the satisfaction of a taste for discrimination or the realization of dollars-and-cents profits) than avoid contributing to a subordinating system.

EQUIVALENT GOALS IN THE CASE LAW

Seen in that light, the connection between antidiscrimination and accommodation is clear. And indeed, commentators and judges have drawn the connection at least since the controversy over pregnancy accommodation in the early 1980s. As Lucinda Finley noted of that debate, "[m]ost feminists agree that one of the crucial issues to be addressed in order to eliminate the economic and social subordination of women [is how] to make the workplace more accommodating to pregnancy and parenting needs."[39] Those who argue for legally mandated workplace accommodations for pregnancy contend that such accommodations "place[] women on an equal footing with men and permit[] males and females to compete equally in the labor market."[40] The Supreme Court seemed to endorse the point in its decision in *California Federal Savings & Loan Ass'n v. Guerra ("Cal Fed").*[41] In *Cal Fed*, the Court upheld a California statute that required employers to provide (unpaid) maternity leave to women but did not require them to provide equivalent paternity leave to men. Rejecting a claim that Title VII and the Pregnancy Discrimination Act barred such "special treatment" of women, the Court reasoned that the state statute "promote[d] equal employment opportunity" and thus served the goal of equal access to the workplace that underlies federal antidiscrimination law: "By 'taking pregnancy into account,'

California's pregnancy disability-leave statute allows women, as well as men, to have families without losing their jobs."[42]

In the disability context as well, the Court has recognized that accommodation serves the goal of equal access to societal opportunities by helping to dismantle a structure of subordination. In *US Airways v. Barnett*,[43] which contains the Court's most extensive engagement with the ADA's mandate of reasonable accommodation in employment, Justice Breyer's majority opinion endorsed the notion of equal access by stating that the statute requires accommodations when they "are needed for those with disabilities to obtain the same workplace opportunities that those without disabilities automatically enjoy."[44]

The Court elaborated on the argument for assimilating accommodation to antidiscrimination in *Olmstead v. L.C.*,[45] a nonemployment ADA case. *Olmstead* involved the ADA's Title II, which prohibits state entities, in any of their operations, from discriminating against people with disabilities. The Court held that Title II's prohibition on discrimination requires states, as an accommodation, to house people with mental disabilities in community settings rather than congregate institutions in certain circumstances.[46] The state had argued that such a requirement of "reasonable accommodation" could not be derived from Title II's prohibition on "discrimination." The state contended that it had not provided community treatment to anyone who lacked a disability, so it could not have discriminated on the basis of disability when it denied such treatment to individuals who had disabilities.[47] But the Court rejected this argument and instead concluded that "unjustified institutional isolation of persons with disabilities is a form of discrimination."[48]

The Court gave two principal reasons for that conclusion. "First, institutional placement of persons who can handle and benefit from community settings perpetuates unwarranted assumptions that persons so isolated are incapable or unworthy of participating in community life."[49] And "[s]econd, confinement in an institution severely diminishes the everyday life activities of individuals, including family relations, social contacts, work options, economic independence, educational advancement, and cultural enrichment."[50] In other words, just as the core applications of antidiscrimination law are justified by the imperative to eliminate group-based stigma and to open opportunities for disadvantaged groups, the requirement of accommodation is justified on precisely the same grounds.[51] Although *Olmstead* did not involve discrimination in employment, its analysis translates readily into the employment context.

Seen from the perspective of the equal-access-to-social-goods argument that animates *Olmstead*, any assertion that accommodation is merely "redistributive" and therefore less morally justifiable than antidiscrimination[52] succumbs to a classic baseline problem.[53] If one wishes to say, as the critics do, that anti-discrimination law simply restores a just distribution but accommodation redistributes, then one must assume that any distribution reflecting intentional discrimination is unjust and therefore an inappropriate baseline for a determination of whether redistribution is occurring. Eliminating intentional discrimination thus restores a just distribution; it does not require redistribution from that normatively appropriate starting point. But that assumption begs the question. For if a distribution reflecting intentional discrimination is unjust and hence an improper baseline for determining whether redistribution has occurred, why can we not say the same thing about a distribution reflecting the creation of institutions inaccessible to people with disabilities (that is, one reflecting the lack of accommodation)? By this account, accommodation requirements (like antidiscrimination requirements) simply restore a just distribution; they do not "redistribute." Indeed, this is one of the central claims of disability rights activists and a key underpinning of the minority-group model.[54] Antidiscrimination and accommodation thus cannot be distinguished on the ground that one requires "redistribution" while the other does not—at least not without a normative argument explaining why (independent of the circular concept of "redistribution") intentional discrimination is unjust while the failure to accommodate is not.

EQUIVALENT MEANS

One possible basis for such a normative distinction involves the different ways in which antidiscrimination and accommodation requirements require employers to act. An antidiscrimination requirement demands that an employer disregard an individual's protected class status and treat that individual as he would anyone else. An accommodation requirement, by contrast, requires that the employer take account of an individual's protected class status and treat that individual in a way he might not treat anyone else.[55] We might therefore be tempted to say that antidiscrimination requirements prohibit certain wrongful acts, while accommodation requirements require employers "to act as Good Samaritans."[56] But invocation of the act/omission distinction can hardly solve the problem here. To the extent that the act/omission distinction has any analytic or normative traction in any context, it does not readily distinguish antidiscrimination from accommodation. If one accepts the act/omission distinction, there is a strong argument that discrimination—no less than the failure to accommodate—is best characterized as an omission rather than an act. The point is easiest to see in the case of hiring discrimination. As Matt Cavanaugh argues, "[A] policy of discrimination does look like a policy of merely omitting to give people something. 'We might happen not to hire any black or female applicants,' employers might say, 'but there is nothing to prevent them starting up their own firms. We wouldn't do anything to stop that—at least, we wouldn't treat them any differently than we treat our existing competitors. That proves we aren't actually trying to do black or female applicants any harm. We have just decided that they aren't going to get any help from us, which is a different thing altogether.'"[57] If hiring discrimination can be so readily characterized as the mere omission to give a benefit, it is hard to distinguish *on act/omission grounds* from the failure to accommodate.

This point connects to David Strauss's observation that antidiscrimination laws can easily be described as being not race- (or gender-) blind but race- (or gender-) conscious.[58] Employers use categorical statistical proxies all the time, but antidiscrimination law brackets out one set of proxies (those based on race, gender, and the other forbidden classifications) and prohibits employers from relying on the proxies in that set.[59] As Strauss argues in the race context, an antidiscrimination requirement "is race-conscious because it singles out race as a special characteristic and forces people to become conscious of race in a way they would not otherwise be."[60] Employers subject to such a requirement are "forced to be race-conscious" themselves: "[T]hey will be aware that racial groups are entitled to different treatment from other groups, because in dealing with them one must alter one's usual patterns of generalizing about people."[61] Accommodation requirements, of course, operate in exactly the same way: they require employers to exempt members of a protected class from the kinds of categorical judgments that employers make about other employees every day.

Even if an act/omission argument does not establish a normative distinction between antidiscrimination and accommodation, perhaps there is a difference of substance in the distribution of the costs of these two modes of civil rights law.[62] As the Supreme Court has emphasized, denial of accommodation is often paradigmatically rational conduct. In the many circumstances where the cost of accommodation makes a worker with a disability less net productive than other workers who are available to fill his position, an employer "could quite hardheadedly—and perhaps hardheartedly—hold to job-qualification requirements which do not make allowance for the disabled."[63] An accommodation requirement therefore imposes costs by requiring employers to act in a way that is (for them at least) irrational.

But this argument cannot distinguish antidiscrimination from accommodation requirements, for antidiscrimination requirements, too, demand that employers act in a way that is (for them at least) irrational. This point follows from the fact that antidiscrimination laws extend beyond prohibiting discrimination motivated by prejudice against, or ignorance of the productive potential of, members of a group.[64] As I noted above, the laws prohibit employers from engaging in intentional race or sex discrimination even when a rational, nonbigoted, purely bottom-line-oriented employer would engage in that conduct. As Christine Jolls has argued, these aspects of disparate-treatment law are "similar to an accommodation requirement in forcing employers to employ certain individuals even though they impose greater financial costs."[65]

Accommodation mandates thus do nothing more than present a special case of the general problem of rational discrimination. The discussion above suggests three basic justifications for imposing on employers the obligation to refrain from rational discrimination against members of subordinated groups. First, what purports to be rational discrimination may frequently be nothing more than animus-based discrimination in disguise. Second, even non-animus-based rational discrimination may reflect the phenomenon of "selective sympathy and indifference." And third, even where rational discrimination does not fall into one of the first two categories, it represents an employer's participation in constructing and maintaining the structure of occupational segregation that undergirds a system of subordination—participation the employer could avoid at relatively modest cost. Under a minority-group model, each of these arguments applies to cases involving the failure to accommodate.

Take animus and selective sympathy first. Many activists and scholars who have provided theoretical justification for the minority-group model hold the view that employers make individualized accommodations for people without disabilities all the time,[66] and that the accommodations required by people with disabilities are frequently no more burdensome or costly.[67] Indeed, the cases contain numerous examples of employers refusing to grant accommodations required by people with disabilities even though they have provided very similar accommodations to nondisabled individuals[68] and of employers refusing accommodations that would entail only de minimis costs.[69] In such cases, two explanations are overwhelmingly plausible. The employer's refusal of accommodation to the individual with a disability may rest on animus against people with disabilities. Alternatively, the refusal may rest on the failure to appreciate the degree to which the requested accommodation is comparable to accommodations the employer gives nondisabled employees all the time—a clear case of selective sympathy and indifference.

In many cases, of course, people with disabilities request accommodations that are clearly more costly than, or otherwise not comparable to, accommodations requested by nondisabled employees. If we expand the time frame of our analysis, though, it becomes apparent that even many of these cases involve selective sympathy and indifference. Requests for modifications to buildings and other physical structures provide the best example here. Physical facilities may be inaccessible to people with disabilities simply because nobody ever considered people with disabilities as possible users of those facilities—and not because it would have been costlier to build accessible structures in the first place.[70] That lack of consideration is the very definition of selective sympathy and indifference.[71] This point itself is in many cases connected to past animus-based discrimination: one reason nobody considered people with disabilities as possible users may be that many employers simply excluded people with disabilities from jobs outright.[72] Just as with intentional discrimination, the present-day failure to accommodate thus perpetuates and entrenches group-based inequalities that resulted from past discrimination. Although these accommodations are costly, the costs are really nothing more than the costs of providing a remedy for the failure to take account of people with disabilities at a time when it would have been essentially costless to do so.[73]

There are still many cases in which people with disabilities require accommodations that entail unique and significant costs and that cannot be deemed remedial in this sense.[74] Even here, however, the justification for accommodation requirements under the minority-group model tracks one of the justifications for prohibiting rational statistical discrimination: the employer is the only party in a position to dismantle the structure of occupational segregation that undergirds a system of subordination. At least where the accommodation "is not likely to impose crippling costs on any single businessman,"[75] mandating the accommodation fits comfortably within the duty to avoid contributing to a subordinating system (where such avoidance can be achieved at reasonable cost) that underlies the prohibition on rational discrimination. Indeed, the "reasonable accommodation" requirement, with its obvious allusion to the kind of "reasonable" care that is the touchstone of negligence law, implements that duty quite precisely.[76]

THE LIMITATIONS IMPOSED BY THE ANTIDISCRIMINATION ANALOGY

To this point, I have argued that (at least when read according to the minority-group model) the ADA's accommodation requirement is normatively quite similar, in its ends and its means, to a classic antidiscrimination requirement. Those who criticize the ADA for being too broad, expensive, and intrusive are therefore incorrect. But those who seek to integrate people with disabilities into the key areas of economic and civic life should not be satisfied, for antidiscrimination law is a very limited tool that lacks significant power to attack broad-gauged inequalities.[77] That is because antidiscrimination law is a fault-based regime that imposes on employers a responsibility to eliminate (some subset of) barriers to workplace equality that are understood to result in some way from an employer's own conduct.

For many people with disabilities, however, the barriers to full participation in the workplace are structural and difficult to attribute to the fault of any particular employer. Those barriers include the unavailability of personal assistance and assistive technology to help some people with disabilities get out of bed and to work in the morning, the lack of accessible transportation to the workplace, and the structure of our health insurance system (which drives people with disabilities out of the private insurance system and into programs such as Medicare and Medicaid that heavily penalize work).

By employing two key doctrines I will discuss in the pages that follow—the "job-related" rule and the access/content distinction—courts have assimilated the ADA's accommodation mandate very closely to traditional antidiscrimination requirements. In so doing, they have drained the accommodation requirement of significant power to eliminate the deep-rooted structural barriers that keep so many people with disabilities out of the workforce. These doctrines categorically exclude certain classes of accommodation from the purview of the ADA—even if the requested accommodations could be provided reasonably and without undue hardship. They do so by drawing on the notions of employer fault and duty that underlie more traditional antidiscrimination laws. As I demonstrate below, the evident limitations of the doctrine shed light on the underappreciated limitations of the minority-group model.

THE JOB-RELATED RULE

The job-related rule quite directly relieves employers of responsibility for alleviating broad structural barriers to the employment of people with disabilities. Under that rule, which has been endorsed by both the Equal Employment Opportunity Commission and a number of courts, the ADA requires employers to provide only those accommodations that are "job-related" and are not "personal item[s]."[78] Thus, an employer might be required to provide a disabled individual with an accommodation that "specifically assists the individual in performing the duties of a particular job" (so long as the accommodation is reasonable and can be provided without undue hardship).[79] But the employer will never be required to provide "an adjustment or modification [that] assists the individual throughout his or her daily activities, on and off the job."[80]

The job-related rule plainly rules out a number of accommodations that could be provided at reasonable cost and without undue hardship and that, while necessary to enable many individuals to work, also provide off-the-job benefits. For example, the rule excuses employers from any obligation to provide assistive technology that people with disabilities need to get to work—at least if that technology also helps them outside the workplace.[81] Nor need employers provide medical treatment or rehabilitation that would make an individual with a disability able to work,[82] paid leave to attend training for a new service animal that would enable an individual with a disability to come to work,[83] or training that would enable an individual to perform a new job when he has become unable to perform his old job because of a disability.[84] In all of these cases, the accommodation might enable an individual with a disability to work, and it might be provided at "reasonable" cost and without "undue hardship." But because the accommodation would also provide benefits that extend beyond the individual's relationship with his particular employer, the job-related rule excludes it from the ADA's requirements.

By similar logic, the statute does not require employers to provide the home-based personal assistance that many individuals with disabilities need to get out of bed and ready for work, because such assistance also enhances those individuals' independence more generally.[85] It bears emphasis that the problem here is not the expense or burden of personal-assistance services, which might be relatively cheap. The problem is that such services help the disabled individual off the job as well as on. When an individual with a disability needs the assistance of an aide in performing on-the-job tasks, an employer might well be required to provide it.[86] That is true even if the cost is substantial.[87] But an employer will never be required to provide aides who offer off-the-job help, no matter how inexpensive.

The EEOC and at least one lower court have gone even further and concluded that an employer's accommodation obligation does not even begin until the individual with a disability arrives at the workplace. Accordingly, the employer need not provide transportation to help the individual get to the workplace in the first instance.[88] The case law is not uniform on this issue, however.[89] But whether it affects access to transportation or not, the job-related rule represents a significant limitation on the accommodation requirement's power to disestablish deep-rooted structural obstacles to employment for people with disabilities.

THE ACCESS/CONTENT DISTINCTION

In addition to applying the job-related rule, courts have consistently employed what I will call the access/content distinction in adjudicating accommodation claims under all three substantive titles of the ADA: Title I, which prohibits discrimination in private employment; Title II, which prohibits discrimination by state and local governments; and Title III, which prohibits discrimination by places of public accommodation. These courts have held that an accommodation can be required only if it provides people with disabilities "access" to the same benefit received by nondisabled individuals; an accommodation that would alter the "content" of the benefit will not be required, even if it can be provided at reasonable cost and without undue hardship. In practice, this distinction has largely drained the statute of effectiveness in attacking what may be the single most significant employment barrier faced by people with disabilities as a group—the current structure of our health insurance system.

Although the ADA contains a specific safe harbor provision for certain insurance practices, the cases that have rejected ADA challenges to condition- and treatment-specific exclusions and benefits caps have not typically relied on that provision. Judge Posner's leading decision in *Doe v. Mutual of Omaha Insurance Co.*[90] is exemplary. The plaintiff, who had HIV, challenged AIDS caps that Mutual of Omaha had imposed on its health insurance policies. Defending the caps, the insurer made no effort to claim the protection of the safe harbor provision; indeed, it conceded that the safe harbor *did not* apply.[91] Despite that concession, the court rejected the plaintiff's ADA claim on the basis of the access/content distinction. Because Mutual of Omaha offered people with HIV the same product it offered everyone else (health insurance with an AIDS cap), the court concluded that it had not denied the plaintiff access to the goods or services it offered and therefore could not be liable under the statute.[92] In seeking to lift the AIDS caps, the court held, the plaintiff impermissibly sought to change the content of the insurance policies Mutual of Omaha offered.[93]

Judge Posner made clear that the access/content distinction was not an insurance-specific doctrine. Rather, it reflected a general limitation on the ADA's accommodation requirement: "The common sense of the statute is that the content of the goods or services offered by a place of public accommodation is not regulated. A camera store may not refuse to sell cameras to a disabled person, but it is not required to stock cameras specially designed for such persons."[94] Like Judge Posner, courts adjudicating ADA cases frequently say that an accommodation may be required only if it provides a disabled individual access to the same opportunity provided to others (the same job in the employment context, the same government benefit in the public services context, or the same good or service in the public accommodations context). If an accommodation provides nothing more than such access, then the defendant must provide it to the extent reasonable. But no accommodation will be required—no matter how reasonable—if it would alter the content of the opportunity the defendant offers generally.[95]

Although the insurer does not usually stipulate itself out of the ADA's safe harbor, *Doe*'s analysis is typical of the case law in this area. The cases have consistently rejected challenges to disability-related caps or exclusions on insurance, and they have typically done so on access/content grounds: so long as the insurer offers people with disabilities the opportunity to purchase policies on the same terms as everyone else, it has not denied them access to the benefit received by the nondisabled. That is true even if the policy terms cap or exclude coverage for specific disabling conditions, or for specific treatments that only people with disabilities can use.[96] The ADA has proven ineffective in challenging the limits on private health insurance for people with disabilities, and the access/content distinction has been largely responsible for that result.

LIMITING ACCOMMODATION AND ASSIMILATING IT TO ANTIDISCRIMINATION

The job-related and access/content rules serve a discernible agenda. Both operate to assimilate the accommodation requirement very closely to a classic antidiscrimination requirement. In that sense, they have a strong resonance with—though they were not the inevitable result of—the stark opposition disability rights advocates drew between antidiscrimination and charity or welfare.

As we have seen, the accommodation requirement seems on its face to take us far beyond a conception of discrimination as animus. That requirement demands that an employer bear a "reasonable" cost to alter its facilities and routines to promote the participation of people with disabilities—even if the employer clearly had a sound business reason for not making those alterations in the first place.[97] It may still be easy to see how the employer might have acted wrongfully when it failed to provide something like a wheelchair ramp that both is necessary to permit many people with disabilities to work at the employer's facilities and is something that only the employer is in a position to provide. But if an employer is required to provide personal-assistance services or transportation to enable an employee with a disability to get to work, or health insurance coverage that meets the employee's particular needs, the accommodation requirement seems much more like a requirement that the employer do something to "make up for" the disadvantage that people with disabilities experience because of broader societal decisions about the allocation of social services.[98]

Accommodation skeptics could readily see such a broad reading as presenting in particularly dramatic terms two of the basic challenges they have leveled against the requirement in general. First, such a reading requires an employer to bear a financial burden not because of any particular fault on its part but simply because of the fortuity that this particular worker with a disability applied for one of its positions.[99] Second, such a reading threatens to turn the accommodation requirement into an essentially standardless vehicle for ad hoc wealth redistribution to individuals with disabilities.[100]

But it is not just accommodation skeptics who might feel that way. The minority-group model itself imposes pressure to reject the broader reading of the accommodation requirement. The exponents of that model explicitly and emphatically rejected charity and welfare as responses to disability. They argued that it was only a denial of civil rights, and not the lack of charitable largesse, that kept people with disabilities out of the workforce. But the more that individual employers are required to counteract broad structural obstacles that they did not themselves create, the more it appears they are being required to provide charity.[101]

Both the job-related rule and the access/content distinction appear to respond to these concerns by limiting the reach of the accommodation requirement to circumstances in which the traditional justifications for antidiscrimination rules apply. The job-related rule rests on an implicit act/omission distinction in which employers can be held responsible for their "own" choices but cannot be required to make up for broader failures of social provision. Although that act/omission distinction is not especially convincing analytically, it is precisely the same kind of distinction that seems to underlie the requirement of intentional discrimination in equal protection cases.[102]

The access/content distinction seems to serve a similar function. Indeed, the Supreme Court has been quite open on the point: in *Alexander v. Choate*, the case that introduced the access/content distinction to disability discrimination law, the majority expressly stated that the distinction was necessary to "keep [the accommodation requirement] within manageable bounds."[103] The distinction limits required accommodations to those cases in which the defendant has imposed an obstacle that prevents people with disabilities from availing themselves of the same opportunities open to the nondisabled. Like the job-related rule, it assimilates the accommodation requirement very closely to an antidiscrimination requirement.

As I have argued in previous work, the job-related and access/content doctrines are formally indeterminate in substantial respects. Courts and advocates committed to broader social welfare provision for people with disabilities could easily read those doctrines in a way that would require employers to dismantle structural barriers to employment for people with disabilities. In particular, sympathetic courts could define the "benefit" at a higher level of generality—in the AIDS cap case, for example, as insurance that meets important health care needs—so that a wider swath of conduct is understood as denying "access" to that benefit.[104]

But the courts' current applications of these doctrines suggest that efforts to achieve social welfare redistribution through the ADA—a statute that bills itself as an antidiscrimination measure—will meet with substantial resistance. The accommodation requirement has the potential to serve as an open-ended tool of redistribution to people with disabilities, and judges uncomfortable with such a redistributive role will look for some principle to constrain and guide their application of that requirement. The current case law shows that they have, quite naturally, looked to settled tools of antidiscrimination law—including notions of employer fault and disparate treatment—for such a principle. So long as courts interpreting the accommodation requirement feel compelled to focus on the fault of individual employers, as opposed to that of society as a whole, that requirement will lack significant power to undo the deep-rooted structural barriers to employment for people with disabilities.[105] And so long as courts interpreting the accommodation requirement feel compelled to limit the statute's redistributive potential by employing the access/content distinction, the same desire to limit the ADA's sweep will likely lead them to continue to define the "content" of the relevant opportunity at a low level of generality. If they do, the ADA will remain virtually useless as a means of attacking the private insurance limitations that impose the greatest practical burden on many people with disabilities.

CONCLUSION

The ADA's accommodation requirement has been regarded as a "profound" innovation[106] that represents an effort to shift the baseline against which we measure "discrimination."[107] But my discussion in this chapter should demonstrate that any differences are at best ones of degree and not of kind. The accommodation requirement does shift the baseline of analysis somewhat, for it does not limit its scrutiny to those acts taken with the intent to discriminate; taking a wider view, the requirement asks whether an employer has reasonably accounted in its actions for potential employees with disabilities. But it serves essentially the same goals and uses means that are, as a normative matter, similar to those of traditional antidiscrimination law. And the job-related and access/content doctrines make the accommodation requirement even more similar to an antidiscrimination requirement. The job-related rule, like the intentional discrimination requirement, focuses attention on the responsibility of the individual defendant as opposed to that of society as a whole, and the access/content distinction, like a formal nondiscrimination rule, asks whether people with disabilities have been denied access to the same opportunities as similarly situated nondisabled persons.

Those who criticize the ADA's accommodation requirement as going well beyond traditional antidiscrimination requirements are wrong. But the similarity between the ADA and those antidiscrimination requirements is double-edged. Many of the most important contributors to disability inequality are deep-rooted and structural. Antidiscrimination requirements have little power to attack such structural barriers to equality. The minority-group model, which adopts antidiscrimination rules as the response to disability inequality, once again proves insufficient. As I explain in chapter 8, an effective response must go beyond antidiscrimination and accommodation to incorporate, in addition, a significant social welfare component.

5

DISABILITY AND SAFETY RISKS

Much disability-based discrimination is motivated by the fear of safety risks. Consider a few examples drawn from prominent cases filed under the ADA: A dentist refuses to treat a patient who has HIV out of fear that the disease will be transmitted by accident during the treatment process.[1] A truck company refuses to hire a driver with insulin-dependent diabetes out of fear that he will experience insulin shock and wreck his vehicle.[2] An oil refinery refuses to hire an individual with a chronic liver disease out of fear that toxins present in the plant's atmosphere will be dangerous to his health.[3] A manager fires a person with a mental illness out of fear that she will physically attack her coworkers.[4] These examples are not unusual. Indeed, a brief glance at the ADA and Rehabilitation Act cases decided by the Supreme Court shows that they are quite common.[5] Unlike in other areas of civil rights law,[6] disability discrimination law is repeatedly called upon to respond to intentional discrimination that is motivated by a concern for private or public safety.

These cases raise important questions for advocates of disability rights. Although those advocates have often sharply criticized professional communities for seeking paternalistically to dominate people with disabilities, professionals who assess and respond to risk can be important allies. But not all professional communities will be responsive to disability rights interests. As I will argue, current disability rights law ignores these complexities by broadly deferring to expert judgments about risk. It also unjustifiably permits employers to engage in their own form of paternalism. Some elements of the law's approach to risk-motivated discrimination take appropriate account of the important concerns that are present in this context, but disability rights advocates should find a great deal to criticize as well. As with the other issues I discuss in this book, the issue of risk-motivated discrimination highlights some of the key tensions within disability rights thinking. I explore those tensions in the discussion that follows.

PROFESSIONALISM AND PATERNALISM

In general policy debates concerning risk regulation, a populist, democratic position is often set in opposition to an expert, technocratic one. Scholars who advocate the technocratic position contend that members of the general public demand irrationally large investments to reduce risks to life,[7] are inconsistent in their treatment of numerically identical risks,[8] and often support policies that have the perverse effect of increasing aggregate risks.[9] The work of these scholars traces the irrationalities to systematic cognitive errors that affect the public's perceptions of risk: overestimates of small risks and underestimates of large ones; overreaction to prominent or sensational sources of risk; status quo biases, framing effects, and the irrational desire to eliminate all risk from a given source; and fear of "new" or involuntarily imposed risks even where other risks are just as great.[10] Technocratic risk regulation scholars have thus argued that the analysis and management of risks should be the responsibility of "expert" institutions attuned to "scientific" understandings of risk.[11]

But these technocratic arguments have come under fire from democratic risk regulation scholars. Those scholars contend that differences between lay and "expert" perceptions of risk do not reflect public irrationality so much as different value judgments. Democrats argue that people rationally distinguish among different risks based on differences of context—and that those contextual differences are the primary explanation for the supposed "irrationalities" identified by the technocrats.[12] Democratic risk regulation scholars respond to the difficulties with the technocratic position by urging deference to the value judgments of the public, both for reasons of popular sovereignty and because those value judgments seem normatively attractive on their merits.[13]

The democratic position is typically espoused by liberal supporters of health, safety, and environmental regulation. It also resonates strongly with many disability rights advocates' skepticism of professional communities.[14] One might, therefore, think that disability rights advocates would embrace that position. But matters are more complicated. A basic premise of American disability rights activism, as embodied in the minority-group model, is that people with disabilities constitute a socially stigmatized group. If the goal of disability rights advocates is to impose a check on the prejudices of the majority, then a regime that aims simply to transform the majority's views into policy seems instantly problematic.

Indeed, in a number of circumstances it seems quite difficult to disentangle the public's views about disability-related risks from the stigma that disability rights advocates aim to combat through such laws as the ADA. To the extent that people find disability-related risks more salient or "available," for example, that availability is likely to have a significant connection to the stigma and stereotypes that disability rights law aims to eliminate. Both the fear of HIV transmission during the height of the AIDS epidemic and the continuing fear of violence by workers with psychiatric disabilities clearly seem to fit this pattern.[15] Similarly, to the extent that people fear disability-related risks because they are thought to be new, that novelty is likely the direct result of past discrimination (discrimination that has prevented people with disabilities from working in allegedly risky settings).

Here, as elsewhere, skepticism of professionals and professional communities cannot be the whole story. Given the public fear of disability, it should not be surprising that at least some professionals will be more likely than the general public to support efforts to integrate people with disabilities into jobs and opportunities. But as I demonstrate below, not all professionals will be reliable allies in these efforts. The task for disability rights activists is to identify the professional communities that will prove reliable and to advocate for legal deference to those, and only those, communities. The law has, by this standard, deferred too broadly to professionals.

The context of risk-motivated discrimination also raises important questions about paternalism. As I discuss below, much risk-motivated disability discrimination stems from an employer's paternalistic concern that a person with a disability will hurt herself if she works on a particular job. Paternalism that denies opportunities to people with disabilities "for their own good," has long been a principal target of disability rights activists. But outside the disability context, the law governing workplace safety is pervasively paternalistic — it displaces the choices of workers to accept a premium for working in a risky environment by prohibiting employers from imposing certain risks. The task for disability rights advocates is to articulate a reason to treat disability-related paternalism differently from the general and widely accepted paternalism in this context. So far, the courts have ruled in favor of extending the general attitude of paternalism toward workers to the disability context.

THE ROLE OF PROFESSIONALS IN ASSESSING RISKS

If employers are ever permitted to exclude individuals with disabilities because of safety risks, two key questions arise: How much risk is enough to justify exclusion, and who decides? The Supreme Court has answered these questions by requiring a "significant" risk and deferring heavily to public health officials on the question. Although the Court's deference to professionals stands in some tension with the antiprofessionalism espoused by many disability rights activists, I will argue that deference in these circumstances actually serves disability rights goals. But extending deference beyond public health officials to frontline safety regulators—as the Court has done—does not serve those goals.

DEFERENCE TO PUBLIC HEALTH OFFICIALS UNDER CURRENT LAW

To balance the imperative of public safety with the obligation to eliminate unfounded stereotypes, the federal courts developed a set of principles under the Rehabilitation Act that have come to be known as the "direct threat" doctrine.[16] Congress subsequently codified that doctrine in the ADA (in a somewhat convoluted way that I will describe when it becomes important later in the chapter).[17] Unlike the bona fide occupational qualification doctrine applied in the sex and age discrimination areas, the direct threat doctrine does not allow employers to make a categorical judgment that a given disability is always unsafe.[18] Rather, the employer must engage in an individualized inquiry into the plaintiff's unique abilities, to determine whether it would be unsafe to hire her.[19] An exclusion must meet stringent standards: a perceptible risk—even of serious harm—is not enough; the risk must be a "significant" one.[20] And employers may not stop after determining that hiring the plaintiff would pose such a safety risk in the job as currently structured; they must also consider whether any reasonable accommodation could be implemented that would reduce the risk to insignificance.[21] The doctrine also protects people with disabilities against archaic stereotypes by requiring employers to rely on the best available objective evidence, and it ensures that incomplete information will not lead to exclusion by forcing the employer to bear the burden of proving the existence of a significant risk.[22]

The Supreme Court has not left judges and juries to their own devices in making the "significant risk" determination. Rather, the Court has said that "the views of public health authorities, such as the U.S. Public Health Service, CDC, and the National Institutes of Health, are of special weight and authority" in determining whether affording an opportunity to the plaintiff would pose a significant risk,[23] and that "courts normally should defer to the reasonable medical judgments of public health officials" on these questions.[24] If public health officials say it is safe to hire or serve a particular individual with a disability, the Court has said, that individual generally may not be excluded unless the defendant shows that the judgments of those officials are "medically unsupportable."[25] Although this rule of deference is not absolute,[26] it is strong.

The Supreme Court's rule of deference to public health officials stands in some tension with the skepticism toward professionals expressed by many disability rights advocates. But many disability rights advocates have supported that rule nonetheless. I believe that they are correct to do so. But that is because of the political balance of power in public health agencies as much as any generalized reason for deference to expertise.

THE ALTERNATIVE TO DEFERENCE: JUDGES AND JURIES DECIDE

In ordinary litigation, judges and juries have the responsibility for applying open-ended legal standards like "significant risk" to the particular facts. A natural first question to raise about the doctrine of public health deference, then, is why the ordinary practice should not apply in disability discrimination cases.

One reason should be obvious, for it played a significant role in molding the institutional structure for implementing Title VII of the Civil Rights Act of 1964[27]—one of the models for the ADA. Judges and juries may be especially susceptible to the public prejudices that lead to discrimination. The same prejudices and fears that lead a restaurant to determine that it is unsafe to hire people with HIV may also influence the judge or (particularly) the jury who decides that the restaurant acted properly in refusing to hire people with that condition.[28]

Prejudice aside, there is a structural reason for disability rights advocates to distrust significant risk determinations made by actors whose focus is limited to a single case with a single defendant. Judges and jurors might agree, when considering the question in the abstract, that trade-offs must be made between risks and opportunity—that just as we wouldn't spend $100 million to save one statistical life, we also wouldn't confine all people with HIV to unemployment to save one statistical life.[29] But when asked whether the particular defendant sitting in the courtroom should bear the risk, it is easy to ignore this more global analysis and treat any risk to life—no matter how small—as sufficient to warrant exclusion.[30] The identification of the party who must bear the consequences only exacerbates the "zero-risk mentality" that leads people to demand an elimination of all risk. Many HIV cases decided in the early and middle 1990s provide an excellent example of this mentality. They held that *any* risk of transmitting the disease—no matter how infinitesimal—was "significant" and therefore warranted exclusion. These courts argued that "'the victim of infection with this rare but fatal infection can hardly be consoled by the odds,' or '[s]urely it is no consolation to the one or two individuals who become infected . . . that they were part of a rare statistic.'"[31]

A strong rule of deference to public health officials can overcome the antirisk bias plaintiffs face in challenging risk-based discrimination. If juries are particularly likely to be influenced by community prejudices, and particularly unlikely to see beyond the facts of the particular cases before them, a rule of deference should seem especially apt. Under the Supreme Court's rule of deference, for example, the judge will take the case away from the jury if the consensus of public health officials is on the plaintiff's side and the defendant has not carried the heavy burden of showing that the consensus is "medically unsupportable." Such a rule imposes significant constraints on the judge as well, by requiring the judge to state with some certainty that the public health consensus is wrong, rather than allowing her to indulge her own zero-risk mentality.

PROBLEMS WITH PUBLIC HEALTH OFFICIALS

There thus appear to be substantial reasons for disability rights advocates to shy away from leaving the determination of "significant" risk to the unfettered judgment of judges and juries. But why should such advocates think that public health officials are any better?

One might attempt to answer this question in technocratic terms: the statute requires deference to public health officials because they possess the expertise necessary to undertake the "scientific approach to risk assessment."[32] But such a justification is quite problematic. Even if we assume that public health officials are uniquely capable of determining the "true" extent of the risk imposed by allowing a person with a disability to participate in a given opportunity, we still need to know something else: Is the risk worth running? That is at bottom a value question. Public health officials may have unique expertise in quantifying risks, but such expertise can give disability rights advocates no normative justification for vesting those officials with authority to resolve questions of value.[33]

The history of public health practice belies any notion that public health officials are apolitical "experts." Public health is as political as any other government activity. Indeed, people with disabilities would seem to have a lot to fear from a policy of leaving safety determinations to the public health "experts."[34] Public health officials have made almost astoundingly broad claims about the reach of their jurisdiction. Because virtually everything in life may have an effect on the public's health, the logic of public health imposes pressure to expand the scope of the enterprise to regulate virtually all human activities.[35] Within this potentially limitless jurisdiction, public health officials frequently have a range of discretionary coercive powers, including powers of involuntary isolation and quarantine.[36] And "[s]ome of the worst abuses against vulnerable groups have occurred in the name of public health."[37] Public health measures have been marked by racism, classism, homophobia, and the hysteria associated with whatever epidemic is most dreaded at the moment.[38] These problems do not lie wholly in the past. One might wonder, then, why many disability rights advocates believe people with disabilities will be well served by a regime that defers so strongly to "expert" public health officials.

DISABILITY RIGHTS AND THE
POLITICS OF PUBLIC HEALTH

Any justification for the doctrinal deference to public health officials must therefore start by acknowledging the inherently political nature of the public health enterprise. I believe that disability rights advocates can make a strong political case for public health deference in the disability discrimination context.

That the public health process is political does not imply that public health agencies simply reflect the inclinations of the broader community. For a number of reasons, the political balance of power in such agencies is likely to make them unusually receptive to the claims of people with disabilities. For disability rights advocates, then, the best justification for public health deference is that the deference rule allocates authority to adjudicate disputes over risk-based discrimination to an entity that is uniquely likely to act in a manner that furthers those advocates' integrationist goals.

Why might public health officials be particularly likely to take account of the interests of people with disabilities? One reason relates to institutional culture and professional norms—factors that can have a crucial effect on the actions of even the most political agencies.[39] Although public health officials come from a variety of professional disciplines, the institutional culture of public health agencies is distinctive in its central concern with the probabilistic nature of risks and harms. The epidemiological-probabilistic orientation of modern public health practice exerts a strong pressure on public health officials to gather enormous amounts of information from a variety of sources and then to tally up and weigh the society-wide costs of a proposed course of action against the society-wide benefits.[40] That tallying exercise itself operates as a guard against cognitive biases that might otherwise result in the unjustified denial of opportunities to people with disabilities.[41]

Moreover, the fear of driving risks underground has recently given public health officials a keen interest in eliminating unjustifiable discrimination against those who are believed to pose risks to others. Those officials have come to recognize that discrimination in this context is often quite shortsighted. Allowing doctors to refuse treatment to people with HIV (for example) might eliminate a (tiny) risk to the individual doctors, but only at the expense of creating greater risks to society as a whole (by, for example, depriving people with HIV of the care they need for opportunistic infections that may themselves be contagious, or by eliminating other opportunities to provide people with HIV the means to mitigate the risks they might pose to others).[42]

In addition, one of the aspects of public health agencies that may seem the most threatening to people with disabilities—the agencies' potentially all-encompassing jurisdiction—may ironically provide the greatest assurance that the interests of people with disabilities will be heeded. The point connects to the argument, advanced by prominent risk regulation scholars, that risk producers are likely to have disproportionately better access to the administrative process than are risk consumers. In this view, risk producers—often a concentrated group with a large stake in agency decisions—will typically have great ability to organize and attempt to influence an agency-run risk regulation process.[43]

That argument is typically framed as a critique of proposals to vest greater authority for risk regulation in administrative agencies. But advocates may find that the point cuts in the opposite direction in the disability discrimination context. If private market decisions are likely to be driven by discrimination against and undervaluing of the interests of people with disabilities, then disability rights law should operate as a corrective to that tendency. Allocating decisionmaking authority to an institution to which people with disabilities have disproportionate access is one way to correct the antidisability bias.

Because of the expansive, society-wide jurisdiction of broad-based public health agencies like the Centers for Disease Control and Prevention (CDC), people with potentially risky disabilities are particularly likely to have disproportionate access to them. People with potentially risky disabilities like HIV and insulin-dependent diabetes have an enormous stake in making certain that public health officials are fully informed of and sensitized to their conditions. If those officials overstate the risks, any particular person with such a disability will most likely be excluded from a very broad array of activities. Private employers or places of public accommodation, by contrast, lack a similar incentive to become involved in the public health decisionmaking process. If public health officials understate the danger associated with hiring or serving individuals with particular disabilities, any given private business—indeed, any given sector of the economy—is likely to bear only a small part of the risk. Depending on the impairment at issue, any given private business may be unlikely ever to encounter an individual with that condition.[44] People with disabilities (and disability rights organizations) therefore will have an unusually strong incentive to monitor and become involved in the decisionmaking processes of public health agencies.

And, indeed, that is exactly what happened during the first decade of the HIV/

AIDS epidemic, as Ronald Bayer has shown. Keenly attentive to the health costs of using coercive measures to attack the epidemic—even when those measures might have had some short-term payoff—public health officials rejected broad-scale mandatory HIV screening, opposed calls for mass quarantine of people infected with HIV, and generally shied away from targeted isolation of specifically identified infected individuals who deliberately engaged in repeated high-risk behavior.[45] Despite the array of coercive powers that were at their disposal, public health officials typically sought out alternative means of addressing the problem "even in the face of the challenge of individuals whose deliberate behavior posed a threat of HIV transmission."[46] As Bayer and Amy Fairchild-Carrino have noted, "public health officials from states bearing the greatest burden of the AIDS epidemic" tended to view restrictive measures "as a kind of 'fool's gold'—costly, time consuming, and ultimately of little public health significance."[47]

The restraint of public health officials was not limited to their own response to the epidemic. Rather, because unjustified discrimination against people known to have HIV threatened the public health regardless of who perpetrated the discrimination, public health agencies like the CDC took a strong stand against exclusion of people with HIV (or restriction of their activities) by schools and workplaces.[48] And public health officials remained in close contact with gay community groups and other representatives of people with HIV throughout this process. Nearly all observers acknowledge that this relationship had a significant effect on public health policy.[49]

To be sure, some have seen the public health response to the HIV epidemic as an example of unjustified capitulation to or capture by supposedly powerful gay rights and civil liberties groups.[50] Bayer himself criticizes public health officials for their apparent timidity in pressing policy positions at odds with those urged by gay community leaders in some instances.[51] But the overall picture of a public health establishment held captive to the desires of gay groups does not ring true.[52] For one thing, public health officials took positions opposed to those of gay community leaders on some high-profile issues in responding to the AIDS epidemic—notably the questions of blood donations by members of high-risk groups before the development of an effective HIV antibody test and of widespread HIV testing of members of such groups.[53] More fundamentally, when public health officials forewent coercive measures in their responses to AIDS, their position reflected less a capture by an important interest group than a hardheaded calculation that an epidemic spread by the intimate conduct of particular segments of the community simply could not be brought under control by measures that failed to pay attention to the interests of those segments of the community.[54] In many cases of risk-based disability discrimination, a similar dynamic is likely to play on public health agencies.

AGAINST TECHNOCRATIC
DEFERENCE TO "EXPERTISE"

I have argued that disability rights advocates seem correct to embrace the technocratic rule of public health deference as a means of advancing their goal of full integration of people with disabilities into our nation's civic, economic, and social lives. I have sought to explain the apparent inconsistency between this conclusion and the general hostility of disability rights advocates to technocratic arguments by pointing to factors specific to public health agencies that indicate that those entities are particularly likely to be solicitous of the interests of people with disabilities. But embrace of the technocratic rule of public health deference should not slide into an endorsement of technocratic decisionmaking processes more generally. Such a general endorsement of technocratic approaches would ignore the highly contextual and institution-specific nature of the disability rights case for public health deference.

The Supreme Court's decision in *Albertson's, Inc. v. Kirkingburg* provides an example of unwarranted deference to government "experts." In that case, the Court held that no "direct threat" inquiry was necessary when an employer refused to allow a person with monocular vision to work as a truck driver.[55] Federal Highway Administration (FHWA) regulations, in force since 1971, require drivers of commercial motor vehicles in interstate commerce to have corrected vision of 20/40 or better in both eyes. Although the regulations allowed the FHWA to grant waivers to people with monocular vision who had good driving records, and the FHWA had in fact granted the plaintiff such a waiver, the Court held that the employer was entitled to rely on the basic vision standard set forth in the regulation. Accordingly, the Court held that the plaintiff was not a "qualified" individual, and that he was not entitled to demand that the employer make an individualized showing that hiring him would pose a significant risk.[56]

Simply from the standpoint of proper interpretation of the ADA, the *Albertson's* opinion seems exceptionally problematic.[57] What is notable here, however, is the Court's willingness to defer to the FHWA's determinations regarding whether people with monocular vision could be excluded from truck driving jobs. Disability rights advocates could legitimately argue that deference to such frontline regulatory agencies, no matter how expert, is far less likely to advance their interests than is deference to public health agencies. Unlike with broad-portfolio public health agencies, people with disabilities are likely to have disproportionately little access to industry-specific or subject-matter-specific agencies like the FHWA. Such industry-specific agencies are most likely to be responsive to the concerns of the industry, labor union, and public interest groups (in this instance, safety advocates) that confront them on a daily basis.[58] And their organic statutes may bar them from considering (or be read to bar them from considering) the effect that their decisions will have on people with disabilities.[59] As a result, it seems quite likely that they will take actions that fail to account for—and may even affirmatively disserve—the interests of people with disabilities.

Paula Berg has illustrated this point by examining decisions made by the Occupational Safety and Health Administration (OSHA).[60] Berg identifies several instances in which the exclusive focus on the interests of employers and employees has led OSHA to disregard the interests of—and even encourage discrimination against—people with disabilities. Most notably, the agency allows employers to escape the most costly aspects of its tuberculosis (TB) standard if they simply forbid people with actual or suspected TB from entering their facilities. Such a rule serves the interests of employees without TB in OSHA-covered workplaces, but it encourages covered employers to exclude people with that condition—even in cases where reasonable accommodations could eliminate any safety risk.[61] A case like *Albertson's*, which holds that the regulations adopted by industry-specific or subject-matter-specific regulatory agencies displace the ADA's direct threat requirement, might simply encourage businesses to seek the promulgation of such regulations as a shield against ADA liability.

While public health agencies "such as the U.S. Public Health Service, CDC, and the National Institutes of Health"[62] appear to possess institutional attributes that make them particularly likely to take seriously the interests of people with disabilities, there is strong reason to believe that other regulatory agencies do not. Disability rights advocates should pause, then, before allowing their embrace of the technocratic rule of public health deference to extend unquestioningly to deference to other "expert" agencies.

PATERNALISM AND RISKS TO THE PERSON WITH A DISABILITY HERSELF

One type of risk-motivated discrimination presents unique questions—discrimination on the basis of a fear that a person with a disability will injure herself alone. Ought the employer be permitted to substitute its judgment about the risk for that of the individual with a disability? Even if the employer is correct about the extent of the risk, can the employer decide that a job is too risky for an individual with a disability over the objection of the individual herself? The Supreme Court addressed this question in *Chevron U.S.A., Inc. v. Echazabal*,[63] and it came down squarely on the side of employer paternalism. As I will show, there are strong arguments that the *Chevron* decision was wrong as a matter of formal legal analysis. That decision also failed to heed, inappropriately in my view, the generally antipaternalistic approach taken by most disability rights activists.

PATERNALISTIC DISCRIMINATION AND THE LAW

The *Chevron* case was brought by Mario Echazabal, who had chronic liver disease.[64] Chevron rejected his application for a position at its refinery because it believed that exposure to the hepatotoxic substances present in the workplace environment would pose a risk of further liver damage.[65] The case presented the question of whether an employer could reject an applicant on the ground that employment would pose a direct threat to the health or safety of the applicant himself.[66] As a formal legal matter, the answer to that question required a rather technical consideration of the convoluted structure of the ADA's employment title.

Although the statute provides a defense to an employer that refuses to hire an individual who presents a "direct threat,"[67] the provisions establishing that defense are not straightforward. The statute requires plaintiffs to prove, as a threshold matter in all ADA employment cases, that they are "qualified" for the position they seek—that is, that they "can perform the essential functions of the employment position."[68] This requirement, which seems to focus entirely on the present ability to perform job tasks, says nothing about safety risks. Rather, safety risks are treated under the section of the statute that establishes defenses.[69] That section first provides, in a generally phrased provision, a defense for "qualification standards" that are "job-related and consistent with business necessity."[70] The statute then provides that "[t]he term 'qualification standards' may include a requirement that an individual shall not pose a direct threat to the health or safety of other individuals in the workplace."[71] According to the statutory definition, "[t]he term 'direct threat' means a significant risk to the health or safety of others that cannot be eliminated by reasonable accommodation."[72] ADA Title I thus establishes the "direct threat" defense not through a provision creating the defense in its own right but as a gloss on the general defense for "qualification standards."

The statutory "direct threat" provision says nothing about risk to the health or safety of the disabled employee herself; both it and its companion definitional provision speak exclusively of risks posed to "others."[73] But the EEOC adopted a regulation that extended the direct threat defense to cases in which the employee with a disability poses a risk only to herself.[74] Echazabal argued the EEOC's threat-to-self regulation was inconsistent with the limited language of the statutory direct threat provision.[75] The absence of threat-to-self language from the statute was particularly telling, Echazabal argued, because the EEOC's regulations interpreting the Rehabilitation Act—the predecessor statute to the ADA— explicitly included such language.[76] By rejecting the threat-to-self language of the earlier EEOC regulations, Echazabal contended, Congress made a clear decision to adopt the same rule that applies under Title VII, which forbids an employer from excluding protected-class employees for their own safety. (The issue came up most prominently in cases challenging employers' exclusions of women from jobs thought to be too risky for them.)[77] Such a decision would be in keeping with the recognition in statutory findings and legislative history that, just as it was with women before the enactment of Title VII, paternalistic exclusions had been a major contributor to the disadvantage experienced by people with disabilities.[78]

The Court rejected that argument. It began by stating that the terms "job-related and consistent with business necessity" establish "spacious defensive categories, which seem to give an agency (or in the absence of agency action, a court) a good deal of discretion in setting the limits of permissible qualification standards."[79] Given the permissive language of the direct threat provision (namely, "may include"), the Court concluded that a requirement that an employee not pose significant risks to others was merely an example of the qualification standards that might be embraced by the statute's general business justification provision.[80] The Court held that the EEOC permissibly interpreted that general business justification defense to include cases where the employee would pose a significant risk to his own health.[81]

But the inclusive language of the direct threat provision is hardly dispositive: what Congress includes also gives a clue as to what Congress excludes. Can there be any doubt, for example, that by saying qualification standards "may include" a requirement that the employee pose no "direct threat" or "significant risk," Congress prohibited employers from refusing to hire individuals with disabilities based on indirect threats or insignificant risks?[82] The carefully crafted textual limitations in the direct threat provision, coupled with the express statutory purpose of eliminating discrimination based on "stereotypic assumptions,"[83] strongly imply that the circumstances in which a safety-risk defense may be asserted are limited to those involving a "direct threat" and a "significant risk." Similarly, one can make a strong argument that the textual limitation of the direct threat provision to cases involving risks to others, when considered in the light of the prohibition of paternalistic discrimination under Title VII[84] and Congress's recognition of paternalism as a major target of the ADA, implies a clear rejection of the EEOC's earlier endorsement of a threat-to-self defense under the Rehabilitation Act.

The Court answered this point by arguing that in the law prior to the enactment of the ADA, there was no "clear, standard pairing of threats to self and others" such that the inclusion of a defense for one in the statute would ordinarily be taken to imply an exclusion of a defense for the other.[85] Indeed, the Court asserted, the threat-to-self language in the EEOC's Rehabilitation Act regulation itself represented an effort to give content to the Rehabilitation Act's own direct threat language—language that, like the ADA's direct threat provision, applied by its express terms only in cases involving a threat to others: "Instead of making the ADA different from the Rehabilitation Act on the point at issue, Congress used identical language, knowing full well what the EEOC had made of that language under the earlier statute."[86]

But both steps of that argument are flawed. First, there has indeed been a long-standing "pairing of threats to self and others"[87] in disability law—most notably in the law governing civil commitment. "General civil commitment statutes ordinarily require mental illness and dangerousness to self or others as criteria of commitment."[88] When the normative justification for involuntary commitment based on "dangerousness to self" has been challenged, the challenges have been framed and understood as attacks on paternalism.[89]

Second, the Court was simply wrong to assert that the EEOC's threat-to-self regulation under the Rehabilitation Act represented an interpretation of the direct threat language in that earlier statute. To the contrary, that regulation expressly purported to interpret the Rehabilitation Act's requirement that the plaintiff be "qualified" for the position she seeks[90]—while the statutory direct threat provisions appeared in a portion of the statute that defined the term "handicapped person."[91] Indeed, the EEOC's Rehabilitation Act regulation had a far broader scope than the direct threat provisions that existed in that earlier statute. The statutory provisions expressly applied only to two classes of people with disabilities: (1) alcoholics or drug abusers "whose employment, by reason of such current alcohol or drug abuse, would constitute a direct threat to property or the safety of others"[92]; and (2) individuals with a "currently contagious disease or infection," who, "by reason of such disease or infection, would constitute a direct threat to the health or safety of other individuals."[93] The EEOC's Rehabilitation Act regulation applied to all individuals with disabilities who posed risks to themselves or others—not just alcoholics, drug abusers, and people with contagious diseases.[94] Moreover, the Rehabilitation Act's two direct threat provisions were not adopted until after the EEOC had promulgated its regulations.[95] It is therefore implausible to suggest that the EEOC's threat-to-self regulation in any way interpreted the direct threat language in that statute.

Thus, by defining the term "qualified individual with a disability" in the ADA solely by reference to present abilities to perform job tasks,[96] Congress removed the statutory basis on which the EEOC had rested its threat-to-self regulation. Congress moved consideration of safety risks from the threshold "qualified individual" inquiry, where the EEOC's Rehabilitation Act regulation had put it, to the new general direct threat defense. And Congress expressly tailored that defense—in contrast to the EEOC's earlier approach—to cases involving threats to others. When viewed in this light, the omission of threat-to-self language from the ADA seems far more telling than the *Chevron* opinion suggests.

PATERNALISTIC DISCRIMINATION AND DISABILITY RIGHTS IDEALS

There is a decent argument, then, that the Court got the law wrong in *Chevron*. And the Court's decision clearly ran counter to positions broadly held by disability rights activists. As the discussion in chapter 2 demonstrated, virtually all participants in the disability rights movement have united in their opposition to paternalism—to nondisabled people acting to deny opportunities to people with disabilities "for their own good." But that consensus among disability rights activists can obscure a tension among different bases for opposition to paternalism. *Chevron* is an ideal vehicle for exploring that tension.

As I explained in chapter 2, the dignity of risk is a central notion for many disability rights activists. But that notion can be expressed in more libertarian or more egalitarian ways. As chapter 2 shows, the libertarian version played a crucial part in the campaign to enact the ADA, and it was probably key to at least some of the support the ADA received from conservative Republicans. That version suggests that dignity inheres in making one's own choices about the risks one should assume. Permitting someone else to decide what risks an individual can take thus disrespects that individual's autonomy.

Note that, in the libertarian version of the dignity-of-risk argument, there is nothing particularly special about people with disabilities. It would be just as inconsistent with autonomy to deny a nondisabled person the right to choose what risks she will assume. But, of course, the law denies individuals that right to choose all the time. Modern occupational safety law, exemplified by the Occupational Safety and Health Act (OSH Act), requires employers to comply with any number of health and safety standards. The law does not permit workers to consent to violations of these standards. Thus, it forbids workers to negotiate a premium for working in risky conditions. Two basic justifications have been offered for this rule. Some contend that workers face an imbalance of bargaining power, and that their decisions to work in risky conditions, even for a premium, are not truly voluntary.[97] Others place less emphasis on voluntariness and bargaining power; they simply argue that some choices are sufficiently harmful for them to be denied to individuals.[98] Either way, modern occupational safety law seems to violate the libertarian version of the dignity-of-risk principle.

For this reason, a number of commentators have seen the position taken by disability rights activists in the *Chevron* case as a direct challenge to modern occupational safety law—and indeed, the entire structure of modern public health policy. Ronald Bayer has made this argument in its strongest form. Criticizing those who advocated for Mario Echazabal,[99] Bayer contends that their position entailed a "root-and-branch rejection of paternalism" that "reflected a fundamental rupture with a central tenet of labor legislation."[100] He finds it troubling that "organizations with a long history of struggling to protect the interests of the vulnerable have embraced the antipaternalism that is more typically given voice by the proponents of privilege."[101] That situation, he concludes, "not only suggests the profound influence of individualism in American culture but also reveals the tension between that influence and a robust view of social justice."[102]

If the dignity-of-risk argument takes a libertarian form, then Bayer's points are well taken. The libertarian dignity-of-risk argument would call occupational health and safety legislation into question, and it clearly is in tension with a robust view of social justice. This should not be surprising. Libertarian approaches, by their very nature, conflict with efforts to use government power to achieve social justice. Indeed, even though libertarian-conservative arguments were a key part of the campaign to pass the ADA, acceptance of those arguments will, as I showed in chapter 3, limit the reach of the ADA itself.

But one need not read the dignity-of-risk argument as reflecting a libertarian concern with individual autonomy or a generic antipaternalism. The dignity-of-risk argument might instead reflect a practical egalitarianism. In this view, the problem is not paternalism per se; the problem is paternalistic *discrimination*. The problem is singling out a particular, historically disadvantaged class of people for exclusion based on safety concerns. When "individuals with disabilities [a]re being deprived of the opportunity to assume the standard workplace risks that others [a]re permitted to assume,"[103] history gives reason to be concerned that prejudice and stereotypes, rather than careful, dispassionate analy-

sis, are motivating the exclusion. Concern with such paternalistic discrimination does not in the least call into question paternalistic laws that set minimum
workplace standards that apply across the board to all workers.

This point was not novel to the disability rights movement. To the contrary,
it had been the basis for the feminist campaign against sex-specific protective
labor legislation after the enactment of the Civil Rights Act of 1964. States had
adopted a number of different kinds of laws targeting women for special labor
protections. In an article published shortly after the Civil Rights Act's enactment, Pauli Murray and Mary Eastwood described some major categories of
these laws: "[L]aws prohibiting the employment of women in certain occupations, such as employment in bars and mines; maximum hour laws for women;
minimum wage laws for women; laws prohibiting the employment of women
during certain hours of the night in certain industries; [and] weight lifting
limitations for women."[104] Those laws had a tremendously harmful effect on
women's opportunities to participate independently in economic life. But they
were justified as protecting women from physical risks, among other things.

The Supreme Court offered such a justification in *Muller v. Oregon*,[105] which
upheld sex-specific protective legislation at a time when the Court was invali-
dating more general regulations of the employment relationship as violating
freedom of contract: "That woman's physical structure and the performance
of maternal functions place her at a disadvantage in the struggle for subsistence
is obvious. This is especially true when the burdens of motherhood are upon
her. Even when they are not, by abundant testimony of the medical fraternity
continuance for a long time on her feet at work, repeating this from day to day,
tends to injurious effects upon the body, and, as healthy mothers are essential to
vigorous offspring, the physical well-being of woman becomes an object of public interest and care in order to preserve the strength and vigor of the race."[106] As
feminist activists and lawyers demonstrated, *Muller*'s analysis was entirely typical. Sex-specific protective laws typically rested on overbroad, false, and often
ridiculous stereotypes in exactly the same way.[107] And courts applied *Muller*
itself to justify "jury exclusion, differential treatment in licensing occupations,
and the exclusion of women from a state-supported college."[108]

When feminists challenged state protective laws, and later extended their challenge to employers' own policies that paternalistically excluded women from
particular jobs on safety grounds,[109] they were not challenging "central tenets of
labor law" or taking the side of "proponents of privilege."[110] Still less were they
choosing "individualism" over "social justice."[111] To the contrary, they were seeking equality of opportunity and attacking policies that singled out women for

exclusion on the basis of safety concerns—concerns that typically were either based on stereotypes or equally applicable to men who were not excluded.

Bayer discusses the feminist campaign against protective labor legislation.[112] He does not criticize that campaign per se. But he does not appear terribly sympathetic to it, either. Thus, in criticizing "organizations with a long history of struggling to protect the interests of the vulnerable" for having "embraced the antipaternalism that is more typically given voice by the proponents of privilege" in the *Chevron* case, Bayer laments "[h]ow long a distance had been traveled" since *Muller*.[113] But if one accepts the feminist challenge to protective labor legislation, one will not see *Muller* (as Bayer appears to) as a case of "social justice" trumping "individualism."[114] Rather, one will see *Muller* as a case in which the Court blessed a regime that, in the name of protecting women from harm, denied them, on the basis of sexist stereotypes, the same economic opportunities that were available to men. To reject *Muller*, then, is not necessarily to reject paternalistic occupational health and safety rules that govern an employer's treatment of *all* of its employees. Nor is it to reject "social justice." Most people would contend that the feminist campaign against sex-specific protective legislation struck an incredibly important blow *for* social justice. On the egalitarian antipaternalist view, disability rights advocates sought the same thing in *Chevron*.

Even accepting that the antipaternalism of disability rights advocates follows that of feminist advocates in being rooted in egalitarianism rather than libertarianism, one might attempt to salvage Bayer's argument by contending that disability is different from sex. We might find stereotypes about women as weaker and more likely to harm themselves on the job ridiculous. But disability-based stereotypes may resonate more strongly. Don't disabilities often in fact make people more likely to injure themselves? (Notice that this is a variation of the argument, discussed in the previous chapter, that unlike in the race and sex context it is often rational to discriminate on the basis of disability.)

There is good reason to think that disability is not so different, however. Fears that people with disabilities will injure themselves on the job are typically overblown, and the risk is often nonexistent. (It certainly was in *Chevron*: on remand from the Supreme Court's decision, the court of appeals ruled that Mario Echazabal had presented "evidence that there was no scientific basis" for the company's conclusion that working in the refinery would pose a risk to his health and that the district court had erroneously granted summary judgment to the company.)[115] Norman Daniels has astutely pointed out the implications of the widespread stereotypes about disability. Allowing employers to show that an employee with a disability will "in fact" injure himself or herself could, he says, "end up providing an individualized, scientific cover to stereotyping and thus discrimination. Who will be forced to undergo such risk assessment, and what kinds of bias will be brought to that task?"[116] To respond to that prospect by forbidding paternalistic discrimination is not at all to undermine the basis for occupational safety regulation — even paternalistic occupational safety regulation.

The threat-to-self context is yet another area in which the differences among disability rights advocates matter. Those who take a more individualistic or libertarian view of the dignity-of-risk concept will have a hard time explaining why their position does not call into question all of modern occupational safety regulation. Those who take a more egalitarian view of the concept will have a much easier time, though they still will confront difficulties in persuading people that disability-based stereotypes are often false.

CONCLUSION

The problem of risk-motivated discrimination offers an ideal context in which to explore the tensions within disability rights thinking. In particular, it demonstrates the value and limits of skepticism of professional communities. It also highlights a fault line between two ways of giving content to an antipaternalist concern with the dignity of risk. The next chapter considers another legal context that offers additional light on these and other tensions within the disability rights movement's antipaternalism.

6

DISABILITY, LIFE, DEATH, AND CHOICE

In the previous chapter, I examined some of the complexities of the disability rights movement's antipaternalism by considering two very different ways of cashing out the notion of the "dignity of risk." In this chapter, I will examine a set of issues on which disability rights advocates have in some cases clashed publicly with one another—with both sides invoking the notion of antipaternalism. That set of issues involves life-and-death questions such as whether to treat newborns with disabilities and whether terminally ill adults should have the right to obtain assistance in suicide. When such issues are discussed in American public discourse, the question of abortion rights often lurks close by. So it is here. As the Theresa Schiavo case highlighted in 2005, on these life-and-death issues a fair number of very vocal disability rights activists—many of whom consider themselves to be neither conservative nor opponents of abortion rights—have joined forces with antiabortionists against supporters of abortion rights.

Of particular import for my argument, the disability rights advocates who have allied themselves tactically with antiabortion advocates explicitly invoke the principle of antipaternalism. These disability rights advocates embrace the principle of "choice," but they contend that societal stigmas and other social pressures effectively coerce people into making decisions that reflect biases against people with disabilities. On assisted suicide, for example, these advocates believe that a flat ban on the practice is necessary to protect people with disabilities against the paternalism of family members, medical professionals, and insurance companies.

Once the issue is framed this way, however, the antipaternalist position loses much of its analytic (and political) traction. To prohibit the exercise of a choice based on the presumption that people with disabilities will be unable to resist

pressure to make the "wrong" choices can itself quite plausibly be characterized as paternalistic. And, indeed, a number of vocal disability rights advocates
(who probably represent a minority of disability rights advocates but a majority of
people with disabilities) have argued in favor of the right to assisted suicide based
on the same principle of antipaternalism that drives disability rights opponents
of the practice.

The life-and-death issues I discuss in this chapter thus highlight an important tension within the disability rights movement's notion of antipaternalism.
But the issues have much broader resonance as well, because of their connection with abortion rights. Just as they have in the assisted suicide context, many
disability rights advocates have argued that social pressures and stigmas weigh
heavily on pregnant women who undergo prenatal testing that reveals a fetal
disability. Although these women might, if fully informed, choose to carry their
fetuses to term, many disability rights advocates contend that the paternalistic
interference of medical professionals overrides their choices. Most of those advocates have pointedly refrained from advocating any *regulation* of prenatal testing
or disability-selective abortion, however.

Even if most disability rights advocates do not seek to regulate abortions, their
arguments provide a tool that antiabortion activists can use to seek such regulation. As I show in this chapter, current Supreme Court abortion doctrine—particularly since the Court's 2007 decision in *Gonzales v. Carhart*—practically
invites antiabortion activists to justify regulation on the "pro-choice" ground
that it overcomes private and social obstacles to "truly" free choice. That prospect presents a dilemma for the many disability rights advocates who are firm
supporters of abortion rights. Although the logic of their critique of selective
abortion might seem naturally to justify regulation of that practice—just as they
believe that the parallel critique justifies a ban on assisted suicide—disability
rights advocates cannot endorse regulation in the abortion context without setting a precedent that may be applied to scale back abortion rights in areas that
go far beyond disability.

In the remainder of this chapter, I explore these issues with an eye to what they
can tell us about the antipaternalist principle articulated by so many disability
rights advocates. I begin by closely examining the arguments of those disability
rights advocates who, although they support abortion rights, have tactically allied
with antiabortion forces in controversies over the nontreatment of newborns
with disabilities, assisted suicide and "letting die," and (to a lesser extent) prenatal testing. I then highlight the stakes of the position of these disability rights
advocates by showing how—even if they do not seek this result—their position
could readily be used under current doctrine to justify significant restrictions on

abortion. Finally, I explore the views of those disability rights advocates who have defended the right to assisted suicide.

INTERSECTIONS BETWEEN DISABILITY RIGHTS AND ANTIABORTION ADVOCACY

In three related issue areas, a number of prominent disability rights advocates have allied themselves with either arguments or policy prescriptions associated with the antiabortion movement. In each of these three areas—the withholding of treatment from newborns with disabilities, physician-assisted suicide and the "right to die," and prenatal testing for fetal disability—disability rights advocates have challenged practices that are also the targets of antiabortion advocates. But they have done so on the basis of a distinctively disability-oriented argument—one that many of them believe does not entail opposition to abortion rights generally. In each of these areas, disability rights activists contend that the challenged practices reflect discriminatory attitudes about disability, and that any "choice" will not be a free one in light of social pressures, particularly those imposed by powerful professional cultures. I label that position the "disability rights critique."

By referring to *the* disability rights critique, however, I do not mean to imply that the set of arguments I explore in this part of the chapter represents the only position within the disability community. To the contrary, I intend to show that there is no single consensus disability rights position on these matters. The life-and-death issues that are the subject of this chapter are among the most contentious among disability rights advocates. I consider here the views of those disability rights advocates who take positions that intersect with those of abortion opponents, before turning, at the end of the chapter, to the views of those disability rights advocates who disagree with them.

SELECTIVE REFUSAL TO TREAT INFANTS WITH DISABILITIES

Disability rights activists first seriously allied themselves with abortion opponents in the early 1980s.[1] The occasion was a set of cases known as the "Baby Doe" cases, which involved challenges to the denial of treatment to infants with disabilities who had life-threatening medical conditions.[2] The Bloomington, Indiana, case, which commenced in 1982, was the first to draw significant political and legal attention to the issue, and its facts are representative. The case involved a child who was born with Down syndrome, as well as a tracheoesophageal fistula (a condition in which the upper part of his esophagus was not connected to the lower part of his esophagus). Surgery to connect the esophagus had a high prospect of success, and the baby was sure to die without the surgery. The obstetrician who delivered the baby "pointed out to the parents that if the surgery were performed and if it were successful and the child survived, that this still would not be a normal child. That it would still be a mongoloid, a Down [s]yndrome child with all the problems that even the best of them have." Based on the obstetrician's advice, the baby's parents "agreed not to authorize surgery, food, or water for the child." Nurses at the hospital initiated legal proceedings to override the parents' decision, but the Indiana courts ruled that the parents had the right to follow the obstetrician's recommendation. The baby died when he was six days old.[3]

The Bloomington Baby Doe case aroused substantial concern among abortion opponents, who saw the case as proof that society was "now falling down the slippery slope" of disrespect for life.[4] The Reagan administration, not usually one to indulge a broad interpretation of civil rights statutes protecting minority groups,[5] responded by attempting to employ Section 504 of the Rehabilitation Act as a tool to prohibit similar denials of treatment in the future. Section 504 prohibits recipients of federal funding—which include most hospitals—from discriminating on the basis of disability. The administration argued that the refusal to perform surgery to reconnect the esophagus of an infant with Down syndrome constitutes disability-based discrimination, because an infant without Down syndrome would surely receive similar surgery if he needed it.[6]

The courts, however, rebuffed the administration's position. Two cases were particularly significant. The first involved an infant with spina bifida, who died after her parents chose not to perform corrective surgical procedures that "were likely to prolong the infant's life, but would not improve many of her handicapping conditions, including her anticipated mental retardation."[7] In a lawsuit by the Reagan administration's Department of Health and Human Services seeking to investigate the baby's treatment as a possible violation of Section 504, the Second Circuit held that the statute was never intended to apply to medical treatment decisions, and that it could not intelligibly be read to apply "[w]here the handicapping condition is related to the condition(s) to be treated."[8] In the other significant case, the Supreme Court sustained a facial challenge to the regulations the Reagan administration adopted to apply Section 504 to future Baby Doe cases.[9] A plurality of four justices who strongly supported *Roe v. Wade*[10] concluded that Section 504 provided no basis for regulating hospitals' failure to treat newborns with disabilities because the administration had not identified any cases where "a hospital failed or refused to provide treatment to a handicapped infant for which parental consent had been given."[11] The plurality concluded that a "hospital's withholding of treatment when no parental consent has been given cannot violate § 504, for without the consent of the parents or a surrogate decisionmaker the infant is neither 'otherwise qualified' for treatment nor has he been denied care 'solely by reason of his handicap.'"[12]

The Baby Doe cases became a major cause for the antiabortion movement. But they also became a major cause for the still-developing disability rights movement. Although some disability rights activists balked at allying themselves with right-to-lifers,[13] many others held the view advanced by the Disability Rag (the mouthpiece of the more radical grassroots participants in the disability rights movement): "We want the disability rights movement to be liberal, but liberals, in this issue, are siding with parents who want to withhold food from 'deformed' infants so they will die."[14]

When the Supreme Court heard the challenge to the Reagan administration's Baby Doe regulation, a number of disability rights groups joined several anti-abortion groups as amici supporting the administration.[15] The briefs filed by the disability rights organizations had two major themes, which formed a template for later disability rights critiques of assisted suicide and prenatal testing. First, they contended that the decision to withhold treatment from an infant with a disability is often based on an erroneous, if not prejudiced, understanding of the "quality of life" experienced by individuals with disabilities.[16] The brief of (what was then called) the Association of Retarded Citizens was particularly blunt on this point: "This difference in the treatment of handicapped and non-handicapped children directly reflects the physician's judgment that the life of the handicapped infant is of significantly less value than is the life of the non-handicapped infant."[17] The brief filed by the American Coalition of Citizens with Disabilities and numerous other self-advocacy groups urged that physicians' judgments about the quality or value of life for infants with disabilities were "counterfactual" and "based on ignorance and prejudice."[18] And the brief filed on behalf of several professional organizations that supported disability rights urged that "[s]peculation about a child's future 'quality of life' typically involves an insidious combination of both dubious predictions about the course of that life and subjective value judgments about what kinds of lives are worth (or not worth) living."[19]

Second, the disability rights groups urged that it was the physicians' biases and not an unconstrained exercise of parental choice that led to the withholding of treatment from newborns with disabilities. The briefs argued extensively that parents' decisions to withhold treatment from their disabled infants cannot be understood as free choices. Parents necessarily rely on the specialized knowledge and experience of physicians.[20] Parents who must make treatment

decisions for newborn children with disabilities are also mentally and emotionally vulnerable,[21] and they are often told that they must make their decisions
quickly.[22] Moreover, the briefs argued, physicians take advantage of parents'
vulnerability by "misinform[ing] them about the nature of their child's handicapping condition and the prospects for the child's development, education,
and future,"[23] and by "resort[ing] to medical nomenclature to disguise the nonmedical grounds of the recommendation."[24] Two of the briefs referred to "the
suggestion of one physician that parents should not be encouraged to nurture
their newborn handicapped baby lest a bond be established that might cause the
parents to make a 'selfish' decision to order the provision of life-saving treatment,
and the admonition by a leading pediatrician that physicians who believe it to be
desirable to withhold treatment from a child should be patient since '[f]irm rooting of a parental death wish for a defective child usually takes days, at least; and
it is never free of ambivalence.'"[25] In the end, the briefs argued, "'what passes
today for disclosure and consent in physician-patient interactions is largely an
unwitting attempt by physicians to shape the disclosure process so that patients
will comply with their recommendations.'"[26]

ASSISTED SUICIDE

At around the same time that the Baby Doe cases initiated the tactical alliance between disability rights and antiabortion activists, the two groups began
to come together again to oppose physician-assisted suicide and the so-called
right to die. Activists from both camps worked together on a number of prominent cases in the 1980s and 1990s in which people with disabilities sought to
terminate their own lives.[27] When Dr. Jack Kevorkian began using his "suicide
machine" to assist people, many of whom had disabilities,[28] in ending their lives,
disability rights activists formed Not Dead Yet, an organization that opposes assisted suicide and euthanasia from a disability rights perspective. In most major
cases involving right-to-die issues—including the Schiavo case—Not Dead Yet
has filed briefs arguing that the recognition of such a right threatens the lives and
interests of people with disabilities.[29]

As in the Baby Doe cases, opponents of abortion object to assisted suicide
because it is inconsistent with their understanding of the sanctity of human life.
But disability rights activists have again articulated a critique that is distinct from
the arguments of the antiabortion movement.[30] In an argument that parallels
their position on the Baby Doe cases, disability rights activists like those affiliated with Not Dead Yet contend that the practice of assisted suicide reflects a
discriminatory belief that life with a disability is not worth living. They further

argue that if the law recognizes a right to die—no matter how stringently regulated—people with disabilities will be pressured into exercising it.

Disability rights activists argue that if a person without a disability chooses to commit suicide, society treats that choice as the product of an irrational decision-making process that should not be given effect.[31] But "when a person 'chooses' death over an 'undignified' life with a disability, the system sympathizes with that individual's plight and supports his right to die, assuming his disability is the root of his supreme despair."[32] That difference, disability rights advocates argue, reflects biases about the quality of life experienced by individuals with disabilities.[33] Both medical professionals and nondisabled members of the lay public believe that disability has a more negative effect on life quality than people with disabilities themselves report.[34] People without disabilities thus "readily conclude that the disabled person's wish to die is reasonable because it agrees with their own preconception that the primary problem for such individuals is the unbearable experience of a permanent disability."[35] Their biases can be seen in the "intensely stigmatized language" in which the right-to-die debate proceeds, where "disabled people are defective, damaged, debilitated, deformed, distressed, afflicted, anomalous, helpless and/or infirm," while "nonhandicapped persons are 'normal.'"[36]

In the view of many disability rights advocates, supporters of assisted suicide fail to understand that "the greatest suffering of people with disabilities is the socially stigmatized identity inflicted upon them."[37] As chapter 2 shows, disability rights advocates have long argued that the proper remedy for such stigmatization is not medical treatment to eliminate disabilities—and certainly not medical interventions to eliminate people with disabilities—but is instead guarantees of civil rights to change the hostile and inaccessible aspects of society. "If society alleviated the suffering of facing prejudice," writes Paul Miller, "perhaps life with a disability would be recognized as not only worth living but as valuable as that of anyone else."[38]

Moreover, disability rights advocates who oppose assisted suicide argue that the "choice" by a person with a disability to end his life will rarely be a truly free one. Once recognized, they contend, "the right to die will inevitably become a duty to die. People with major disabilities will be pressured into 'choosing' to end their lives."[39] Free choice in this context may be limited by a physician's advice that is based on inaccurate understandings about the quality of life enjoyed by people with disabilities or erroneous predictions about the future course of an individual's medical condition.[40] It may also be limited by financial pressures, particularly in a world of managed care, and by the related desire not to impose financial or psychological burdens on one's family.[41] And free choice may be limited by the societal stigma attached to disability—stigma that people with disabilities may themselves have internalized. In Miller's words, "[W]hen people with disabilities make a 'choice' to seek their right to die, they do so from the position of a society that fears, discriminates against, and stigmatizes disability as undignified. Facing a life of societal exclusion, prejudice, and fear, in conjunction with self-deprecation and devaluation based on those same irrational assumptions, is there really a choice at all?"[42]

Importantly, disability rights advocates who have developed the critique of assisted suicide do not believe that there is any regulation that could adequately protect people with disabilities against being coerced into committing suicide.[43] Accordingly, they urge that a flat ban on the practice is necessary.[44] The Supreme Court largely vindicated that position in the *Glucksberg* and *Vacco* cases, which upheld Washington's and New York's absolute bans on assisted suicide.[45]

PRENATAL TESTING

The Baby Doe and assisted suicide cases were merely proxy battles in the abortion rights wars. But since at least the 1960s—even before the rise of a self-conscious disability rights movement—disability issues have frequently arisen as well in debates about abortion itself. In 1962, Sherri Finkbine's widely publicized effort to obtain an abortion catalyzed public support for the liberalization of abortion laws; Finkbine sought an abortion because she had been taking Thalidomide, which had recently been associated with a high risk of fetal disability.[46] A few years later, an epidemic of rubella—which, when contracted by a pregnant woman, will frequently cause disabilities in the fetus—created additional momentum for liberalization in California particularly.[47] And in the years since *Roe v. Wade*, abortion rights activists and politicians have frequently and successfully invoked "fetal deformity" as a circumstance in which abortions should clearly be permitted.[48] At the same time, a number of antiabortion advocates seem to oppose abortions based on fetal disability even more strongly than they oppose abortions generally. As Kristin Luker reported, "To defend a genetically or congenitally damaged embryo from abortion is, in their minds, defending the weakest of the weak, and most pro-life people we interviewed were least prepared to compromise on this category of abortion."[49] And, indeed, concerns about permitting abortion in cases of "fetal deformity" slowed passage of liberalized abortion laws in California and New York.[50]

Despite the centrality of disability to general debates over abortion rights, for a long time many disability rights activists sought to "side-step[ ]" those debates.[51] In recent years, however, the rise of prenatal testing has spurred many supporters of disability rights to enter the discussion. Prenatal genetic testing now permits the discovery of "gene mutations associated with some 400 conditions, from those universally viewed as severe, such as Tay-Sachs, to those that many might describe as relatively minor, such as polydactyly (a trait involving an extra little finger)," and the number of tests continues to grow.[52] Although such tests are in some cases used to identify conditions that may be treated in utero, their primary use is "as the basis of a decision to abort fetuses that carry mutations associated with disease and/or disability."[53] Often, the tests are used to identify and abort fetuses whose disabilities would not prevent them from living long and fulfilling lives.[54]

Troubled by these developments, many advocates of disability rights have developed a critique of prenatal testing that parallels their critiques of the non-treatment of infants with disabilities and of assisted suicide. They contend "that prenatal testing followed by selective abortion is morally problematic, and that it is driven by misinformation."[55] These advocates believe that testing for—and abortion of—fetuses with disabilities is morally problematic because it reflects a view that life with a disability is not worth living. To them, prenatal testing and selective abortion represents a significant step toward ultimate achievement of "the eugenicist's dream of eliminating disabilities" by eliminating people with disabilities.[56] Selective abortions will inevitably reduce the numbers of people with disabilities and their attendant visibility in the community—visibility that has been crucial to overcoming a legacy of prejudice and fear.[57] Moreover, if fewer people with disabilities are born, and it becomes easier to prevent them from being born, the social and political commitment to treatment, social services, and nondiscrimination protections for people with those conditions may weaken substantially.[58] And the availability of selective abortions may also entrench discrimination and prejudice against people with disabilities by "reinforcing the general public's perception that disability is a tragic mistake (that could and should have been avoided) and that disabled people are therefore justifiably marginalized."[59] To these advocates, the medical detection and elimination of fetuses with disabilities thus represents the ultimate triumph of the "medical model" against which the disability rights movement has mobilized.

In addition to believing that selective abortion decisions are morally problematic, disability rights critics of prenatal testing also believe that those decisions are misinformed, if not coerced. As in the Baby Doe cases, they contend that doctors and genetic counselors have a tendency (subtly or not) to urge pregnant women to subject their fetuses to prenatal testing and abort fetuses with disabilities.[60] As Adrienne Asch diplomatically puts it, "Despite the professional commitment to non-directiveness in genetic counseling, it is clear that many professionals do not practice in a way that legitimates the choice to maintain a pregnancy of a fetus affected by a disabling trait."[61] Too often, disability rights advocates contend, the advice pregnant women receive after discovering a fetal disability focuses on (often unduly) negative predictions about short life expectancies and extensive medical needs rather than on the ways children with disabilities "can participate in the life of family, school and community."[62] They argue that this skew in advice rests on health professionals' uninformed beliefs about disability: "Recent studies suggest, for example, that many members of the health professions view childhood disability as predominantly negative for children and their families, in contrast to what research on the life satisfaction of people with disabilities and their families has actually shown."[63] And skewed advice—even if presented in a "nondirective" manner—can effectively coerce women into choosing abortion.[64] As Mary Mahowald observes, "Although decisions for prenatal testing and termination are usually thought to be autonomous, some individuals report they feel pressured by physicians and others to undergo prenatal testing and encouraged to terminate when the result is positive."[65]

Adherents to the disability rights critique of prenatal testing do not oppose abortion generally; many of them strongly endorse abortion rights.[66] Indeed, the most vocal disability rights critics of prenatal testing and selective abortion do not even urge that those practices be subject to legal regulation to prohibit disability-based discrimination. They aim, instead, to persuade medical professionals to provide pregnant women with full information—including information about the positive aspects of living (and parenting a child) with a disability—before offering prenatal tests and suggesting selective abortions.[67] In Asch's words, they seek "to facilitate true reproductive choice for women by urging changes in the way prenatal testing occurs and the rhetoric that surrounds it."[68] But once prospective parents have full information, presented in a noncoercive manner, many of these advocates urge that we must "endorse the choices people make about their reproductive and family lives."[69] Although the disability rights critique of selective abortion has the same structure as the critiques of nontreatment and assisted suicide, the critics in this context endorse a very different policy prescription.

THE IMPLICATIONS OF THE DISABILITY
RIGHTS CRITIQUE

Although those who have articulated the disability rights critique have pointedly refused to endorse regulation of abortion, their arguments can readily be used to support just such regulation. Current constitutional doctrine relating to abortion is rooted in a principle of autonomy. The Supreme Court has held, most notably in *Planned Parenthood of Southeastern Pennsylvania v. Casey*,[70] that a choice of such profound moral and practical significance for a woman must be made by her, freely. But the Court also has recognized—in the mode of the disability rights critique—that private as well as public pressure can inhibit free choice. Accordingly, it has upheld regulations of abortion that are justified as removing obstacles to the woman's authentic choice. But once we allow government to regulate the abortion decision in the name of removing private obstacles to free choice, we confront a classic Legal Realist baseline problem: all choices are made under an array of constraints, so the government will always have some plausible argument for regulating to promote choice. And the notion of autonomy, by itself, will not provide a basis for rejecting any such regulation.

The disability rights critique could thus serve as a model for those who wish to defend ever more stringent abortion regulations. Like the disability rights critics, antiabortion activists need only identify private, social, or professional forces that, by pressuring women to have abortions, create obstacles to "truly" free choice.[71] Regulation can then be justified as overcoming those obstacles and promoting choice. Indeed, although many disability rights critics specifically disavow any desire to impose regulations on the abortion decision, their arguments would readily justify regulations under the Supreme Court's post-*Casey* jurisprudence. The tension between the disability rights critique and support for broad abortion rights is therefore greater than some of the critics seem to believe. I elaborate on these points in the remainder of this section.

The Supreme Court has rooted constitutional protection of abortion rights in the guarantee of "liberty" in the Due Process Clause of the Fourteenth Amendment.[72] The liberty protected by the Constitution, the Court has ruled, includes freedom in making "the most intimate and personal choices a person may make in a lifetime, choices central to personal dignity and autonomy."[73] In what Justice Scalia later derided as the "famed sweet-mystery-of-life passage,"[74] the Court in *Planned Parenthood v. Casey* rested squarely on a concept of freedom of choice, stating that "[a]t the heart of liberty is the right to define one's own concept of existence, of meaning, of the universe, and of the mystery of human life. Beliefs about these matters could not define the attributes of personhood were they formed under compulsion of the State."[75] Despite Justice Scalia's criticisms, the Court has reaffirmed that language, as well as *Casey*'s understanding that the constitutional protection of abortion rights rests on "the respect the Constitution demands for the autonomy of the person in making these choices."[76]

The disability rights critique is, as a logical matter, entirely consistent with the Supreme Court's protection of the right of free choice. Indeed, many of the most important exponents of that critique have sworn allegiance to the right to choose. But, in a classic Legal Realist move, the disability rights critique insists that private actors can limit free choice at least as much as the government can. In each of the areas discussed above, disability rights critics have emphasized the way societal stigmas and powerful social and financial pressures can effectively compel particular choices—whether the choice of a parent to withhold treatment from a newborn with a disability, the choice of an individual with a disability to exercise his right to die, or the choice of a pregnant woman to test her fetus for disabilities and have an abortion if a disability is discovered. To the extent that the disability rights critics have sought to regulate individuals' choices in these areas, they have justified their regulatory proposals as serving, rather than undermining, freedom of choice. Regulation is necessary, disability rights critics have argued, to provide a counterbalance to the strong social forces that will otherwise lead people to accord less value to the lives and potential lives of individuals with disabilities. By counteracting a coercive social setting, regulation helps to ensure that the choices made in this context are authentic exercises of an individual's will.

Of course, this move—regulating to remove obstacles to choice—cannot be limited to matters that touch on disability. As the Legal Realists demonstrated in their successful attack on freedom of contract, the move is available whenever the reigning legal principle is one involving the liberty to choose.[77] And, indeed, it is a move that has played a significant role in the Supreme Court's abortion jurisprudence.

It was abortion rights activists who first urged that constitutional doctrine should be attentive to private restrictions on choice. In the abortion funding cases,[78] abortion rights lawyers contended that the government's failure to fund abortions for indigent women, particularly when the government funded childbirth, coerced them into forgoing abortions.[79] The Court, however, rejected the argument. Although the Court acknowledged that *Roe v. Wade* had recognized "a constitutionally protected interest 'in making certain kinds of important decisions' free from governmental compulsion,"[80] it held that the state's failure to fund abortion did not constitute compulsion. Rather, the Court concluded that any constraint on the woman's exercise of free choice resulted from her indigency, neither a condition that is attributable to the government nor one that the government has a constitutional obligation to alleviate.[81] The Due Process Clause, the Court held, protects against "unwarranted government interference with freedom of choice" but "does not confer an entitlement to such funds as may be necessary to realize all the advantages of that freedom."[82]

Although the abortion funding cases rejected the conclusion that indigence imposed the kind of constraint on free choice that requires the state to counter-act it, the Court accepted a more modest understanding of the Legal Realist point in *Casey*. There, the Court held that states may adopt regulations that are "calculated to inform the woman's free choice, not hinder it."[83] Indeed, the cen-tral aspect of *Casey*'s retooling of the Court's post-*Roe* abortion jurisprudence was the case's explicit recognition that states may "tak[e] steps to ensure that [the woman's] choice is thoughtful and informed" and may "enact laws to provide a reasonable framework for a woman to make a decision that has such profound and lasting meaning": "Even in the earliest stages of pregnancy, the State may enact rules and regulations designed to encourage her to know that there are philosophic and social arguments of great weight that can be brought to bear in favor of continuing the pregnancy to full term and that there are procedures and institutions to allow adoption of unwanted children as well as a certain degree of state assistance if the mother chooses to raise the child herself."[84] *Casey* thus recognized that states may constitutionally remove private restrictions on free choice, even if they impose new restrictions in doing so. The case adopted what might be thought of (ironically) as a pro-choice rationale for regulation.[85]

The *Casey* joint opinion applied these principles to uphold a number of sig-nificant restrictions on abortions. One such restriction was the so-called in-formed consent provision, which required a physician, twenty-four hours in ad-vance of performing an abortion, to provide the woman with information about the fetus's gestational age and the risks of abortion and childbirth; the state also required the physician to make available printed materials "describing the fetus and providing information about medical assistance for childbirth, information about child support from the father, and a list of agencies which provide adop-tion and other services as alternatives to abortion."[86] As Justice Stevens high-lighted, the printed materials seemed "clearly designed to persuade [a woman] to choose not to undergo the abortion."[87] Also, the twenty-four-hour waiting period imposed significant restrictions on the ability to obtain an abortion in a state with a limited number of abortion clinics, some of which were open only a few days a week.[88] But the Court nonetheless upheld the provision as (in the words of the lead opinion) one that "facilitates the wise exercise" of the "right to decide to terminate a pregnancy."[89]

The lead opinion appeared to presume that, absent the informed consent law, many women would decide precipitously, without full information about the alternatives to abortion or consequences of abortion on the woman and fetus. The opinion concluded that "attempting to ensure that a woman apprehend[s] the full consequences of her decision" serves legitimate interests in "reducing the risk that a woman may elect an abortion, only to discover later, with devastating psychological consequences, that her decision was not fully informed."[90] It also concluded that the twenty-four-hour waiting period helps to ensure that the abortion decision "will be more informed and deliberate" by requiring "some period of reflection."[91]

If one believes that the decisions of individual women typically are informed, deliberate, and not influenced by social pressures to have abortions, then the informed consent restrictions upheld in *Casey* appear as nothing more than gratuitous interference with the right to choose abortion.[92] And the interference may be severe: the restrictions upheld in *Casey* may have a powerful effect on the practical ability of women to have abortions.[93] But the justices who jointly wrote the lead opinion in *Casey* evidently thought otherwise. Some insight into their thinking can be found in two subsequent opinions written by Justice Kennedy (one of the three authors of the *Casey* joint opinion): his dissent in *Hill v. Colorado*[94] and his majority opinion in *Gonzales v. Carhart.*[95]

Hill involved a state law that imposed an eight-foot floating buffer zone around people within one hundred feet of a health care facility; the Court rejected the claim by a number of antiabortion "sidewalk counselors" that the statute violated their First Amendment rights. Dissenting from that ruling, Justice Kennedy urged that the majority's opinion not only "undermin[ed] established First Amendment principles" but also "conflict[ed] with the essence of the joint opinion in [*Casey*]."[96]

In explaining the latter point, Justice Kennedy made clear his view that women seeking abortions often have not fully reflected on or obtained information about the decision. He referred to "the argument[ ] by proponents of abortion" that "a young woman might have been so uninformed that she did not know how to avoid pregnancy," and contended that antiabortion counselors merely "seek to ask the same uninformed woman . . . to understand and to contemplate the nature of the life she carries within her."[97] Justice Kennedy emphasized "the profound difference a leaflet can have in a woman's decisionmaking process."[98] He quoted extensively from "the account of one young woman who testified before the Colorado Senate."[99] That woman, who decided not to have an abortion after being presented with a pamphlet by sidewalk counselors, testified that before she received the pamphlet she thought "abortion [was] the only way out because of [*sic*] it's all I knew."[100] If the buffer zone law had been in effect when she was pregnant, she said, "I would not have got any information at all and gone through with my abortion because the only people on my side were the people at the abortion clinic" who "knew exactly how I was feeling and what to say to make it all better."[101] But receiving the pamphlet from the antiabortion counselors, she said, "helped me make my choice. I got an informed decision, I got information from both sides, and I made an informed decision that my son and I could both live with."[102]

In *Carhart*, Justice Kennedy wrote for the Court in a ruling that upheld the federal ban on the procedure known as "partial-birth abortion." Of most importance here, his opinion relied in part on informed consent grounds to uphold the ban. Although he recognized the lack of "reliable data to measure the phenomenon," Justice Kennedy stated that "it seems unexceptionable to conclude some women come to regret their choice to abort the infant life they once created and sustained" and that "[s]evere depression and loss of esteem can follow."[103] Speculating that "some doctors may prefer not to disclose precise details of the means" used in the so-called partial-birth procedure, he found it "self-evident that a mother who comes to regret her choice to abort must struggle with grief more anguished and sorrow more profound when she learns, only after the event, what she once did not know: that she allowed a doctor to pierce the skull and vacuum the fast-developing brain of her unborn child, a child assuming the human form."[104] Accordingly, he concluded that the ban was a proper means of "ensuring so grave a choice is well informed"—that is, that the procedure could be banned because some women who choose it ultimately come to regret the choice and believe that it was not fully informed.[105]

Especially when read in the light of Justice Kennedy's arguments in these subsequent cases, it is apparent that the *Casey* joint opinion's rationale for upholding the informed consent requirement had exactly the same structure as the disability rights critique discussed above. Both arguments can be used to justify government restrictions on choice, but neither argument rejects choice as the governing principle. To the contrary, both openly embrace the view that the Constitution protects freedom of choice. They simply assert that the government is not the only—or perhaps even the most important—threat to free choice. Both the disability rights critics and the Casey joint opinion point instead to social pressures and the lack of information as significant obstacles to free choice. Although government regulation may in some ways restrict choice, it does so in an effort to remove even greater obstacles to free choice.[106]

The obvious problem for abortion rights advocates is the same one confronted by advocates of freedom of contract in the face of the Legal Realist critique. If the only basis for abortion rights is individual autonomy, and government can regulate to remove private or societal threats to free choice, then courts can be expected readily to defer to any number of restrictions on abortion.[107] At the limit, such an argument could even justify a rule that flatly prohibits abortions. (*Carhart*, which upheld a flat ban on a particular type of abortion, is clearly a step in that direction, and antiabortion activists are certain to press further.)[108]

Many women who have abortions do so because of social pressures (such as stigmas against unwed motherhood), financial pressures, or threats of domestic violence. It is easy enough, applying the Legal Realist logic, to argue that an abortion chosen under the influence of such pressures may not reflect the woman's "true" or "uncoerced" choice: if most abortions occur under such conditions, the argument would go, autonomy may be best served by prohibiting abortion entirely—particularly if the pressures that operate on a woman's choice are subtle and hard to detect in any particular instance.[109]

That argument may seem farfetched, if not Orwellian. For one thing, most of the women whose abortions are "coerced" by social or financial pressures or threats of violence face those same sorts of pressures in other areas of their lives. Of greatest import here, those sorts of pressures (instantiated through dependence on men) will often lead women to become pregnant in the first place. Laws truly concerned with women's autonomy would not focus so asymmetrically on avoiding coercion in the choice to have an abortion; such laws would attempt to remove private and social obstacles to women's choices (or at least their reproductive choices) across the board. And on a doctrinal level, *Casey* seems clearly to say that although states can regulate abortion, they cannot prohibit it entirely or even place an "undue burden" on it[110]—permit but discourage, as Roger Rosenblatt described Americans' views on abortion at around the time the case was decided.[111]

For these reasons, I do not support the pro-choice argument for banning abortion. But my point in this chapter is not to attack or defend the normative or policy prescriptions espoused by any particular set of activists. My goal is to examine—and explore the stakes of—the positions taken by disability rights advocates on both sides of these questions. And for that purpose, it is crucial to note that the seemingly perverse argument for banning abortion in the name of choice would parallel the argument made by disability rights critics of assisted suicide. Those critics accept that autonomy is the basic goal of the disability rights movement, and many agree that an autonomous choice to commit suicide should, in principle, be protected. But they contend that if assisted suicide is allowed at all, the pressures will be so powerful that many people with disabilities will be forced to "choose" to end their lives—and that the pressures will be so subtle that they will not be reliably detected in any individual case. In those circumstances, disability rights critics argue, autonomy is best served by prohibiting assisted suicide altogether.[112]

Justice Souter—another author of the *Casey* joint opinion—adopted that very reasoning in his concurring opinion in the *Glucksberg* case.[113] The plaintiffs had argued that Washington's prohibition on assisted suicide denied individuals with terminal illness the right, guaranteed by *Casey*, to make choices concerning major life decisions. In rejecting that claim, Justice Souter agreed with the plaintiffs that the Constitution accords some protection to the choice of a patient with terminal illness regarding when and how to die.[114] But he concluded that the state's interest in, among other things, "protecting patients from mistakenly and involuntarily deciding to end their lives" was sufficient to justify the flat prohibition on assisted suicide.[115] Justice Souter argued that the recognition of such a state interest was fully consistent with the autonomy principle that underlay the plaintiffs' claims—it did not reflect "a moral judgment contrary to" that asserted by the plaintiffs.[116] Rather, it reflected an empirical view (which Justice Souter believed to be well grounded) that the legalization of assisted suicide in any form would inevitably lead many people to "choose" to die under coercive circumstances—a result that even strict regulation could not prevent.[117] The state's ban on assisted suicide thus did not reflect disrespect for the principle of autonomy. Even though a ban necessarily impinges on autonomy in cases where an individual would truly voluntarily choose to end his life, the failure to adopt a ban impinges on autonomy in cases where an individual's "choice" to die reflects coercion. If, as disability rights critics believe, coerced suicide reflects the greater threat, then a ban on the practice is the policy most consistent with promoting autonomy. The same kind of analysis could readily be applied to abortion—and, indeed, Justice Kennedy's opinion for the Court in *Carhart* goes a long way down the road toward doing just that.

Although many who have articulated the disability rights critique have pointedly disavowed governmental regulation of the abortion decision, their arguments lend themselves to being used in support of such abortion restrictions. If the goal is free choice, and stigma against people with disabilities filtered through powerful professional culture makes choice unfree, regulation to overcome those powerful private forces is a straightforward response. As the discussion above demonstrates, it is a response that could easily be blessed under the Supreme Court's post-*Casey* abortion doctrine.

THE AUTONOMY ALTERNATIVE

As I have shown, disability rights critics in each of three areas—selective nontreatment of infants with disabilities, assisted suicide, and prenatal testing followed by selective abortion—have urged that powerful social biases may significantly constrain people's choices. But their policy prescriptions are very different in the different areas. For selective nontreatment and assisted suicide, the critics believe that government action—in the form of a flat ban on those practices—is the only way to protect people from coercion. For selective abortion, however, the critics urge a nonregulatory path of changing social norms. I went on to show that the arguments of the disability rights critics could readily justify restrictions on selective abortion under the Supreme Court's current abortion jurisprudence, notwithstanding the critics' nominal support for abortion rights.

One group of disability rights activists has avoided this internal tension. That group—which probably constitutes a minority of disability rights activists but a majority of people with disabilities—supports the right to assisted suicide. The most prominent exponents of this position are the individuals affiliated with Autonomy, Inc., which is an organization of people with disabilities who oppose the position of Not Dead Yet. The late Andrew Batavia, who had quadriplegia and played a key role in the passage of the ADA, was the central figure in the organization's founding. Batavia explained his views in an amicus brief he filed in the 1996 Term Supreme Court assisted suicide cases on behalf of a number of prominent individuals with disabilities—including the distinguished historian Hugh Gregory Gallagher and Michael Stein, who today is one of the leading disability-law scholars in the world.

The Autonomy brief argued in explicitly disability rights terms for a right to assisted suicide. The brief noted poll results indicating that a majority of people with disabilities support such a right, and it contended that those results are consistent with the core disability rights principles of independence and antipaternalism: "Where for generations, almost every aspect of their existence was defined by a paternalistic society that labeled them inferior and relegated them to institutions, [people with disabilities] are unwilling to relinquish their autonomy."[118] The brief had harsh words for disability rights activists, like those associated with Not Dead Yet, who oppose a right to assisted suicide: "In essence," the brief contended, those advocates "appear to be saying that the individual with a disability should have control over every decision in his or her life, except for the decision of whether to live in the face of a terminal illness. This blatant contradiction is glaring and unacceptable to a substantial majority of people with disabilities."[119]

As Batavia explained in a subsequent article, disability rights supporters of the right to assisted suicide "do not necessarily contest the[] empirical evidence" assisted suicide opponents muster regarding "physicians' (and other health professionals') training, treatment behavior, attitudes on quality of life, and biases concerning persons with disabilities."[120] But to go from that empirical observation to the conclusion that assisted suicide should be prohibited, in his view, is to deny people with disabilities all choice in the matter. Accordingly, although Batavia endorsed regulation to ensure that the decision "is the will of the individual seeking death after being adequately informed of all available alterna-tives," and he criticized Dr. Jack Kevorkian for following a procedure that "did not ensure the competence of the patient and the voluntariness of the process," he defended a right to assisted suicide.[121]

The Autonomy position is appealing, because it seems to avoid the internal inconsistencies of the disability rights critics. But some tensions remain. As the previous paragraph shows, disability rights activists who defend a right to assisted suicide support substantial regulation of that right to ensure informed consent. They do not take a laissez-faire position to match their position on abortion rights.

Informed consent requirements like those upheld in *Casey* are typically seen by abortion rights supporters as doubly problematic: not only do they assume (paternalistically) that women cannot be trusted to make informed choices, they also are designed to obstruct the woman's exercise of her choice. There is no doubt that informed consent requirements for assisted suicide can be criticized on the same grounds: they displace the expressed choices of individuals with dis-abilities on the assumption that those individuals would not make those choices if they were *really* thinking about it. They also make it harder to exercise the choice of death. How can disability rights activists who support a right to assisted suicide get on their high horse about autonomy and antipaternalism when they are willing to endorse those requirements?

There are possible justifications for treating abortion and assisted suicide dif-ferently, but they point up the limited traction the antipaternalist principle has in resolving these questions. One might be more willing to accept informed con-sent requirements in the assisted suicide context because more is at stake than with abortion—the life of a person instead of the potential for that life. Or one might justify the difference by comparing the strong evidence that people with disabilities often get over their suicidal thoughts with the relatively weak evi-dence (some call it "junk science") that women who have abortions ultimately believe they made the wrong choice.[122] To similar effect, one might believe that informed consent requirements for assisted suicide are less often designed to impede the exercise of the right than are informed consent requirements for abortion. Indeed, I would wager that most disability rights activists who support abortion rights—including those who support assisted suicide—would favor in-formed consent requirements for disability-selective abortions, if they believed those requirements would not be used simply as part of a campaign to deny women the right to choose abortion.[123]

These are powerful reasons to accept informed consent requirements for as-sisted suicide where one would not accept them for abortion (even disability-selective abortion). But far from rejecting paternalism, these arguments recognize that paternalism *is* sometimes appropriate in the assisted suicide context. Even those who oppose an assisted suicide ban on putatively antipaternalist grounds, then, recognize the need for *some* paternalism in this context. None of the participants in this debate is purely an antipaternalist.

CONCLUSION

The life-and-death issues discussed in this chapter demonstrate the limits of the antipaternalist principle as a guide to the goals of the disability rights movement. Disability rights activists who seek a ban on assisted suicide invoke the antipaternalist principle—they seek to liberate people with disabilities from the paternalistic interference of family members, medical professionals, and insurance carriers. But disability rights activists who support a right to assisted suicide invoke the antipaternalist principle as well—they seek to liberate people with disabilities from the paternalistic interference of vitalists and others who believe they cannot make considered choices about how and when to end their lives. The antipaternalist principle alone cannot resolve this dispute—at least once we accept that private as well as government actors can limit free choice. Moreover, both those disability rights activists who support and those who oppose assisted suicide defend some degree of paternalistic government regulation.

The antipaternalist principle, therefore, is doubly limited. Multiple, even opposing, policy outcomes are likely to be consistent with it, and paternalism will sometimes be justified in any event. Resolution of the issues discussed in this chapter—even from a disability rights perspective—requires more than antipaternalism. Whether one follows the line of the disability rights critics or takes the autonomy position depends in part on empirical questions (How frequently are individuals pressured into one or another decision, and by what kinds of pressures?), in part on which kind of paternalism one believes is worse (for example, government or private), and in part on one's broader views about individual liberty and bodily integrity. I find myself more sympathetic with the autonomy position, but I cannot deny that *both* positions have strong resonances in the disability rights principles of antipaternalism and independent living.

It is important to emphasize that, regardless of whether one endorses the disability rights critique or the autonomy position, the critique of the nontreatment of infants with disabilities stands on its own. Infants, unlike fetuses, are clearly "persons,"[124] but unlike adults who seek assistance in suicide they have no say over the nontreatment decision. There is therefore no inconsistency in permitting assisted suicide for adults with disabilities or disability-selective abortions while at the same time prohibiting selective nontreatment of infants with disabilities.[125] Nor, obviously, is there any inconsistency between banning assisted suicide and selective abortion while at the same time prohibiting the nontreatment of infants with disabilities. Although the disability rights critique of selective nontreatment has the same structure as the critiques of assisted suicide and selective abortion—and it has a similar resonance with antiabortion advocates—the selective nontreatment critique is quite distinct. Unfortunately, the Baby Doe issue has become so firmly associated with abortion politics[126] that it is often hard for judges to dissociate the two.

7

THE LIMITS OF THE
ANTIDISCRIMINATION MODEL

The preceding four chapters have focused on legal doctrine. I hope I have shown that significant controversies in the interpretation of the ADA and other laws implicating disability rights highlight important tensions internal to the goals of the disability rights movement. In this chapter, I shift my focus to assessing the success of the antidiscrimination model (best reflected in the ADA) in achieving the goals of the disability rights movement.

As the previous chapters have shown, identifying the goals of the disability rights movement is not an easy or uncontroversial task. But amid all the tensions about independence, professionalism, and antipaternalism, and the disagreement as to whether it is best to approach disability as defining a discrete minority group or as reflecting a universal human condition, a core goal constitutes the overlapping consensus of disability rights activists: expanding employment and a full life in the community for people identified as having disabilities. On that score, the record after nearly two decades of the ADA is mixed at best.

SOBERING STATISTICS

Outside the employment area, little reliable data exist regarding the integration of people with disabilities into the life of the community. But what data exist are sobering. Since 1986, the National Organization on Disability (NOD) has commissioned periodic surveys of Americans with disabilities; among other questions, those surveys ask about the respondents' participation in a number of activities of ordinary community life.[1] Since the adoption of the ADA, people with disabilities are significantly more likely to report that they eat out in restaurants at least twice a month: 48 percent of people with disabilities reported that they did so in 1986, but the percentage steadily grew after the passage of the ADA to reach 57 percent in 2004. That is a significant improvement, though the number remains far below what would be necessary for full integration into community life. (A full 73 percent of people without disabilities reported that they ate at restaurants at least twice a month.)

But the percentage of people with disabilities who reported participation in other important community activities actually went *down* slightly between 1986 and 2004: in 1986, 81 percent of people with disabilities reported that they socialized at least twice a month with close friends, relatives, or neighbors; in 2004, the number was 79 percent. In 1994 (the first year the survey posed the question), 27 percent of people with disabilities stated that they considered inadequate transportation to be a problem; in 2004, the number was 31 percent. And the percentage of people with disabilities who reported that they are very satisfied with life in general went down from 39 percent in 1986 to 34 percent in 2004. (By contrast, the percentage of people without disabilities giving the same response rose from 50 percent to 61 percent over the same period.) These are hardly major decreases (and the satisfaction numbers may not reflect an actual decrease as much as rising expectations), but they do suggest that the ADA has not succeeded in integrating people with disabilities fully into the life of the community.

Much more data exist regarding the effects of the ADA on employment. There, any discussion must begin with a striking fact, which virtually no knowledgeable observer disputes: the statute has failed significantly to improve the employment position of people with disabilities. Indeed, by virtually all reports the employment rate for Americans with disabilities has declined over the time the statute has been on the books. A number of scholars have provocatively argued not only that the employment position of people with disabilities has deteriorated but also that the ADA has in fact *caused* that deterioration. There is strong (though not incontrovertible) evidence that the statute (at least initially) imposed some negative pressure on employers' decisions to hire some people with disabilities, but I contend that critics of the statute have argued well beyond their data in urging that the ADA be abandoned. To the contrary, the data suggest that much (though perhaps not all) of the employment decline for people with disabilities resulted from factors extrinsic to the statute. In particular, I will argue, it is quite plausible that the 1990–1991 recession pushed an unusually large number of people with disabilities out of the workforce and onto the Social Security Disability Insurance (SSDI) rolls. Moreover, whatever the ADA's short-term effects, it seems likely that the statute's net long-term effects on employment for people with disabilities will be positive. But the statute has hardly been the solution to the incredibly low employment rates for people with disabilities.

Although the variety of definitions of "disability" makes precise conclusions hazardous, it seems clear that the employment picture for Americans with disabilities did not improve during the 1990s. To the contrary, the employment rate for men with disabilities pretty clearly fell, and the employment rate for women with disabilities either fell, stayed the same, or increased only a small amount.[2] Here is a rough-and-ready summary of the relevant statistics:

> When "disability" is defined as an impairment that imposes limitations on any life activity, the employment rate for working-age people with disabilities declined from 49% in 1990 to 46.6% in 1996, according to the federal government's National Health Information Survey (NHIS). When "disability" is defined more broadly—as a diagnosed impairment simpliciter—the employment rate for working-age men with disabilities fell from 84.7% in 1990 to 77.3% in 1996, while the employment rate for working-age women with disabilities stayed relatively stagnant at just over 63% during that period, according to the NHIS. And when "disability" is defined more narrowly, as an impairment that specifically limits the life activity of working, the employment rate for working-age men with disabilities fell from 42.1% in 1990 to 33.1% in 2000, according to the federal government's Current Population Survey, which provides data that can be compared across the entire decade; the employment rate for working-age women with disabilities fell from 34.9% to 32.6% over that period, according to the same measure.[3]

These data are especially striking, because the 1990s saw not just the implementation of the ADA but also the rising tide of an economic boom. With overall employment rates rising sharply, and employment rates for people with disabilities stagnant or falling, the disabled employment rate fell sharply relative to the nondisabled employment rate.[4]

These facts should be sobering for those who believed the ADA would move people off the welfare rolls and into the workforce in large numbers. Even more sobering are the findings of three prominent studies which conclude that the initial implementation of the statute was associated with a significant decrease in employment for people with disabilities—a decrease that could not be explained by other factors.[5] Although that may seem a strange result for a statute designed to improve employment outcomes for people with disabilities, the point is straightforward: disappointed applicants are likely to have a hard time enforcing the prohibition on disability discrimination in hiring, because hiring discrimination is very difficult to prove. Incumbent employees with disabilities, by contrast, will have a much easier time enforcing the requirement that they receive accommodations.[6] Employers thus will have an incentive to reject applicants with disabilities, in order to save on accommodation costs.

The data, supported by a fairly straightforward economic theory, thus seem to suggest that it is no accident that employment for people with disabilities fell or stagnated at the same time that the ADA went into force. Instead, those outcomes may be the predictable effect of imposing an accommodation mandate on employers. At least on its face, the picture does not look good for supporters of the ADA. If one wants to bring people with disabilities into the workforce, perhaps the statute's accommodation mandate is not the tool that will achieve that goal.

A DEFENSE OF THE ADA

Some scholars take that point a step further to contend that the ADA is actually counterproductive and should be abandoned. For reasons I discuss below, I believe that their argument is overblown. But one should not be complacent. It is also wrong to suggest, as have some ADA supporters, that there is nothing essentially wrong with the statute, or at least nothing that a more enlightened Supreme Court could not solve. It makes sense to consider that complacent argument first.

Scholars who defend the ADA have argued, first, that a careful review of the data shows that the ADA did not cause a decline in employment for people with disabilities, and that employment among at least some subgroups of people with disabilities has actually increased. In addition, some have argued (or at least suggested) that the limited tangible results of the ADA stem from restrictive decisions by the Supreme Court, rather than anything inherent in the statute's accommodation mandate approach. These are thoughtful arguments. In the end, though, they do not defeat the case for reform of the ADA.

CHALLENGING THE STATISTICS

Defenders of the ADA have offered three basic reasons why the data showing a decline in employment for people with disabilities do not tell the full story. First, they argue that the data rely on a definition of "disability" that focuses on people with impairments that limit the kind or amount of work they can do; when definitions that focus on non-work-related impairments are used, employment for people with disabilities seems to have increased since implementation of the ADA.[7] Second, they note that the data showing a decline in employment rely on self-reports of disability status; if the ADA changed attitudes toward disability by encouraging more people who have jobs to shed the "disability" label and more people who are unemployable to assert that they have disabilities, the data may mask an increase in employment for the target population.[8] Third, they contend that the expansion of eligibility for SSDI beginning in the mid-1980s, combined with the recession of the early 1990s, was most responsible for moving people with disabilities out of the workforce.[9]

These are important arguments, but each has weaknesses. First, the ADA may well have helped individuals whose disabilities do not limit the kind or amount of work they can do (and who thus are unlikely to need accommodations), but that finding is basically consistent with the story that the statute has perversely encouraged discrimination against people whose disabilities require accommodation.[10] If the statute helped people who need no accommodation but hurt those who do need accommodation, it can hardly be deemed a success even on its own terms. Second, it is possible that the ADA changed attitudes toward disability so quickly and profoundly that people altered their self-reports of whether they had disabilities, but it is unlikely that such attitudinal changes occurred to a degree (or in the direction) that would lead studies of disability employment to mask job growth.[11] Third, although the expansion of SSDI was likely pulling people with disabilities out of the workforce, the ADA was not succeeding in pulling or keeping them in.[12]

The arguments challenging the decline-in-employment data do help make the case against the position that the ADA should be scrapped. But they do not make the case for standing pat. From the very beginning, advocates of the ADA urged that a principal goal of disability policy should be to move people with disabilities into the workforce.[13] The statute has simply not achieved that goal in significant numbers, if at all. As Ruth Colker notes, "No study has been able to establish that the ADA has had any positive impact on the employability or poverty rate of individuals with disabilities."[14] At best, the disaggregated data suggest that the statute has moved people whose disabilities do not need accommodation into the workforce, but that it has left behind those people whose disabilities need accommodation. And even if SSDI expansion has made leaving work more attractive, it is still the case that the ADA has not created sufficient opportunities to expand work among people with disabilities. Policymakers who wish to maximize work opportunities for people with disabilities, while at the same time providing for those who are left behind by the job market, should not be satisfied with the job the ADA is doing.

BLAMING THE SUPREME COURT

Perhaps, though, the ADA is doing a poor job because the Supreme Court and lower courts have read it so narrowly. It is clear that the courts have been hostile to ADA employment claims. As previous chapters have shown, the Supreme Court has issued a number of high-profile rulings against ADA employment plaintiffs. Colker, among others, has suggested that those Supreme Court decisions have contributed to the ADA's failure to improve the employment picture for people with disabilities.[15]

I agree, by and large, that the courts have read the ADA too narrowly, particularly in the employment context. But that likely has very little to do with the statute's failure to improve employment opportunities for individuals with disabilities (as Colker admits). As I have shown in previous chapters, the restrictive judicial decisions have roughly confined the statute's coverage to those individuals who need the ADA's protections to remain in the workforce. In its definition-of-disability cases, for example, the Supreme Court has read the ADA as protecting individuals whose impairments prevent them from performing "a broad class of jobs," but it has held that the statute offers no protection "[i]f jobs utilizing an individual's skills (but perhaps not his or her unique talents) are available."[16] Although that holding clearly (and improperly, in my view) excludes some individuals from the statute's protection, the excluded individuals are likely to be those who can find other (though not as good) jobs without the ADA. Restrictive judicial decisions, therefore, are unlikely to explain the persistently high non-employment rate for people with disabilities.[17]

There is, then, no good reason to assume that the ADA is working fine, or that it will be working fine if only the new ADA Amendments Act leads the courts to change course. Whatever one's view of the evidence suggesting that the statute has *decreased* employment for people with disabilities, it is clear that the statute hasn't *increased* employment for people with disabilities to any significant extent. The nonemployment rate for people with disabilities remains exceptionally high—at roughly the same rate as it was in 1990 when Congress enacted the ADA. And the restrictive judicial interpretations of the statute are not likely to have contributed meaningfully to that problem. To solve the disability employment problem requires going beyond the ADA.

ABANDON THE ADA?

The evidence that the ADA is not improving the disability employment problem is powerful. But one should not cast the statute aside on the basis of that evidence. Before the ink was even dry on the ADA, a number of prominent commentators argued that the law was counterproductive and should be repealed. For example, Richard Epstein argued for repeal in his book *Forbidden Grounds*, published in the year the ADA began to take effect.[18] Jerry Mashaw, while taking issue with Epstein's argument in some respects, similarly pronounced the ADA to be "a deeply-flawed statute" in need of a radical overhaul.[19] The evidence suggesting that the ADA caused a decline in employment for people with disabilities has only added fuel to the fire. Thomas DeLeire, who produced one of the key studies, has argued that his results demonstrate that the ADA should be replaced by a tax credit for workers with disabilities.[20]

But that conclusion is premature. It is quite possible that the ADA initially had (at least somewhat of) a negative effect on the employment of (at least some subset of) people with disabilities—though there is genuine reason for doubt on this score.[21] There is good reason, however, to believe that any such negative effect was a short-term phenomenon. In their study of the statute's effects, Christine Jolls and J. J. Prescott found that the ADA caused a decline in disability employment in 1993 and 1994, but that it had no effect thereafter.[22] Daron Acemoglu and Joshua Angrist similarly found "that the negative effects of the ADA seem to peak in 1994 or 1995."[23] And the NOD surveys discussed above, which showed the employment rates of people with disabilities decreasing from 1986 through 1998, reveal a steady increase since. In the 2004 survey, 35 percent of respondents reported that they were employed, 6 percentage points higher than in 1998, and 1 percentage point higher than in 1986.[24] The employment rate remains quite low, but the trend does not suggest that the ADA has been *counter*productive.

These results should not be surprising. If the ADA encourages hiring discrimination because employers fear the cost of providing accommodations, that incentive is likely to dissipate (though perhaps not completely) over time. In many cases, accommodations involve one-time expenditures (like installing a ramp) that will benefit an entire class of prospective employees with disabilities; once such an accommodation is made to one employee, an employer will have no reason to refuse to hire other employees who will benefit from the same accommodation.[25] Moreover, as the ADA's mandate matures, employers, employees, and courts can be expected to develop, implement, and disseminate practices that will reduce the costs of finding and providing an appropriate accommodation.[26]

Although the ADA has not done a great job of moving people with disabilities into the workforce, then, there is no good reason to believe that its long-term effects will be counterproductive. To the contrary, the statute has probably already had a demonstrably positive effect on the employment of individuals whose disabilities do not require accommodation, and it is likely ultimately to have a positive effect on the employment of individuals whose disabilities require accommodation as well. Judging from the periodic NOD surveys, the statute has already reduced discrimination against incumbent employees with disabilities (in promotions, assignment of responsibilities, pay, and other benefits) as well.[27] A great deal of reform is necessary—and I discuss in the next chapter some of the forms it might take—but for now it is sufficient to conclude that the case for abandonment of the statute has simply not been made.

SOME EXPLANATIONS

Although the ADA has not had a significantly negative effect on the employment and community participation of people with disabilities, the statute's *positive* effects have been limited at best. What can explain this limited success? In the remainder of this chapter, I offer two major explanations. The first rests on the difficulty in effectively enforcing the ADA given the limited remedies available for violation of the statute. The second rests on the limits of antidiscrimination law in achieving broad and deep social change. Each of these factors, I believe, has played a role in the ADA's limited success in achieving the core goals of the disability rights movement.

ENFORCEMENT DIFFICULTIES

For a statute that is often accused of being a font of abusive and frivolous litigation, the ADA is remarkably underenforced. Because of the limited remedies available for violation of the statute, as well as the incentive structure facing plaintiffs' lawyers, too few ADA cases get brought. At the same time, those limits and incentives skew the types of cases that get brought. The result is in some ways the worst of both worlds. The story is slightly different for public accommodations suits and for employment suits, so I treat the two contexts separately.

In public accommodations cases, the key fact is that the ADA does not provide a damages remedy; successful plaintiffs can obtain forward-looking injunctive relief only.[28] The lack of a damages remedy out of which to carve a contingent fee gives plaintiffs' lawyers a disincentive to take ADA public accommodations cases. In employment cases, where money damages and back pay are available, the problem is one that exists (to a lesser extent) in employment discrimination litigation outside the disability context as well. Because it is difficult to prove hiring discrimination and much easier to prove discrimination against an incumbent employee, plaintiffs' lawyers are likely to take far fewer hiring cases than discharge cases. Unfortunately, that skew in case selection may give employers a disincentive to hire workers with disabilities in the first place.

PUBLIC ACCOMMODATIONS

Supporters of the ADA frequently contend that the statute's requirement of accessible public accommodations serves the interests of business by opening up a new market.[29] It is undeniable that accessibility does increase a business's pool of potential customers. And the ADA's requirements in this context are not particularly costly: in new construction, where it is relatively cheap to provide it, the statute requires full accessibility; in existing buildings, where accessibility may be onerous to achieve, the statute requires the removal of barriers only where removal does not entail "much difficulty or expense."[30] One might therefore ask why it was necessary to legislate accessibility: Won't businesses rationally want to remove barriers to access?

For a variety of reasons, however, operators of public accommodations may not voluntarily make their facilities accessible. Even if accessibility is completely rational from the perspective of a business, the owner may lack sufficient information: she may erroneously assume that barrier removal is more expensive than it is, or she may underestimate the amount of new patronage that would result from making her business accessible.[31] The owner's assessment of the costs and benefits of accessibility may be skewed by prejudice against or stereotyping of people with disabilities, even if the prejudice or stereotyping is unconscious.[32]

Barrier removal might not even be rational from the perspective of a particular business. The costs of making a business accessible, while small, might not be matched by increased patronage from individuals with disabilities. One might expect that a business that is the first mover in making its premises accessible could reap significant advantages by cornering the market on customers with disabilities. But those advantages might not be readily realized in practice. Given the availability of phone or Internet shopping and the possibility of asking or paying someone else to go to the store, an individual with a disability may not find it worth her while to expend the time and effort to go shopping in person if only one or a few stores are accessible. If so, one business can reap the benefits of accessible facilities only if many other businesses make their facilities accessible as well. Without some assurance that other businesses will remove barriers, an individual business may lack the incentive to do so itself.[33] And even if most businesses become accessible, not every business will realize a net benefit as a result; for some (perhaps many) businesses, the cost of barrier removal will outweigh the benefit of increased patronage. Requiring widespread accessibility serves an important societal interest in eliminating the stigma against and second-class citizenship of people with disabilities, but it may not be bottom-line rational for any particular business.

The ADA's mandate of accessible public accommodations thus helps respond to problems of bounded rationality and prejudice, problems of collective action and coordination, and socially harmful "rational discrimination." But the statute's good effects depend crucially on enforcement. If a business owner erroneously believes that barrier removal is expensive, she will not discover her error unless she is actually threatened with an enforcement action or the risk and consequences of enforcement are so great as to give her a reason to fear being targeted with litigation. If business owners want to be sure that others will remove barriers before they do so, they will have no incentive to act unless they know that a significant number of those who refuse to act will face enforcement actions. And if businesses rationally serve their bottom lines in refusing to make their premises accessible, only an actual threat of enforcement will make them change their ways.

The problem is that enforcement is akin to a public good: once a business becomes accessible to individuals with a particular disability, all individuals with similar disabilities in the relevant area will benefit. Because an individual who succeeds in forcing a business to remove barriers cannot appropriate all of the benefits of that action, the mere creation of a right of accessibility affords insufficient incentives to achieve full enforcement. And government cannot be counted on to fill the gap. The U.S. Department of Justice has devoted "only a small cadre of lawyers" to disability rights enforcement, and those lawyers must shoulder responsibility for enforcing the ADA against state and local governments as well as against private businesses.[34] A report of the National Council on Disability found that the department's Disability Rights Section "is understaffed in many areas of its responsibility, with significant operational consequences." These consequences include "decisions . . . not to open for investigation a large proportion of [public accommodations] complaints received."[35] As a result, the department has brought relatively few enforcement actions against places of public accommodation.[36]

Because the government does not fully enforce the ADA, private enforcement is essential. But in the private bar "most civil rights litigation is not brought by institutional litigators or by large firms engaging in pro bono activity" but rather is brought by individual lawyers who are trying to make a living.[37] Accordingly, enforcement largely depends on lawyers who need to earn income on their cases to keep their practices viable. As in other areas of public interest litigation, Congress sought to provide an incentive for enforcement of the ADA's public accommodations provisions by giving prevailing plaintiffs the right to recover attorneys' fees. But the incentives to bring ADA accessibility cases are still likely to be too weak to lead to full enforcement.

The statutory provisions limiting private plaintiffs to injunctive relief have two significant consequences that dampen private attorneys' incentive to bring ADA accessibility suits. First, because ADA public accommodations plaintiffs have no prospect of a monetary recovery out of which to carve a contingent fee, statutory attorneys' fees are likely to be the exclusive source of compensation for their lawyers. Practitioners who rely on contingent fees frequently earn effective hourly rates that are slightly higher than the hourly rates similarly credentialed practitioners charge their paying clients.[38] But under the Supreme Court's interpretation of the fee-shifting statutes, practitioners who rely on statutory attorneys' fees will always earn lower effective hourly rates than similarly credentialed practitioners with fee-paying clients. The Court has held that statutory attorneys' fees must be calculated by determining the number of hours plaintiffs' counsel reasonably expended and multiplying that number by a "reasonable hourly rate" for counsel's services.[39] That hourly rate—known in attorneys' fees jurisprudence as the "lodestar"[40]—is set according to the "prevailing market rates" that lawyers of similar skill and experience charge to fee-paying clients.[41] The Court specifically rejected a rule that would enhance the lodestar "to compensate for risk of loss and of consequent nonpayment."[42] As a result, plaintiffs' lawyers in statutory fee cases, who get paid only for hours expended in cases they win, are paid for those hours at the same hourly rate as lawyers with fee-paying clients, who get paid for all of the hours they work, win or lose. That difference in compensation tends to deter lawyers from taking cases like those under the ADA's public accommodations title, in which compensation comes only from statutory fees.[43]

Second, under the Supreme Court's controversial decision in *Buckhannon Board and Care Home, Inc. v. West Virginia Department of Health and Human Services,* plaintiffs' counsel can recover fees only when the litigation results in a "judicially sanctioned change in the legal relationship of the parties"—not an out-of-court settlement or voluntary compliance.[44] If a business owner can moot an ADA accessibility suit by removing the challenged barriers before the court issues a judgment, the plaintiff's counsel will recover no fee. It is true, as the Court emphasized, that "'voluntary cessation of a challenged practice does not deprive a federal court of its power to determine the legality of the practice' unless it is 'absolutely clear that the allegedly wrongful behavior could not reasonably be expected to recur.'"[45] But plaintiffs in ADA accessibility cases will often be unable to avail themselves of this principle. Where defendants respond to a plaintiff's complaint by constructing a ramp or removing some other structural barrier in a durable way, they will often be able to convince judges that there is no chance that the challenged behavior will recur.[46] That is true even when the lawsuit was the clear motivation for the decision to remove the barriers.[47]

The *Buckhannon* Court suggested that its rule would offer defendants an incentive to voluntary compliance because "the possibility of being assessed attorney's fees may well deter a defendant from altering its conduct."[48] That analysis may be correct *ex post* (once a case is brought), but it ignores the *ex ante* effect of the Court's ruling on plaintiffs' lawyers' choices of what cases to take. If a defendant's voluntary compliance can moot a purely injunctive lawsuit and deprive the plaintiff of the right to recover attorneys' fees, plaintiffs' counsel who depend on statutory fees are likely to take far fewer purely injunctive cases in the first place—which means far fewer ADA public accommodations cases. To the extent that businesses remove barriers to access only in response to litigation—and the absence of a damages remedy gives businesses little reason not to take this "wait and see" approach—the *Buckhannon* decision will cause a net decrease in voluntary compliance with the ADA.

The foregoing discussion should suggest a big part of the reason why, nearly two decades after enactment of the ADA, noncompliance with the statute's public accommodations title is widespread: there is not a sufficient incentive for private attorneys to bring ADA public accommodations suits. All other things being equal, an attorney will choose to work for a fee-paying client, or to bring damages actions in which a contingent fee can be recovered, rather than bring the purely injunctive cases that the ADA's public accommodations title authorizes. ADA public accommodations litigation simply pays a lower effective hourly rate than do those alternatives because a plaintiff's counsel will be unable to recover attorneys' fees if she loses or if she succeeds too easily. And the government cannot and will not fill the enforcement gap.

A major reason for the lack of effectiveness of the ADA's public accommodations title, then, is the statute's failure to provide a damages remedy to successful plaintiffs. As I have shown in earlier work, that same limitation on remedies has, perhaps perversely, led to the kinds of litigation tactics businesses consider abusive.[49] Despite its reputation as a font of abusive litigation, the public accommodations title of the ADA is extremely underenforced—and the lack of a damages remedy is responsible for both the reputation and the underenforcement.

EMPLOYMENT

The story in the employment area is somewhat different. There is no shortage of ADA employment litigation, but it overwhelmingly focuses on the discharge of employees with disabilities rather than the failure to hire them. As Steven Willborn showed a few years ago, "the ratio of discharge to hiring cases has been about 10 to 1" under the statute.[50] The tilt in favor of discharge cases can be readily understood as a response to the incentives facing plaintiffs' lawyers. Incumbent employees are more likely to be able to pay retainers to plaintiffs' attorneys than are disappointed applicants, their damages are likely to be higher, and it is typically easier to prove discrimination in a case where the plaintiff has been successfully performing the job for years than in a case where the plaintiff has never worked at the job.[51] Under the ADA, it is especially difficult to prove hiring discrimination, because of the diverse array of disabilities covered by the statute and the concomitant difficulty in mustering statistical proof of discrimination against any particular disability.[52] ADA hiring cases are therefore not particularly attractive to plaintiffs' attorneys.

Although the skew in favor of discharge cases under the ADA is understandable, it may well be impeding the statute's ability to improve the employment rate for people with disabilities. The more that employers believe they are at risk of discharge suits instead of hiring suits, the more likely are they to discriminate at the hiring stage.[53] The skew in litigation is therefore a likely contributor to the limited effectiveness of the ADA's employment title.

THE LIMITS OF ANTIDISCRIMINATION LAW

Underenforcement (and misdirected enforcement) has certainly contributed to the ineffectiveness of the ADA in achieving the core goals of the disability rights movement. But even if it were perfectly enforced, the statute could not achieve those goals. That is because of the limited nature of antidiscrimination law.

As I argued in chapter 4, antidiscrimination law focuses on the discrete acts of identifiable, faulty actors. In the employment discrimination context, antidiscrimination law prohibits discrete acts or omissions by employers when those acts or omissions amount to "discrimination"—whether those acts or omissions involve intentional discrimination against protected-class members, the adoption of job selection criteria with an unjustified disparate impact on them, or the refusal to make a reasonable accommodation that a protected-class member requests.[54]

Unfortunately, many of the most significant barriers that keep people with disabilities from entering the workforce are not readily attributed to the discrete, faulty acts and omissions of particular employers. Although—as the discussion in much of the rest of this book should demonstrate—discrimination is plainly a major problem for people with disabilities, many individuals with disabilities face significant barriers to employment that operate well before they are ever in a position to be discriminated against by an employer.[55] Many people with disabilities need personal-assistance services—attendants who assist with personal hygiene and other activities of daily living—to help them get out of bed and get to work.[56] Many others need assistive technology to perform work-related (and other) tasks, as well as structural modifications to their homes to enable them to leave for work in the morning.[57] And the lack of accessible transportation remains a crucial issue for people with disabilities.[58]

But far and away the most significant barrier to employment for people with disabilities is the current structure of our health insurance system.[59] For two major reasons, health insurance is a matter of especial importance for those who have disabilities. First, because our society's response to disability has historically been so heavily medicalized, many of the services people with disabilities need for independence and participation in the labor force—personal assistance and assistive technology being the most obvious—are typically regarded as "medical" services for which the health insurance system is responsible. Second, even without considering those services (which might more appropriately be provided in a nonmedical context), it is nonetheless true that people with disabilities, on average, have greater health needs than do those without disabilities.[60]

In its current form, our health insurance system affirmatively disserves the interest of people with disabilities in moving into the workforce. The problem is not that people with disabilities are disproportionately uninsured; they are not.[61] The problem is that private insurance—on which most nondisabled people rely for their health needs—fails to cover the services people with disabilities most need for independence and health.[62] And public insurance is saddled with requirements that lock people with disabilities out of the workforce.[63]

It is not impossible to attribute these barriers to the faulty acts or omissions of particular employers—or of government agencies suable under the ADA's public services title. But such attribution presses against widely held understandings of the limited nature of antidiscrimination law's intervention in society. Thus, as I showed in chapter 4, courts have used the access-content distinction to assimilate the ADA's accommodation requirement closely to an antidiscrimination rule that requires likes to be treated alike. In the process, they have deprived the statute of much utility in attacking the health insurance practices that keep so many people with disabilities out of the workforce. As applied to cases challenging limitations on public welfare benefits, too, the access-content distinction has made it much harder to use the statute to demand new services that would break down the structural barriers that keep people with disabilities out of the workforce. And the job-related rule, by limiting the accommodation obligation to in-the-workplace practices, has made it difficult to use the ADA as a tool to require private employers to break down structural barriers—like the lack of personal-assistance services and accessible transportation—that are not easily seen as the fault of the individual employer.

As I showed in chapter 4, the access-content and job-related limitations are not necessary readings of the ADA or the antidiscrimination paradigm, and they are substantially indeterminate as a formal matter. But when courts invoke those limitations to narrow the scope of the ADA's accommodation requirement, they reflect a broadly held view that antidiscrimination law is itself an inherently narrow tool, one that does not command large-scale social change. As a historical matter, of course, that view of antidiscrimination law is wildly wrong. But antidiscrimination law has been domesticated, the price of obtaining broad societal consensus supporting it.[64] As I showed in chapter 2, many disability rights activists argued that antidiscrimination law was all that was necessary to ensure disability equality. But they did not appreciate just how limited a tool antidiscrimination law had become. The limits of their strategy have become painfully apparent. In the next chapter, I offer some thoughts about how that strategy can be retooled to achieve the core goals of the disability rights movement, while heeding the lessons that led disability rights activists to turn to antidiscrimination law in the first place.

8

FUTURE DIRECTIONS IN DISABILITY LAW

As I demonstrated in the previous chapter, the nearly two decades since the enactment of the ADA have seen real successes for disability rights—but those successes have been limited. On important measures, Americans with disabilities remain roughly where they were at the time President George H. W. Bush signed the statute into law. The previous chapter identified two basic reasons for that state of affairs: the lack of effective enforcement of the ADA, and the limits of antidiscrimination law as a tool for achieving broad and deep social change.

To make the core goals of the disability rights movement a reality, then, requires a two-pronged approach: improving the enforcement of the ADA, and adopting new interventions that go beyond the ADA's antidiscrimination/accommodation model. In this chapter, I offer some rather wonkish thoughts about that approach, what forms each prong might take, and the difficulties each prong poses for disability rights activists. I begin by discussing some means for improving the enforcement of the ADA. As I hope to show, there are a number of possibilities here; those possibilities may be politically difficult to obtain from Congress or the executive branch, but they are ones on which all disability rights activists, at least, can agree. Interventions that go beyond the ADA's antidiscrimination/accommodation model, which I discuss next, are in some ways the opposite. They may be politically easier to obtain from Congress and the executive branch, but they raise difficult dilemmas for disability rights activists who sought to move from welfare rights to civil rights. Much of the future task of disability rights advocacy will involve efforts to manage these dilemmas.

IMPROVING ENFORCEMENT OF THE ADA

PUBLIC ACCOMMODATIONS

The way to improve enforcement of the ADA's public accommodations title is straightforward: Congress should authorize a remedy of damages, and not just a forward-looking injunction, for violations of that title. As I showed in the previous chapter, the absence of a damages remedy has deprived plaintiffs' lawyers of an incentive to bring ADA public accommodations suits. In part, that is because the rules governing statutory attorneys' fees give plaintiffs' lawyers a relative disincentive to bring injunctive civil rights cases of any kind. But the disincentive is even greater in the ADA context, where accessible businesses can make changes to their physical structures while a lawsuit is pending and deprive the plaintiff's lawyer of *any* fees. A damages remedy would solve these problems, by giving plaintiffs' lawyers the chance to earn a contingent fee on ADA public accommodations cases, and by depriving businesses of the chance to render those cases moot by making changes after a lawsuit is filed.

Unfortunately, businesses and their political allies have recently devoted a great deal of energy to efforts to impose even further limits on the remedies for violation of the ADA's public accommodations title. They have done so out of concern for what they believe to be abusive litigation brought under that title. In particular, the concern focuses on serial litigation—individual lawyers or plaintiffs bringing hundreds of cases each, against dozens of businesses in each town they visit, without notifying a business of the problem before filing suit. As I have shown in other work, those sorts of litigation tactics are the direct result of the limitations Congress already placed on remedies for violation of the public accommodations title. The best response to those tactics—and to the widespread lack of enforcement of the statute—would be to (a) authorize a damages remedy, (b) require ADA public accommodations plaintiffs to provide presuit notice, and (c) pay attorneys' fees to plaintiffs who succeed in eliminating ADA violations by providing such presuit notice.[1] That response would require Congress to amend the ADA, and it may be difficult to secure such an amendment in the current political climate. But such an amendment is essential to achieving the goal of ensuring that people with disabilities have full and equal access to our civic life.

EMPLOYMENT

In the employment context, some possible means of improving enforcement are equally straightforward. The basic problem is the lack of incentive for plaintiffs' attorneys to bring hiring cases. One obvious solution would be to increase the damages available under the ADA for hiring-stage discrimination.[2]

The ADA caps compensatory and punitive damages at $300,000 (less for employers with fewer than one hundred employees),[3] and no damages are available in a reasonable-accommodation case if the employer demonstrates a good-faith effort to accommodate.[4] To remove these restrictions would require legislative action—which would likely face political hurdles similar to those faced by the proposal to authorize a damages remedy for ADA public accommodations cases.

Another possibility could be implemented without legislative action: the Equal Employment Opportunity Commission could devote more of its resources toward bringing hiring-stage cases. Now that the Civil Rights Act of 1991 has created a damages remedy for employment discrimination—which has attracted a large number of private plaintiffs' lawyers to the field—the EEOC's enforcement generally ought to focus on the kinds of cases that private lawyers are *not* bringing.[5] In the disability context, where private attorneys are bringing discharge cases that may actually create a *disincentive* to hire members of the protected class, government action to bring hiring cases that would counteract that disincentive is particularly imperative.[6]

The EEOC has brought some high-profile hiring cases under the ADA.[7] Unfortunately, however, the agency continues to bring a large number of individual discharge cases.[8] Those cases can generally attract the private bar, and far from giving employers an incentive to hire applicants with disabilities, they may have the opposite effect. The EEOC should make it a priority to bring more hiring cases—cases that the private bar has proven unwilling or unable to bring. Because the EEOC does not rely on contingent fees or statutory attorneys' fees to fund its litigation practice, it can bring the small-recovery hiring cases that are not profitable for the private bar. Those cases will directly help the individual charging parties to get jobs. More important, they will help to ensure that ADA litigation creates incentives to hire, rather than reject, applicants with disabilities. Even if the damages an employer ultimately must pay when it loses a hiring case are small, it must waste time and resources on litigation to defend its position; the threat of that litigation will give employers reason to avoid discrimination at the hiring stage.

To be sure, increased hiring-stage enforcement will not have the right incentive effect if the EEOC loses too many of its cases. And although the commission has the financial resources to bring hiring discrimination cases regardless of the likelihood of success, it will face many of the same barriers to success that private attorneys do. In particular, the EEOC, like private attorneys, will still encounter difficulty in proving that the employer refused to hire the applicant because of a disability. While the EEOC will have more resources with which to collect and analyze data regarding the employer's hiring decision, the employer will still be able to offer nondiscriminatory reasons, which may be difficult to discredit without a trial, regarding why the applicant with a disability was passed over. There are therefore likely to be few "easy-to-win suits."[9] And statistical proof, which was so important to proving systemic disparate treatment in the race and gender contexts, will be difficult to muster in the disability context. The problem, after all, is not so much private counsel's lack of technical statistical skills as the fact that there are so many diverse conditions covered by the ADA's disability definition, which "makes comparisons between an employer's treatment of people with different disabilities largely meaningless."[10] If a rejected applicant with paraplegia complains of discrimination, and at most a handful of other people with paraplegia had ever applied for similar positions, the EEOC is not going to be able to draw statistically meaningful conclusions about the existence of intentional discrimination.[11]

Because hiring-discrimination suits depend on the typically contestable question of whether the defendant intentionally discriminated—and statistical proof is likely to be of less-than-usual help—they present a higher risk of failure than do reasonable-accommodation suits brought on behalf of incumbent employees. That risk may be an obstacle to convincing the EEOC to bring more hiring cases, for the agency has set a goal of a 90 percent success rate in its litigation.[12]

But there are ways for the EEOC to improve its chances of success in ADA hiring-stage litigation. In particular, the commission could begin a program of using testers to ferret out hiring discrimination.[13] Testers have been used extensively in fair housing litigation[14] and to some extent in other employment discrimination litigation.[15] But they have been virtually absent from ADA employment litigation. That is too bad, because testing is likely to be particularly useful at the hiring stage—the very stage where ADA enforcement should be expanded.[16] When a private complainant files a charge of disability-based hiring discrimination with the EEOC, the agency could respond by sending disabled and nondisabled testers to confirm the charge—at least if the alleged discriminator is a business that makes large numbers of entry-level hiring decisions each year. If the employer not only refused to hire the individual with a disability who filed the EEOC charge but also refused to hire disabled testers while offering to hire similarly situated nondisabled ones, that would be powerful evidence of intentional discrimination.[17]

It would be even better to use testers in a more affirmative way, in advance of the filing of any individual charge of discrimination. The commission could identify the large industries or employers that generate per capita the highest number of ADA hiring discrimination charges. It could then periodically choose from those employers at random and send disabled and nondisabled testers to apply for open, entry-level positions. If the tester investigation found discrimination, the results could be the basis for a commissioner charge or a pattern-or-practice claim against the employer. Such precomplaint investigations, if performed by the EEOC itself, might require an amendment to the ADA,[18] but the commission almost certainly has the authority to work with private parties who conduct testing-based investigations.[19]

Even using testers simply to investigate complaints would require a significant commitment of resources (which is why private plaintiffs' attorneys do not use them),[20] but increased use of testing would pay significant dividends. Employers would know that there is an ever-present possibility that they are being monitored for disability bias when they make hiring decisions.[21] That knowledge, and the risk that they will be forced to defend themselves in possibly protracted litigation if they pass over applicants with disabilities, will give employers an incentive to avoid any bias against those applicants in the hiring process. And that incentive will help temper the aspects of the ADA that tend to suppress employment for people with disabilities.

Unfortunately, there are substantial political obstacles to the EEOC's implementing a hiring testing program under the ADA. In the employment context, testing has been highly controversial. Many employers object to the deception inherent in testing, and they believe that government-sponsored testing amounts to entrapment.[22] Moved by these arguments, the then EEOC chair Evan Kemp (whom readers might recall from chapter 2) withdrew an effort at fair employment testing in the early 1990s,[23] and a Republican Congress in the late 1990s all but forbade the commission to spend funds on testing.[24] The controversy over testing, combined with the pressure on the domestic budget these days, will make it difficult to implement an ADA hiring testing program.

Those obstacles need not be insurmountable, however. The Department of Justice has conducted a fair housing testing program for more than a decade now—in Republican administrations as well as a Democratic one.[25] The Supreme Court has also approved of testing as a means of enforcing the Fair Housing Act.[26] There is no reason testing should be substantially more problematic in the employment setting.

In the end, it may not be possible politically for the EEOC to engage in more vigorous hiring-stage enforcement. But the effort is likely to be essential to orienting the ADA toward improving the employment rates for people with disabilities.

MOVING BEYOND ANTIDISCRIMINATION
AND ACCOMMODATION

Even if they were politically feasible, efforts to expand enforcement of the ADA could have only a limited effect. As I showed in chapter 7, the deeper problem is not a lack of enforcement; the deeper problem is antidiscrimination law's focus on the discrete, faulty acts and omissions of particular defendants. Especially in the employment area, the limits of antidiscrimination law pose acute problems. Accordingly, disability rights activists must move beyond antidiscrimination law to embrace social welfare interventions if they are to achieve the goals of employment and integration into community life. As the discussion in chapters 2 through 4 should suggest, however, this move poses problems for disability rights activists whose goal was to seek "independence" from government largesse.

One ought not to overstate the novelty of this tension. Disability rights activists, after all, have long invoked the power of the state to enforce a principle of antidiscrimination and accommodation. As chapter 4 showed, many members of the public have in fact understood the accommodation mandate as a form of forced charity or welfare. And much of the judicial effort to narrow the ADA can be seen as an attempt to manage the tension between disability rights activists' opposition to charity and welfare and those same activists' embrace of a mandate that looks, to many people, like welfare.

In my view, the effort to avoid an association with "charity" or "welfare" at all costs is an effort that makes no sense. Even the purest of antidiscrimination measures can be characterized as creating "special rights," as reactions to the struggle for gay and lesbian rights have shown. And the effort to keep the ADA from becoming charity or welfare has deprived the statute of much power to eliminate the deep-rooted structural barriers that keep so many people with disabilities out of the workforce. Where the disability rights movement's projects of employment and community participation come into conflict with the movement's welfare reform project, I would contend, employment and community participation should prevail.

This does not mean that disability rights activists should embrace a return to the old days, where charity and cure were seen as the preferred response to disability. Any move to social welfare approaches must take account of the important critiques disability rights activists raised against the earlier round of those approaches. Social welfare interventions must be tailored to promote employment, integration, and community participation, and to avoid unnecessary paternalism and dependence. In the sections below, I describe a number of areas in which people affiliated with the disability rights movement have turned toward advocating for social welfare policies. I begin with what I believe to be a false start before turning to some initiatives that are more promising.

A FALSE START:
EMPLOYMENT QUOTAS AND SUBSIDIES

Most countries in Europe, and others around the world, have historically adopted employment quotas for people with disabilities.[27] In a typical form, a quota policy requires all employers over a certain size (sixteen or more employees under the German statute) to set aside a certain percentage of their job slots (about 6 percent under the German statute) for people who fit some definition of disability. Employers who do not meet their quota must pay a fine or tax that goes to promote employment among people with disabilities, often by subsidizing employers who exceed their quota.[28]

A number of American commentators have suggested adopting a version of the European tradable quota system in the United States to augment or replace the ADA.[29] Yet quota systems have not been particularly successful in increasing employment or achieving integration in Europe.[30] Indeed, the trend in Europe—in part the result of advocacy by politically active people with disabilities—is to abandon quotas in favor of ADA-like antidiscrimination and accommodation laws.[31] There is no reason to expect that quotas would work any better in the United States. Even if mandatory, tradable quotas were a political possibility in America—which I believe they are not—they would not be good policy.[32]

A proposal more moderate than a quota system would use subsidies to encourage employers to hire workers with disabilities.[33] A number of commentators have suggested that the federal government should adopt a "Disabled Worker Tax Credit" modeled on the Earned Income Tax Credit.[34] To the extent that some people with disabilities require accommodations that are so costly as to be un-"reasonable" under the ADA, a subsidy regime is attractive.[35] But there are a number of reasons to be skeptical about such a regime. Some of these reasons are technocratic. It is hard to design a subsidy that goes only to the marginal employers who would not have hired workers with disabilities in the absence of the subsidy. Indeed, there might not be many marginal employers who will be moved to hire workers with disabilities once they receive a subsidy. The regime may therefore end up "buying the base" at a high price, without having much of an effect on the disability employment rate.[36] For this reason, among others, the history of subsidy policies for disadvantaged workers yields few success stories.[37]

Moreover, subsidies raise especial ideological concerns in the disability context. A long-standing aim of disability rights activists has been to assert that people with disabilities are full citizens, for whom work opportunities should be a matter of civil rights rather than charity.[38] Although social welfare provision that reduces the stigma of dependence associated with disability remains essential, employment subsidies will likely do nothing but reinforce that stigma.[39] Indeed, there is evidence that employment subsidies outside the disability context have stigmatized their recipients and actually harmed job prospects.[40] These points suggest a particular need for care before pursuing the subsidy route.

A MORE PROMISING EFFORT:
EXPANDING PUBLIC HEALTH INSURANCE

Proposals for employment quotas and subsidies have tended to come from policy wonks rather than disability rights movement activists. But movement activists have used social welfare interventions in a much more promising way in their efforts to expand the coverage of public health insurance. As I discussed in chapter 7, our current health insurance system constitutes the most significant barrier to employment and community integration for people with disabilities, and the discussion below shows that activists' efforts to expand public health insurance can help remove those barriers without increasing the stigma of dependency.

ENFORCING THE MEDICAID ACT

Even if disability rights advocates have increasingly turned toward efforts to enact social welfare legislation, one might expect that disability rights litigation would continue to be dominated by the ADA. To a large extent, that is true — especially in the individual-plaintiff lawsuits that make up the vast majority of disability rights cases.[41] But in the systemic-reform dockets of disability rights organizations, there is a notable trend toward a social welfare approach. In dozens of recent cases, those organizations have filed suits to enforce provisions of the Medicaid Act (Title XIX of the Social Security Act).[42] Rather than merely demanding an end to discrimination or seeking an accommodation under the ADA or the Rehabilitation Act, these suits demand specific benefits to which the plaintiffs claim entitlement under the federal Medicaid statute.

Disability rights organizations have not been indiscriminate in the benefits they have sought through litigation. Rather, they have focused on those Medicaid benefits — like community placements and personal-assistance services — that enhance opportunities for people with disabilities to participate in community life (particularly in employment). They have tended to bring Medicaid suits that address two kinds of problems. First, many people with disabilities have been forced to remain on waiting lists for community-based services to which they are entitled under their states' Medicaid plans because the states have refused to provide those services in a timely manner to all who are eligible.[43] Disability rights organizations have frequently brought class action suits that contend, among other things, that such waiting lists violate various requirements of the Medicaid Act.[44] Plaintiffs in these cases have obtained a number of favorable rulings from courts, and they have received significant relief in settlements.[45]

Second, some state Medicaid policies, such as low reimbursement rates for personal assistance and other services, can make it impossible in practice for individuals with disabilities to obtain adequate community-based services even if the state does not place those individuals on a waiting list.[46] Disability rights organizations have challenged these policies under the adequate-payment provision of the Medicaid Act. That provision requires states to "assure that payments are consistent with efficiency, economy, and quality of care and are sufficient to enlist enough providers so that care and services are available under the plan at least to the extent that such care and services are available to the general population in the geographic area."[47] These suits have been less successful than the waiting-list suits, however.[48]

Litigation to enforce the Medicaid Act plainly has serious limitations as a tool to achieve community integration for people with disabilities. Such litigation can be no more effective in achieving those goals than is the Medicaid statute itself. To be sure, Medicaid covers an array of services that are important to people with disabilities — potentially including, at each individual state's option, such services as durable medical equipment and prosthetics.[49] Also at state option, Medicaid may provide home-based and community-based services, including personal assistance, for many people with disabilities.[50] But in two significant respects, Medicaid is a flawed tool. First, the wide discretion accorded to states in the structuring of Medicaid benefits makes the program a less than sure means of promoting the interests of people with disabilities. Tight state budgets can lead to massive reductions in Medicaid benefits.[51] Second, the structure of the Medicaid program itself imposes significant obstacles to the ability of people with disabilities to live and work in the community, because the program has a strong bias toward paying for the needs of institutional rather than community placements.[52]

At best, then, Medicaid litigation can force states to comply with their own decisions to provide optional services. If states respond to that litigation by amending their Medicaid plans to cut back on the services they promise to provide, there is nothing in the statute to stop them.[53] Successes in Medicaid litigation thus may become Pyrrhic victories for disability rights advocates.

But the rise in Medicaid litigation by disability rights advocates is important nonetheless. Despite its limitations, it represents a recognition that antidiscrimination strategies alone cannot achieve employment and community integration for people with disabilities. These goals can be achieved only through state-provided services—core social-welfare-law interventions. As I discuss below, disability rights advocates are increasingly focusing their legislative advocacy on efforts to alter the aspects of existing Medicaid law that limit the program's power to achieve these goals.

EXPANDING ELIGIBILITY FOR PUBLIC HEALTH INSURANCE

As I discussed above, the most significant aspects of our current health insurance system that limit employment opportunities for people with disabilities are the powerful work disincentives built into the major public health-insurance programs, Medicare and Medicaid. To obtain coverage under these programs, people with disabilities must generally show that they are unable to work. In the past, recipients who returned to work often lost their Medicare and Medicaid eligibility as a result. Because private health insurance will not provide the services many people with disabilities need, these eligibility rules effectively lock them out of the workforce. Any effort to move substantial numbers of people with disabilities into jobs must address disincentives like these. In particular, such an effort must sever the link between cash benefits and public health insurance and thereby make work no longer a disqualifying factor for the receipt of Medicare and Medicaid.

Recognizing this point, disability rights advocates in recent years have devoted substantial energy to lobbying for legislation that would extend eligibility for Medicare and Medicaid to a larger number of working people with disabilities. Disability rights advocates were among those who successfully pushed for the passage of the Ticket to Work and Work Incentives Improvement Act (TWWIIA) of 1999.[54] Among other things, TWWIIA extends Medicare coverage for a full eight-and-a-half years to individuals with disabilities who leave the Social Security Disability Insurance rolls to return to work.[55] The statute provides for expedited reinstatement to the SSDI-Medicare or SSI-Medicaid rolls for former recipients who, after a period of time back in the labor force, become unable to work once again.[56] It also limits the degree to which work activity can be used as evidence that a former recipient no longer has a disability.[57] These provisions address a significant fear held by many SSDI recipients: if they leave the benefits rolls to return to work, they will lose their SSDI eligibility—and hence their entitlement to Medicare—once and for all, even if they later cannot find adequate work or private health insurance.

But TWWIIA's extension of Medicare coverage to individuals who leave the SSDI rolls has a number of significant limitations. Although the statute extends Medicare coverage to individuals for a longer period of time after they leave the SSDI rolls, it does not make Medicare available to those who have not yet joined those rolls. To become eligible for Medicare in the first place, individuals with disabilities must still establish that they are unable to work, and they must remain unemployed through the lengthy disability-determination process. As a result, Medicare recipients with disabilities continue to develop a significant psychological investment in the proposition that they cannot work, and they continue to experience long periods of separation from the workforce that make them less employable.[58] A truly effective effort to improve the employment rate of people with disabilities must also focus on individuals who are currently employed but whose attachment to the workforce is shaky.[59]

Moreover, an extension of Medicare benefits may not be sufficient to eliminate disincentives to work. Medicare was designed for a nonworking elderly population and does not well serve the interest of people with disabilities in community integration and access to the labor market.[60] For example, Medicare rules make it difficult to obtain coverage for assistive technology, mobility aids, and power wheelchairs in circumstances in which those devices can aid community integration.[61]

Other provisions of TWWIIA attempt to address these limitations of the Medicare extension. Section 201 of the statute authorizes states, at their option, to create Medicaid buy-in programs for working people with disabilities.[62] Given the substantial budgetary pressures on states to limit optional categories of Medicaid spending, however, it is unlikely that those eligibility expansions will ever be fully implemented.

Despite these limitations, TWWIIA marks a major step forward in promoting independence and work for people with disabilities. And the involvement of disability rights activists in lobbying for the statute marked a major advance as well, for it reflected their recognition that social welfare interventions can be crucial in empowering people with disabilities.

EXPANDING THE SERVICES COVERED BY PUBLIC HEALTH INSURANCE

Even if disability rights activists succeed in expanding eligibility for public health insurance, significant structural barriers to employment will remain. As I discussed above, the coverage formulas for both Medicare and (to a lesser but still important extent) Medicaid give short shrift to those services that would enable people with disabilities to live and work in the community. Disability rights activists have increasingly turned their attention to attacking these limitations on Medicare and Medicaid benefits. Indeed, passage of what was once called MiCASSA (the Medicaid Community-Based Attendant Services and Supports Act), now called more simply the Community Choice Act, is a significant legislative priority for disability rights activists.[63] The Community Choice Act would eliminate Medicaid's institutional bias by mandating that states cover personal-assistance services for recipients with disabilities. The bill would give eligible individuals the choice between receiving community-based attendant services and receiving services in an institutional setting, and it would guarantee persons with disabilities the power personally to hire, fire, and manage their assistants.

Disability rights activists' efforts to expand the services covered by public health insurance have not yet borne much fruit. MiCASSA and the Community Choice Act have now been introduced in six successive Congresses without ever making it out of committee. The nursing home lobby, which carries a great deal of clout on Capitol Hill, is strenuously opposed to the bill.[64] If passed, after all, the statute would likely result in large numbers of people moving from nursing homes to home-based and community-based settings. Some groups of parents of people with disabilities, such as Voice of the Retarded, also oppose the bill. The parents in these groups fear that their (now-grown) children will not receive appropriate care in community settings.[65]

Even if advocates of the Community Choice Act can overcome the resistance to its passage, the bill will not be a panacea for people with disabilities. As I discuss below, the bill could easily leave people with disabilities at the mercy of private home-health-care agencies, which may subordinate the independence of their clients to their own profit-maximizing objectives. And the bill is limited to personal-assistance services; it does nothing to assure access to such important services as assistive technology or home modifications for people with disabilities. Nonetheless, the fact that disability rights activists have placed such a high priority on the enactment of legislation expanding the Medicaid program is itself telling. Like the other developments I have been discussing, it reflects a recognition by disability rights activists that the ADA alone is not sufficient to achieve community integration for people with disabilities.

EMERGING DILEMMAS

As the discussion above demonstrates, disability rights activists have increasingly recognized the limitations of the ADA's antidiscrimination approach. But as those activists turn toward social welfare strategies, new dilemmas will arise—

or rather, old dilemmas will reassert themselves. Although social welfare strategies are essential to achieving the goals of disability rights activists, the disability rights movement's 1970s-era critique of the social welfare system remains powerful. And a number of the new social welfare initiatives potentially raise the same sorts of concerns that disability rights activists voiced in the 1970s. Any return to social welfare law must seek to address those concerns.

In the sections that follow, I discuss two broad questions disability rights advocates will face as they embrace social welfare strategies for achieving their goals. First, they must choose whether to advocate universal social insurance benefits or targeted disability-specific interventions. The choice between universalism and targeting is one that recurs throughout social welfare policy, but, as the discussion in chapters 2 and 3 should suggest, the disability rights movement's critique of welfare gives the choice an unusual character in the disability context. Second, disability rights advocates' critique of professional domination of people with disabilities makes it particularly important that renewed social welfare interventions reduce the medicalization of disability benefits and promote consumer control. At the same time, those interventions must do so without placing people with disabilities at risk of receiving inferior services.

UNIVERSAL VERSUS TARGETED APPROACHES

In social welfare policy generally, policymakers are often said to face a trade-off between targeted and universal interventions.[66] Targeted programs—those that focus benefits on a particular needy group—may more efficiently achieve the goal of alleviating suffering.[67] But universal programs—social insurance programs that provide benefits to broad classes, such as all workers or all citizens— are generally thought to be more politically stable. "Programs for the poor are poor programs," the cliché goes.[68]

Looking at the history of the American welfare state in general, there seems to be a great deal of evidence to support the notion that broad social insurance programs fare better politically than do more targeted interventions.[69] The classic comparison is between the history of the Social Security program and that of the major means-tested welfare program, Aid to Families with Dependent Children (which became Temporary Assistance to Needy Families after passage of the 1996 welfare law). Social Security's universal coverage has largely masked the program's redistributive character, and political support for the program has remained sufficiently strong to scare off any effort to change it fundamentally— a point brought home by President George W. Bush's failed effort to privatize Social Security in 2005.[70] Means-tested welfare, by contrast, has long been a political target, and efforts to limit and condition the benefits it provides have not stopped with the passage of the 1996 reform law, which eliminated the federal entitlement to welfare.[71]

In the disability context, however, it might appear that there is no such trade-off between universal and targeted approaches. People with disabilities, after all, have long been considered to be the "deserving poor." A social welfare program targeted to poor people in general might well be politically vulnerable, but a social welfare program targeted to people with disabilities—toward whom the general public has a charitable disposition—will likely be much stronger politically.[72] As disability rights activists turn back to social welfare strategies, they might well be tempted to seek enactment of targeted programs that will provide enhanced benefits for people with disabilities only. Indeed, all of the legislative proposals I discussed above were disability-specific initiatives. At a time when significant retrenchment in domestic spending seems all but inevitable, the successful passage of the TWWIIA statute and the relatively favorable reception the other disability-specific initiatives have received may suggest that such targeted proposals are politically viable in a way that broader social insurance proposals are not.

But targeted disability-specific social welfare programs have a cost as well. As disability rights activists made clear in the 1970s, one reason disability welfare programs have broad political support is that much of the public holds attitudes that are inconsistent with recognizing people with disabilities as full citizens. Many believe that people with disabilities are especially deserving of charity and public largesse precisely because they believe that people with disabilities are not capable of providing for themselves. If disability rights activists rely on and cater to those attitudes to gain support for disability-specific social welfare initiatives, they may end up reinforcing those attitudes in a way that is extremely damaging to the movement's broader goals.[73]

This point suggests that disability rights activists should, whenever possible, seek to achieve their social welfare goals through "universal policies that recognize that the entire population is 'at risk' for the concomitants of chronic illness and disability."[74] (Just as I argued, in chapter 3, that it would be better for the disability rights cause if the ADA were framed in a universalist manner.) The example of employment quotas and subsidies discussed above—and the poor results those interventions have had when attempted—highlights the point.

Health policy seems an extremely promising area in which to take a universalist approach. Until the 1990s, American disability rights activists were quite averse to urging a broadening of guaranteed health coverage. The movement had "worked so hard for so long to separate the issues of health and disability" that demands for broader health coverage seemed to "resurrect[] harmful stereo-types."[75] Three events led disability rights activists to recognize their important stake in health reform debates: the Oregon Health Plan controversy of 1992, the flurry of activity surrounding President Clinton's proposed Health Security Act in 1993 and 1994, and the rise of managed care in the mid- to late 1990s.[76] But if disability rights activists restrict their goals to disability-specific expansions of health insurance such as those embodied in TWWIIA and the Community Choice Act, their actions risk "reviving the stereotype that all people with disabilities are sick and should be viewed as patients."[77] If disability rights advocates place a greater focus on urging enactment of a universal health care system, though, they may help to blunt that stereotype.

For many of the reasons discussed in chapter 7, people with disabilities would disproportionately benefit from a universal guarantee of health insurance. Most notably, such a guarantee would eliminate the fear of the loss of coverage that is the most significant barrier to employment for people with disabilities. But a universal health care system would very likely not be seen as a disability-oriented program, because it would provide benefits to everyone. Advocacy for and enact-ment of such a system would not send the message that people with disabilities are uniquely in need of caretaking; it would send the message that we all need insurance against contingencies in life.

To some extent, of course, disability rights advocates will necessarily be called upon to defend disability-specific interventions. Even in the context of universal health insurance, activists will want to ensure that the benefits formula provides adequate coverage for those services that are particularly important to people with disabilities. And even when disability activists defend the Medicaid en-titlement generally, they will, by their very participation, trigger the feelings of charity and pity many nondisabled people have toward people with disabilities. The attitudes toward disability that remain prevalent in society are too strong to enable activists to escape them fully by urging universal interventions. But by casting demands for social welfare provision in universal terms as frequently as possible, the disability rights movement can help to erode the notion that people with disabilities are fundamentally separate from the community of citizens.

CONSUMER CONTROL

A second issue disability rights advocates must confront as they embrace social welfare programs is the issue of consumer control. To date, disability rights activ-ists have focused their newfound social welfare advocacy on the implementation and expansion of public health insurance programs. As I described above, those activists have sought to compel states to provide the services mandated by the

Medicaid Act, and they have sought to expand the eligibility criteria for (and the services provided under) both Medicare and Medicaid. That medical focus should hardly be a surprise. Many of the services people with disabilities need to enhance their opportunities to live and participate in the community are typically regarded as medical services that should appropriately be provided through the health care and health insurance systems.

But the medical focus of this new social welfare advocacy carries risks as well, when considered in the light of the antipaternalist project of the disability rights movement. Social welfare interventions financed by the health insurance system tend to be delivered through the infrastructure of the health care system. That infrastructure is controlled by medical professionals and is arranged in a way that can itself deny agency and autonomy to people with disabilities.[78] For that reason, disability rights activists in the 1970s and 1980s urged that there is nothing inherently medical in such services as personal assistance or assistive technology—and that those services should be provided through a demedicalized process in which individuals with disabilities, rather than medical professionals, have control.[79] Yet by seeking those services through health insurance programs like Medicare and Medicaid, today's disability activists may be undermining their own goals.

The proposed Community Choice Act provides an excellent example. The bill would require states to provide "community-based attendant services and supports" as a mandatory Medicaid benefit. Mandated services would include an array of personal-assistance services that would enhance the opportunities for people with disabilities to participate in community life. And the bill takes a number of significant steps in the direction of assuring disabled individuals control of the services provided to them. It would require that individuals with disabilities have the power to "select[], manage[], and dismiss[]" their own assistants. It would also guarantee individuals with disabilities "maximum control of the community-based attendant services and supports, regardless of who acts as the employer of record." These requirements would significantly advance the goals of independence and integration for people with disabilities.[80]

But the Community Choice Act would leave intact a significant expression of the medical model of personal-assistance services—the requirement, in many states' Nurse Practice Acts, that "virtually any hands-on services provided for pay to a disabled or elderly person" be treated "as the practice of nursing, requiring licensure."[81] (The bill would not alter the general rule that the states retain the power to regulate the proper practice of medicine.) This requirement often "makes effective in-home services unavailable," particularly for "those who live in a rural area beyond the reach of a nursing agency, or need an attendant for short shifts throughout the day."[82] And when nursing agencies are available to provide personal assistance, they often impose severe restrictions on the use of their services. Some of these restrictions may result from home health agencies' bureaucratic imperatives of coordinating services to a large number of dispersed individuals. Others may reflect an effort to limit attendant services to those that are "truly medical"—even if more custodial services would be most effective in promoting independence. Disability rights activists in a number of states are currently urging relaxation of the restrictions in their Nurse Practice Acts—and they have won some important victories.[83] But until those efforts fully succeed, a statute like the Community Choice Act will have only limited power to enhance the opportunity for people with disabilities to participate in community life.

To be sure, the crafting of consumer-controlled structures for implementing personal-assistance services raises complex political and policy questions. For the reasons I have discussed, relying on home health agencies to deliver personal-assistance services limits the autonomy of people with disabilities. It may therefore seem attractive from a policy perspective to establish a voucher scheme in which individuals with disabilities serve as employers of their own attendants and receive a fixed amount of money to pay their attendants' wages. Medicaid's recent "cash and counseling" demonstration employed a model like this in three states, and it is set to expand.[84] Other countries have begun to move toward voucherized consumer-controlled personal-assistance services as well.[85]

In addition to its policy benefits, a consumer-controlled voucher scheme may seem attractive from a political perspective: using vouchers to implement a Medicaid-funded personal-assistance benefit would fit in well with the broader conservative agenda to privatize and impose choice principles on social welfare services. It is therefore possible to envision an across-the-aisle compromise in which people with disabilities receive new personal-assistance services (which plays to liberals' interest in expanding social welfare programs) but must use vouchers to do so (which plays to conservatives' interest in privatized, choice-based social services). The disability rights movement's rhetoric of independence and consumer control might in this context lend a liberal patina to the generally conservative policy tool of a voucher system.

But there are substantial drawbacks to the cash-and-counseling model of personal-assistance services. For one thing, only a fraction of individuals with disabilities have the time, inclination, and skills to search for, hire, and train their own personal assistants.[86] In this respect, people with disabilities are no different from anyone else. Many people, disabled and nondisabled, who want to hire household assistance—babysitting, housecleaning, or personal assistance—find that the burdens of becoming an employer are great; they seek help from specialized employment agencies that screen, train, and refer candidates for these jobs. If it is to serve the needs of people with disabilities, a comprehensive personal-assistance policy must leave room for such agencies.

Moreover, disability rights activists should regard the conservative agenda behind the cash-and-counseling program as a threatening one. Such a program would likely reduce the wages paid to personal assistants, as they would move from working for (frequently unionized) home health agencies to working for hard-to-unionize individual household employers. Although one result would be the lowering of costs for personal-assistance services, the lower costs can be double edged. If voucher amounts are pegged to lower wage projections, they may be insufficient to attract a stable, qualified workforce of personal assistants. As the Kaiser Commission on Medicaid and the Uninsured recently reported, low wages have already led to a "shortage of direct care workers who are trained and willing to provide community-based personal assistance and other long-term services."[87] There is thus reason to fear that a cash-and-counseling approach to attendant services would serve as yet another means of using deinstitutionalization to cut costs rather than serve the interests of people with disabilities.

A more promising approach would retain an agency-provider model of service delivery but give people with disabilities a greater voice in the operations of the provider agencies. A handful of independent living centers have operated attendant-services programs for a number of years. Longtime disability rights activist Bob Kafka has proposed that independent living centers across the country take over the personal-assistance business more generally, by setting up home-based and community-based support service agencies that would be controlled by people with disabilities and would deliver attendant services according to the "independent living principles" of consumer control and demedicalization.[88] Although much of this new model of "empowering service delivery" remains to be fleshed out, disability rights activists might fruitfully focus their energies on elaborating and testing that model.

CONCLUSION

The discussion in this chapter has been quite wonkish, but the key point is a broad one. As I have shown throughout this book, the projects of the disability rights movement have always been in tension with each other. The goals of employment and community integration, in particular, have often been in tension with the goal of avoiding paternalism and welfare (a goal that itself is subject to multiple, perhaps conflicting, readings). Movement activists sought to resolve the tension by adopting the view that antidiscrimination and accommodation were all people with disabilities needed to compete and participate in the community. But the experience under the ADA demonstrates the limits of the antidiscrimination/accommodation approach. The ADA is essential, and its enforcement should be enhanced in the ways I have described in this and previous chapters. But antidiscrimination law—even when the notion of reasonable accommodation is tacked onto it—is simply too narrow a tool to get at the deep-rooted structural barriers that keep too many people with disabilities from participating fully in the community. To attack those barriers requires something more—something that looks a lot like social welfare.

To move beyond antidiscrimination to social welfare (as many disability rights activists are already doing) raises all the movement's old concerns about paternalism and charity. But I hope that I have shown throughout this book that those concerns simply cannot be avoided. As chapters 3, 4, and 5 showed, concerns about paternalism and charity repeatedly come to the fore in the application and enforcement of the ADA. And as chapter 6 showed, concerns about paternalism can cut both ways. When disability rights activists seek government intervention, in the form of state-mandated reasonable accommodations, one might readily characterize their actions as a request for charity. As chapters 3 and 4 showed, the widespread perception that the accommodation requirement is a form of state-mandated charity has limited the effectiveness of the ADA by encouraging courts to limit the statute's application. The antidiscrimination/accommodation strategy has not resolved the movement's old dilemmas, and there is no reason to think it ever will.

The American disability rights movement has achieved a great deal, but progress has in many respects stagnated. As I have shown throughout this book, the movement has always been a broad one that has embraced a variety of different and conflicting views of the proper means and ends of disability equality. But the movement's policy agenda in recent decades has been too heavily weighted toward one set of these views. What the movement needs is a renewed emphasis on the approaches that have been eclipsed: approaches that look to universalism as a key element of disability policy, and that embrace social welfare programs as important tools for achieving disability equality. Such a renewed emphasis will not avoid the tensions among the various strands of disability rights thinking— indeed, as this chapter has shown, there is even tension between universalism and the social welfare approach—but it will help the movement make progress in achieving its overlapping-consensus goals of integration and equal citizenship.

In the end, there is probably no way to avoid the contradictions of the disability rights movement—and perhaps little reason for the movement even to try. What the movement can and should do is seek to manage those contradictions, and keep focused on the ultimate goals. At its best, that is precisely what the American disability rights movement has done. The willingness of disability rights activists to support such social welfare interventions as the Community Choice Act shows that the movement's pragmatic spirit still lives. That spirit was key to the movement's great twentieth-century victories—and it will be essential to the movement's success in the twenty-first century.

NOTES

CHAPTER 1. INTRODUCTION

1. *See* The Americans with Disabilities Act of 1990, Pub. L. No. 101-336, 104 Stat. 328 (1990). Senator Harkin's "Emancipation Proclamation" statement appears at 136 Cong. Rec. S17,369 (1990).
2. *See* chapter 7 below.
3. For an excellent collection of articles making versions of this argument, see Backlash against the ADA: Reinterpreting Disability Rights (Linda Hamilton Krieger ed., 2003).
4. 536 U.S. 73 (2002).
5. *See, e.g.,* Toyota Motor Mfg., Ky., Inc. v. Williams, 534 U.S. 184 (2002); Sutton v. United Air Lines, Inc., 527 U.S. 471 (1999).
6. *See* Samuel R. Bagenstos, *"Rational Discrimination," Accommodation, and the Politics of (Disability) Civil Rights,* 89 Va. L. Rev. 825, 827 (2003) (collecting commentators making this argument).

CHAPTER 2. THE PROJECTS OF THE AMERICAN DISABILITY RIGHTS MOVEMENT

1. *See, e.g.,* William A. Gamson & David S. Meyer, *Framing Political Opportunity, in* Comparative Perspectives on Social Movements: Political Opportunities, Mobilizing Structures, and Cultural Framings 275, 283–85 (Doug McAdam et al. eds., 1996).
2. *See* Paul K. Longmore, Why I Burned My Book and Other Essays on Disability 54–101 (2003).
3. *See generally* Deborah A. Stone, The Disabled State (1984).
4. Longmore, *supra* note 2, at 79.
5. *See generally* Jacobus tenBroek, *The Right to Live in the World: The Disabled in the Law of Torts,* 54 Cal. L. Rev. 841 (1966).
6. *See, e.g.,* Edward D. Berkowitz, Disabled Policy: America's Programs for the Handi-

capped 197–207 (1987); James I. Charlton, Nothing about Us without Us: Disability Oppression and Empowerment 130–31 (1998); Chava Willig Levy, A People's History of the Independent Living Movement (Ctr. on Indep. Living, U. of Kan., 1988); Gerben DeJong, *Defining and Implementing the Independent Living Concept, in* Independent Living for Physically Disabled People 4, 8 (Nancy M. Crewe & Irving Kenneth Zola eds., 1983); Joseph P. Shapiro, No Pity: People with Disabilities Forging a New Civil Rights Movement 49–54 (1993); Steven E. Brown, Freedom of Movement: Independent Living History and Philosophy (Inst. on Disability Culture, 2000).

7. The story of the Center for Independent Living has been frequently told. The information in the remainder of this paragraph and the next two is taken from Berkowitz, *supra* note 6, at 200–201; Levy, *supra* note 6; Edward V. Roberts, *A History of the Independent Living Movement: A Founder's Perspective, in* Psychosocial Interventions with Physically Disabled Persons 231, 234–39 (Bruce W. Heller et al. eds., 1989); Shapiro, *supra* note 6, at 44–58; Brown, *supra* note 6.

8. Berkowitz attributes some of the Cowell residents' political consciousness to the fact that many of the people who worked at the hospital in positions as orderlies and the like were conscientious objectors to the Vietnam War who were performing alternative service in lieu of being drafted. *See* Berkowitz, *supra* note 6, at 200.

9. *Id.* at 201.

10. *See* Rita A. Varela, *Changing Social Attitudes and Legislation Regarding Disability, in* Independent Living for Physically Disabled People, *supra* note 6, at 28, 43.

11. *See id.*

12. Berkowitz, *supra* note 6, at 202; *see also* DeJong, *supra* note 6, at 8–9 (stating that "[e]ach center offers its own unique blend of advocacy and consumer services"); Varela, *supra* note 10, at 34 (stating that the "motif of local autonomy became a characteristic of the independent living programs that emerged in Berkeley, Houston, and Boston" and arguing that "[i]ndependent living in America . . . was never an orchestrated campaign" but was instead "a movement").

13. Brown, *supra* note 6; *see also* Roberts, *supra* note 7, at 238–39 (describing basic characteristics of independent living centers as: (1) demanding self-determination and control by people with disabilities; (2) providing education to people with disabilities to improve their self-image and to the public at large to demonstrate "the potential of people with even the most severe disabilities to live independent, productive lives with dignity and respect"; (3) coordinating advocacy to fight discrimination and promote participation of people with disabilities in the community; and (4) providing services to all regardless of age or category of disability).

14. DeJong, *supra* note 6, at 11–20; *see also* Peg Nosek et al., A Philosophical Foundation for the Independent Living and Disability Rights Movements, ILRU 30–31 (Occasional Paper No. 1, 1982) (stating that the "element of administrative and policy control by philosophically sophisticated disabled individuals" was "the most significant difference between the true independent living program and the traditional rehabilitation institutions").

15. Charlton, *supra* note 6, at 132.

16. *See* Sharon Barnartt & Richard Scotch, Disability Protests: Contentious Politics 1970–1999, at 61 (2001); Shapiro, *supra* note 6, at 58. Heumann became a major national leader of the disability rights movement and served in the Clinton administration as assistant secretary of education for Special Education and Rehabilitative Services.

17. For a discussion that focuses on the role of the Berkeley CIL in the successful "sign 504" protest, see Roberta Ann Johnson, *Mobilizing the Disabled, in* Social Movements of the Sixties and Seventies 82 (Jo Freeman ed., 1983). *See* Roberts, *supra* note 7, at 235 ("It was no coincidence that the most effective sit-in occurred in the birthplace of the independent living movement. Here, the coalition of people with varied disabilities was a working reality, not a theory.").

18. *See, e.g.,* Barnartt & Scotch, *supra* note 16, at 60–61; Berkowitz, *supra* note 6, at 207; Charlton, *supra* note 6, at 132; Sharon Groch, *Free Spaces: Creating Oppositional Consciousness in the Disability Rights Movement, in* Oppositional Consciousness: The Subjective Roots of Social Protest 65, 87–93 (Jane Mansbridge & Aldon Morris eds., 2001); Richard K. Scotch, From Good Will to Civil Rights 178 (2d ed. 2001); Richard K. Scotch, Politics and Policy in the History of the Disability Rights Movement, 67 Milbank Q. 380, 394 (1989).

19. Charlton, *supra* note 6, at 132; see also Johnson, supra note 17, at 90 ("The development of an independent living philosophy was essential for birthing a social movement of the disabled—not only because of its emphasis on pride and autonomy for the disabled but because it took disabled people out of their isolation and brought them together in large numbers."). In their extensive empirical analysis of disability protests, Barnartt and Scotch start from the premise that civil rights and independent living represent distinct demands and even distinct social movements. See Barnartt & Scotch, *supra* note 16, at 32–44. For reasons discussed above, I think it clear that civil rights and independent living demands represent intertwined strands of the same disability rights movement. Indeed, Barnartt and Scotch themselves suggest that the messages of civil rights and independent living are intertwined. They note: "People with impairments have to be seen as people who wish for, and can live independent, fulfilling, and self-supporting lives. They have to become viewed as people who constitute a minority group that has suffered from a lack of civil rights in order for an extension of the frame of civil rights to be possible." *Id.* at 35.

20. For a review of the deinstitutionalization movement by someone with less than full sympathy for it, see Paul S. Appelbaum, Almost a Revolution: Mental Health Law and the Limits of Change 4–12 (1994). Classic texts that inspired and capture some of the flavor of the ideas of deinstitutionalization advocates include Erving Goffman, Asylums: Essays on the Social Situation of Mental Patients and Other Inmates (1961); David J. Rothman, The Discovery of the Asylum: Social Order and Disorder in the New Republic (1971); and Thomas S. Szasz, The Myth of Mental Illness: Foundations of a Theory of Personal Conduct (1961). For a present-day discussion of the evidence on the effects of institutionalization, see Susan Stefan, Unequal Rights: Discrimination against People with Mental Disabilities and the Americans with Disabilities Act 104–110 (2001).

21. The number of people institutionalized in the United States for psychiatric disabilities, for example, dropped from more than 550,000 in the mid-1950s to about 110,000 in the mid-1990s. *See* Appelbaum, *supra* note 20, at 50.

22. Doris Zames Fleischer & Frieda Zames, The Disability Rights Movement: From Charity to Confrontation 83 (2001) (internal quotation marks omitted; quoting Blank).

23. 20 U.S.C. § 1400 *et seq.* For a good overview of the IDEA's history, see Thomas Hehir & Sue Gamm, *Special Education: From Legalism to Collaboration, in* Law and School Reform 205 (Jay P. Heubert ed., 1999).

24. *See* Shapiro, *supra* note 6, at 137.

25. Shapiro, *supra* note 6, at 75.

26. Adam Samaha argues that the social model has no particular normative or policy implications and requires some broader normative or political theory. See Adam Samaha, *What Good Is the Social Model of Disability?*, 74 U. Chi. L. Rev. 1251 (2007). I have some quibbles with some aspects of his argument, but I am in general agreement with his broad point. Indeed, a key point of this book is to highlight the tensions among various ways of cashing out the social model. But because the social model is important sociologically—as a key location for the various struggles by and within the disability rights movement—I think it important to elucidate what many disability rights activists believe flows from that model.

27. Claire H. Liachowitz, Disability as a Social Construct: Legislative Roots 11 (1988); *see, e.g.,* Harlan Hahn, *Civil Rights for Disabled Americans: The Foundation of a Political Agenda, in* Images of the Disabled, Disabling Images 181, 183–84 (Alan Gartner & Tom Joe eds., 1987) [hereinafter Hahn, *Foundation*]; Jonathan C. Drimmer, Comment, *Cripples, Overcomers, and Civil Rights: Tracing the Evolution of Federal Legislation and Social Policy for People with Disabilities,* 40 UCLA L. Rev. 1341, 1346–51 (1993). Harlan Hahn refers to this model as the "'functional limitations' paradigm." Harlan Hahn, *Feminist Perspectives, Disability, Sexuality and Law: New Issues and Agendas,* 4 S. Cal. Rev. L. & Women's Stud. 97, 101 (1994) [hereinafter Hahn, *Feminist Perspectives*].

28. Michael Oliver, Understanding Disability: From Theory to Practice 32 (1996); *see also* Simi Linton, Claiming Disability: Knowledge and Identity 11 (1998) (noting that the medical definition of disability "casts human variation as deviance from the norm . . . as an individual burden and personal tragedy").

29. *See* Oliver, *supra* note 28, at 36–37; Len Barton, *Sociology, Disability Studies and Education: Some Observations, in* The Disability Reader: Social Science Perspectives 53, 59 (Tom Shakespeare ed., 1998); Jacobus tenBroek & Floyd W. Matson, *The Disabled and the Law of Welfare,* 54 Cal. L. Rev. 809, 809–10 (1966).

30. Liachowitz, *supra* note 27, at 11; *see, e.g.,* Alan Gartner & Tom Joe, *Introduction* to Images of the Disabled, Disabling Images, *supra* note 27, at 1, 4; John Gliedman & William Roth, The Unexpected Minority: Handicapped Children in America 35 (1980); Drimmer, *supra* note 27, at 1350–55; Robert Funk, *Disability Rights: From Caste to Class in the Context of Civil Rights, in* Images of the Disabled, Disabling Images, *supra* note 27, at 7, 12.

31. *See* Linton, *supra* note 28, at 11; Hahn, *Feminist Perspectives, supra* note 27, at 105; *see also* Susan Wendell, The Rejected Body: Feminist Philosophical Reflections on Disability 40 (1996) ("The more a society regards disability as a private matter, and people with disabilities as belonging in the private sphere, the more disability it creates by failing to make the public sphere accessible to a wide range of people."). This point is not limited to disability. The social choices that construct difference in general, Martha Minow has persuasively argued, will be obscured if we treat differences as residing within the person labeled "different." *See* Martha Minow, Making All the Difference: Inclusion, Exclusion, and American Law 75 (1990).

32. Oliver, *supra* note 28, at 32.

33. Minow, *supra* note 31, at 110–14.

34. For a discussion of the origins and fundamental tenets of the British "social model," see Oliver, *supra* note 28, at 19–42.

35. Hahn, *Feminist Perspectives, supra* note 27, at 101; *see also* Oliver, *supra* note 28, at 33 ("[D]isability, according to the social model, is all the things that impose restrictions on disabled people; ranging from individual prejudice to institutional discrimination, from inaccessible public buildings to unusable transport systems, from segregated education to excluding work arrangements, and so on."); Hahn, *Foundation, supra* note 27, at 182 ("A comprehensive understanding of disability requires an examination of the architectural, institutional, and attitudinal environment encountered by disabled persons."); Anita Silvers, *Reprising Women's Disability: Feminist Identity Strategy and Disability Rights,* 13 Berkeley Women's L.J. 81, 105 (1998) ("Because it attributes the dysfunctions of people with physical, sensory, and cognitive impairments to their being situated in hostilely built and organized environments, the [social] model construes the isolation of people with disabilities as the correctable product of how such individuals interact with stigmatizing social values and debilitating social arrangements rather than as the unavoidable outcome of their impairments.").

36. *See, e.g.,* U.S. Comm'n on Civil Rights, Accommodating the Spectrum of Individual Abilities 97 (1983) ("The assumption that handicapped people are fundamentally different and inherently restricted in their ability to participate becomes self-fulfilling as handicapped people are excluded from education, employment, and other aspects of society by these consequences of the handicapped-normal dichotomy."); Chai R. Feldblum, *Antidiscrimination Requirements of the ADA,* in Implementing the Americans with Disabilities Act: Rights and Responsibilities of All Americans 35, 36 (Lawrence O. Gostin & Henry A. Beyer eds., 1993) ("[B]arriers to people with disabilities have been established because members of society have not historically viewed people with disabilities as part of the societal norm. Thus, no effort has been made to ensure that barriers to people with disabilities are not built into the structural frameworks of society."); Hahn, *Foundation, supra* note 27, at 184 (arguing that "all aspects of the external world—including architecture, communications, and social organizations—are shaped by public policy and that policies are a reflection of pervasive cultural values and attitudes," specifically attitudes "of widespread aversion to the presence of disabled individuals").

37. *See, e.g.,* George A. Covington & Bruce Hannah, Access by Design 15 (1997) ("De-

signers have been very exclusive about who they design for, the statistical 'norm'; Joe & Josephine Smith, both perfect in their entirety. Joe & Josephine never aged, never got fat, never tired, never varied in their daily discipline."); *see also* Wendell, *supra* note 31, at 40 ("Much architecture has been planned with a young adult, non-disabled male paradigm of humanity in mind."). As Wendell's comment indicates, prevailing design practices can lead to gender-based, as well as disability-based, exclusion. For general treatment of this point, see Leslie Kanes Weisman, Discrimination by Design: A Feminist Critique of the Man-Made Environment (1992).

38. Minow, *supra* note 31, at 59.
39. *See, e.g.,* Wendell, *supra* note 31, at 48 ("People with disabilities are often forced to work less than they could, or at less creative and demanding jobs than they are capable of doing, because of inflexible workplaces."); Robert L. Burgdorf Jr., *"Substantially Limited" Protection from Disability Discrimination: The Special Treatment Model and Misconstructions of the Definition of Disability,* 42 Vill. L. Rev. 409, 530 (1997) ("[I]n fashioning their facilities and devising their practices, policies and procedures, public agencies, employers and businesses make assumptions about the characteristics of their workers, customers, clients and visitors. These assumptions are based upon a person with so-called 'normal' physical and mental abilities—the 'ideal user.'"); *see also* U.S. Comm'n on Civil Rights, *supra* note 36, at 93 ("Structuring society's tasks and activities on the basis of assumptions about the normal ways of doing things reflects the idea that there are 'normal' people who can participate and there are people with physical and mental handicaps who cannot.").
40. Alexander v. Choate, 469 U.S. 287, 296 (1985) (quoting 117 Cong. Rec. 45974 (1971) (statement of Rep. Vanik, introducing the predecessor bill to § 504 of the Rehabilitation Act)).
41. *See, e.g.,* Timothy M. Cook, *The Americans with Disabilities Act: The Move to Integration,* 64 Temp. L. Rev. 393, 399-407 (1991); Funk, *supra* note 30, at 10–11.
42. Olmstead v. L.C. ex rel. Zimring, 119 S. Ct. 2176, 2187 (1999).
43. *See, e.g.,* H.R. Rep. No. 101-485, pt. 2, at 34–35 (1990), reprinted in 1990 U.S.C.C.A.N. 303, 316–17.
44. *See, e.g.,* U.S. Comm'n on Civil Rights, *supra* note 36, at 97 n.27 ("Our buildings, communications technologies, modes of transportation, and other programs were developed to meet the needs of people who lived in the community; disabled individuals, who did not, were not considered in the planning of these facilities and services.") (quoting Frank Bowe); Funk, *supra* note 30, at 25–26 (arguing that "the vast majority of environmental and policy barriers have a direct connection to a tradition of exclusion of disabled people from organized society" which has led many facilities and institutions—like multistoried educational facilities—to be "designed on the assumption that disabled individuals will not participate in the offered . . . services"). For a poignant, if perhaps apocryphal, story of the self-perpetuating nature of design features that exclude people with disabilities, see Shapiro, *supra* note 6, at 142 ("The postmaster in a small town was told that he would have to make his post office building accessible to people in wheelchairs. There were twenty formidable steps leading to the only public entrance, and the revolving door there was too narrow for even the

smallest wheelchair. The postmaster objected to any renovation for disabled patrons. He sputtered in protest, 'I've been here for thirty-five years and in all that time I've yet to see a single customer come in here in a wheelchair.'").

45. Minow, *supra* note 31, at 119.

46. On this point, see generally Samaha, *supra* note 26.

47. *See* Hahn, *Foundations, supra* note 27; Hahn, *Feminist Perspectives, supra* note 27.

48. Irving Kenneth Zola, *Toward the Necessary Universalizing of a Disability Policy*, 67 Milbank Q. 401, 401 (1989).

49. William Van Alstyne, *Rites of Passage: Race, the Supreme Court, and the Constitution*, 46 U. Chi. L. Rev. 775, 809 (1979).

50. *See, e.g.*, Oliver, *supra* note 28, at 36–37 ("[M]any disabled people experience much medical intervention as, at best, inappropriate, and, at worst, oppressive."); Anita Silvers, *Formal Justice, in* Anita Silvers et al., Disability, Difference, Discrimination 13, 67–74 (1998) ("[P]rogrammatic normalization—the equalizing strategy promoted by the medical model of disability—lends itself to oppression because it validates and further imposes the dominant social group's preferences and biases.").

51. *See, e.g.*, Harlan Lane, *Construction of Deafness, in* The Disability Studies Reader 153, 159 (Lennard J. Davis ed., 1997) ("In the end, the troubled-persons industry creates the disabled deaf person."). For a particularly affecting expression of this view from a journalist and disability rights activist, see Billy Golfus, *The Do-gooder, in* The Ragged Edge: The Disability Experience from the Pages of the First Fifteen Years of The Disability Rag 165, 165–72 (Barrett Shaw ed., 1994). For an excellent expression of this critique by an important participant-theorist of the disability rights movement, see Irving Kenneth Zola, *Healthism and Disabling Medicalization, in* Ivan Illich et al., Disabling Professions 41 (1977).

52. See Berkowitz, *supra* note 6, at 187–88. For a highly critical discussion of the ideology of rehabilitation professionals, see Ruth O'Brien, Crippled Justice: The History of Modern Disability Policy in the Workplace 27–87 (2001).

53. tenBroek & Matson, *supra* note 29, at 831.

54. *Id.*

55. *See, e.g.*, Longmore, *supra* note 2, at 112–14, 234–46.

56. Scotch, *supra* note 18.

57. Cheryl Rogers, *The Employment Dilemma for Disabled Persons, in* Images of the Disabled, Disabling Images, *supra* note 27, at 117, 120–21.

58. *See* Hahn, *Foundations, supra* note 27, at 197; Rogers, *supra* note 57. Even here, one can hear in disability rights activists' claims the echoes of arguments of welfare rights activists like Frances Fox Piven and Richard Cloward, who contended that public welfare generally serves to blunt lower-class unrest at times of high unemployment and to enforce a regime of low-wage work during more prosperous times. *See* Theodore R. Marmor et al., America's Misunderstood Welfare State: Persistent Myths, Enduring Realities 13–14 (1990) (discussing left-wing criticism of the welfare state by, among others, Piven and Cloward); Frances Fox Piven & Richard Cloward, Regulating the Poor: The Functions of Public Welfare (1971); *see also id.* at 286 ("The political circumstances of the 1960's made it crucial, however, that blacks get some-

thing in order to solidify their allegiance to the national Democratic Party, and in order to quiet them. As it turned out, welfare was the system that was made to do most of the giving—partly, perhaps, because black constituents needed money; more importantly, because it was easier to give welfare than to press for concessions that would challenge the interests of other groups in the cities."). *But cf.* Joel F. Handler & Yeheskel Hasenfeld, The Moral Construction of Poverty: Welfare Reform in America 4–5 (1991) (critiquing the Piven and Cloward critique). Piven and Cloward, however, urged broad welfare entitlements. *See* Piven & Cloward, *supra*, at 348. Disability rights activists, by contrast, were much more hostile to the idea of disability welfare.

59. tenBroek & Matson, *supra* note 29, at 831.

60. *See id.* at 836–40 (discussing what seemed to be the emerging possibility of a reconstructed welfare system).

61. *See* Charles Murray, Losing Ground: American Social Policy, 1950–1980 (1984).

62. Roberts, *supra* note 7, at 239.

63. For discussions of Dart's role, see Nat'l Council on Disability, Equality of Opportunity: The Making of the Americans with Disabilities Act 49–59, 72–79 (1997); and Shapiro, *supra* note 6, at 108–11.

64. Nosek et al., *supra* note 14, at 11.

65. *Id.* at 44.

66. *See* Stone, *supra* note 3, at 29–51 (describing evolution of the disability category in the English Poor Laws); Matthew Diller, *Entitlement and Exclusion: The Role of Disability in the Social Welfare System,* 44 UCLA L. Rev. 361 (1996) (discussing the role of the disability category in the American social welfare system).

67. Harlan Hahn, *Antidiscrimination Laws and Social Research on Disability: The Minority Group Perspective,* 14 Behav. Sci. & L. 41, 43 (1996); *see also* Mary Johnson, Make Them Go Away: Clint Eastwood, Christopher Reeve, and the Case against Disability Rights (2003). In developing these arguments, the disability rights movement plainly drew on the feminist movement's argument that paternalistic policies placed women on a "pedestal" that was in fact a "cage," Frontiero v. Richardson, 411 U.S. 677, 684 (1973) (plurality opinion). See Samuel R. Bagenstos, *Justice Ginsburg and the Judicial Role in Expanding "We the People": The Disability Rights Cases,* 104 Colum. L. Rev. 49, 50–51, 56 (2004).

68. *See, e.g.,* Gerben DeJong, *Defining and Implementing the Independent Living Concept, in* Independent Living for Physically Disabled People, *supra* note 6, at 4, 18. The British sociologist T. H. Marshall made the same point about the English Poor Law of 1834. *See* T. H. Marshall, Citizenship and Social Class 15 (Pluto Press 1992) (1950) ("The Poor Law treated the claims of the poor, not as an integral part of the rights of the citizen, but as an alternative to them—as claims which could be met only if the claimants ceased to be citizens in any true sense of the word."). Marshall contrasted that effective denial of citizenship with the reaffirmation of citizenship that is implicit in universal social insurance systems. *See id.* at 33.

69. Thus tenBroek and Matson's observation that "[w]elfare clients, including the blind and the disabled, have been categorically judged incompetent to manage their lives and affairs." tenBroek & Matson, *supra* note 29, at 831.

70. *See* Talcott Parsons, The Social System 428–79 (1951).

71. *See id.*

72. *See* Gliedman & Roth, *supra* note 30, at 35–42; DeJong, *supra* note 68, at 16–18; Hahn, *supra* note 67, at 45.

73. *See* Oliver, *supra* note 28, at 24–25 (reprinting an edited version of the Union of the Physically Impaired against Segregation's 1976 statement of "fundamental principles of disability") ("'Benefits' which are not carefully related to the struggle for integrated employment and active social participation will constantly be used to justify our dependence and exclusion from the mainstream of life—the very opposite of what is intended. This is why the . . . appeal to the state for legislation to implement a comprehensive, national disability incomes scheme is in reality nothing so much as a programme to obtain and maintain in perpetuity the historical dependence of physically impaired people on charity.") (omission in original); *id.* at 26 ("Experts begging for state charity on our behalf can do nothing but lower our status, by reinforcing out-of-date attitudes.").

74. *See, e.g.,* Longmore, *supra* note 2, at 236; DeJong, *supra* note 68, at 12. To some extent, there may be less of a difference between the positions of British and American disability rights activists on this point than meets the eye. British activists, after all, were operating in a country with universal health care, so the opposition to cash benefits did not entail opposition to all social welfare programs. It is significant, however, that the British National Health Service is a universal, rather than disability-specific, social welfare system.

75. *See* Barnartt & Scotch, *supra* note 16, at 78, 177.

76. *See* Shapiro, *supra* note 6, at 130–41.

77. *See, e.g.,* Nosek et al., *supra* note 14, at 3 ("Judy Heumann states, 'To us, independence does not mean doing things physically alone. It means being able to make independent decisions. It is a mind process not contingent upon a "normal" body.'").

78. Elias A. Cohen, *What Is Independence?*, Generations, Winter 1992, at 49.

79. DeJong, supra note 6, at 24; *see also* Adrienne Asch, *Disability, Bioethics, and Human Rights, in* Handbook of Disability Studies 297, 313 (Gary L. Albrecht et al. eds., 2001) ("Disability rights adherents contend that independence need not be viewed in physical terms; rather, self-direction, self-determination, and participation in decision making about one's life are more genuine and authentic measures of desirable independence or, better, interdependence."); Irving Kenneth Zola, *Developing New Self-Images and Interdependence, in* Independent Living for Physically Disabled People, *supra* note 6, at 49, 58 ("The Independent Living Movement argues that it is more important for us to have full control over our lives than over our bodies. We will give up doing some things for ourselves if we can determine when and how they are to be done.").

80. *See* DeJong, *supra* note 6, at 12 ("[D]isabled persons have become aware that benefit rights are prerequisites to living in a community setting. Without income assistance benefits or attendant care benefits, many disabled persons would be involuntarily confined to long-term care facilities.").

81. *See* Charlton, *supra* note 6, at 127 (arguing, as a veteran leader of the independent

living movement, that self-help and self-determination form the core principles of disability rights); Zola, *supra* note 79, at 49 (describing the independent living movement as "but the latest incarnation of an old theme in American life—the idea of self-help"). Foreign students of the American disability movement have seen this point clearly. *See* Jerome E. Bickenbach, *Disability Human Rights, Law, and Policy, in* Handbook of Disability Studies, *supra* note 79, at 565, 576 ("From the beginning of the movement, disability advocates in the United States adopted and made their own the culture of individualism. . . . To reject stereotypes of infirmity and child-like dependency, they believed it essential that people with disabilities strive for independence and self-sufficiency."); Tom Shakespeare & Nick Watson, *Making the Difference: Disability, Politics, and Recognition, in* Handbook of Disability Studies, *supra* note 79, at 546, 550 ("A large element of the movement in North America has stemmed from consumerism and self-help; for example, in the independent living centers, this emphasis plays a large part. This is a particularly American tradition of self-reliance and individual rights.").

82. For example, Peg Nosek and her coauthors argue: "[T]he individual will benefit by adopting a working hypothesis that he is the locus of the problem and the solution in the sense that he is, within the reality of his conscious universe, the only one who can initiate change and perceive its results. Therefore, the individual can be said to bear a complete responsibility for solving his own and society's problems." Nosek et al., *supra* note 14, at 14 (emphasis omitted).

83. *Id.* at 22.

84. DeJong, *supra* note 6, at 20; see also Charlton, *supra* note 6, at 128 (stating that the principles of self-help and self-determination "are not without risk": "[t]hey tend to promote a go-it-alone approach that would require people to actually take control of their lives, an endeavor for which many people with disabilities are not prepared"); Varela, *supra* note 10, at 44 (noting that when independent living movement leaders write about independence "they stress choice, risk, and self-determination"); Irving Kenneth Zola, *Toward Independent Living: Goals and Dilemmas, in* Independent Living for Physically Disabled People, *supra* note 6, at 351–53 (stressing the importance of risk-taking to fulfillment and independent living).

85. DeJong, *supra* note 6, at 18. British activists with disabilities beginning in the early 1970s took a similar view of disability benefits programs. *See, e.g.,* Michael Oliver & Colin Barnes, Disabled People and Social Policy: From Exclusion to Inclusion 80 (1998) (arguing that disability activists in the early 1970s began to understand "that a national disability income might itself be exclusionary; if disabled people were to be provided with an adequate income without working, there would be no need to include disabled people in the labour market and in the workforce").

86. Roberts, *supra* note 7, at 239–40. Bickenbach similarly notes: "In this environment of individual rights and the rejection of paternalistic state agencies, human rights advocates have tended to be highly suspicious of entitlement programming, especially income support and welfare policies, and have argued instead for economic self-sufficiency, usually in the form of remunerative employment. The aim was to

make people with disabilities competitive in the open labor market and to give them a fair and equal opportunity to get and keep a job." Bickenbach, *supra* note 81, at 576.

87. "Personal responsibility" has long been a buzzword for welfare reformers, one given pride of place in the title of the 1996 welfare reform bill, the Personal Responsibility and Work Opportunity Reconciliation Act of 1996, Pub. L. No. 104-193, 110 Stat. 2105 (codified as amended in scattered sections of 42 U.S.C.). On the focus on "responsibility" among welfare reformers, see Neil Gilbert, Transformation of the Welfare State: The Silent Surrender of Public Responsibility 63–65 (2002).

88. *See* Erving Goffman, Frame Analysis: An Essay on the Organization of Experience (1974).

89. Sources I have found useful include: William A. Gamson, *Constructing Social Protest, in* Social Movements and Culture 85, 89–104 (Hank Johnston & Bert Klandermans eds., 1995) [hereinafter Gamson, *Constructing Social Protest*]; William A. Gamson, *Political Discourse and Collective Action*, 1 Int'l Soc. Movement Res. 219, 220–28 (1988) [hereinafter Gamson, *Political Discourse*]; William A. Gamson, *The Social Psychology of Collective Action, in* Frontiers in Social Movement Theory 53, 65–74 (Aldon D. Morris & Carol McClurg Mueller eds., 1992) [hereinafter Gamson, *Social Psychology of Collective Action*]; Scott A. Hunt et al., *Identity Fields: Framing Processes and the Social Construction of Movement Identities, in* New Social Movements: From Ideology to Identity 185, 185–204 (Enrique Laraña et al. eds., 1994); Hank Johnston & Bert Klandermans, *The Cultural Analysis of Social Movements, in* Social Movements and Culture, *supra*, at 3, 8–9; Bert Klandermans, *The Social Construction of Protest and Multiorganizational Fields, in* Frontiers in Social Movement Theory, *supra*, at 77, 80, 85–94; Doug McAdam, *Culture and Social Movements, in* New Social Movements, *supra* at 36, 37–45; David A. Snow et al., *Frame Alignment Processes, Micromobilization, and Movement Participation*, 51 Am. Soc. Rev. 464 (1986); David A. Snow & Robert D. Benford, *Ideology, Frame Resonance, and Participant Mobilization*, 1 Int'l Soc. Movement Res. 197 (1988) [hereinafter Snow & Benford, *Ideology*]; David A. Snow & Robert D. Benford, *Master Frames and Cycles of Protest, in* Frontiers in Social Movement Theory, *supra*, at 133, 135–41; Sydney Tarrow, *Mentalities, Political Cultures, and Collective Action Frames: Constructing Meanings Through Action, in* Frontiers in Social Movement Theory, *supra*, at 174, 186–92; Sidney Tarrow, Power in Movement: Social Movements, Collective Action and Politics 118–34 (1994); Mayer N. Zald, *Culture, Ideology, and Strategic Framing, in* Comparative Perspectives, *supra* note 1, at 261, 261–74.

90. *See* Zald, *supra* note 89, at 261 ("[T]he notion of strategic framing is quite vague in terms of its constituent elements and general processes.").

91. McAdam, *supra* note 89, at 37–38; *see also* Zald, *supra* note 89, at 266 ("Social movements exist in a larger societal context. They draw on the cultural stock for images of what is an injustice, for what is a violation of what ought to be.").

92. *See* Tarrow, *supra* note 89, at 189–92; *see also* Tarrow, *supra* note 89, at 122 ("Out of a cultural toolkit of possible symbols, movement entrepreneurs choose those that they hope will mediate among the cultural underpinnings of the groups they appeal to, the

sources of official culture and the militants of their movements—and still reflect their own beliefs and aspirations.").

93. *See* Gamson, *Constructing Social Protest, supra* note 89, at 89–90 ("Movements may have internal battles over which particular frame will prevail or may offer several frames for different constituencies."); Gamson & Meyer, *supra* note 1, at 275, 283 ("[I]t is comparatively rare that we can speak sensibly of the movement framing. It is more useful to think of framing as an internal process of contention within movements with different actors taking different positions."); Zald, *supra* note 89, at 270 (discussing intramovement contests over framing).

94. *See, e.g.,* McAdam, *supra* note 89, at 37–38; Snow et al., *supra* note 89, at 465 n.2.

95. Groch, *supra* note 89, at 88.

96. *See* Barnartt & Scotch, *supra* note 16, at 18–20.

97. For an excellent discussion that connects this point to broader difficulties faced by liberals and the Democratic Party, see Thomas Byrne Edsall & Mary D. Edsall, Chain Reaction: The Impact of Race, Rights, and Taxes on American Politics 101–4, 122–29 (1991).

98. *See id.*

99. *See* Berkowitz, *supra* note 6, at 221 (noting backlash against accommodation requirement); Stephen L. Percy, Disability, Civil Rights, and Public Policy: The Politics of Implementation 73–75 (1989) (discussing controversy over accommodation requirement).

100. On the controversy over the removal of architectural and transportation barriers generally, see Berkowitz, *supra* note 6, at 217–22; Percy, *supra* note 99, at 106–28; Scotch, *supra* note 18, at 98–100. On the enormous controversy over accessible public transportation, see Berkowitz, *supra* note 6, at 219–21; Robert A. Katzmann, Institutional Disability: The Saga of Transportation Policy for the Disabled passim (1986); Percy, *supra* note 99, at 129–59.

101. *See, e.g.,* John D. Skrentny, The Minority Rights Revolution 265–75 (2002) (arguing that the ease of the analogy between black civil rights and disability civil rights accounted for the quiet passage of the nondiscrimination provisions of the Rehabilitation Act of 1973, but that the high costs of disability rights became obvious during the statute's implementation in the 1970s and 1980s). Writing in 1987, Edward Berkowitz described the differences between the disability rights movement and "earlier civil rights movements" as "significant," and noted that "[t]he black civil rights movement a decade earlier had reduced the cost of public accommodations in the South by reducing the need to have one facility for blacks and another for whites." Berkowitz *supra* note 6, at 221. He continued: "To admit James Meredith's handicapped counterpart to a university would cost money rather than save it. It would mean that the physical plant would need to be expanded or modified, and it would require the university to pay the administrative costs of complying with the federal regulations. Legal advisors to the American Council of Education warned that Section 504 would produce 'sheaves of unread, unnecessary paper.' Few people argued that way in Meredith's case. In the intervening decade, however, inflation had driven the cost of education to the point where major social initiatives, such as accommodating the

handicapped, were subjected to substantial criticism because they were perceived to be costly." *Id.* at 221–22.

102. *See* Berkowitz, *supra* note 6, at 222 (noting that the disability rights movement "was increasing its political sophistication by learning how to temper and tailor its rhetoric"); *id.* ("In the past, leaders had spoken of entitlements and inherent rights. Now, with the arrival of Reagan and George Bush, who led an important Task Force for Regulatory Relief, the leaders stressed independence."); *see also* Gareth H. Williams, *The Movement for Independent Living: An Evaluation and Critique*, 17 Soc. Sci. Med. 1003, 1005 (1983) (arguing that the popularity of the independent living idea "is given strength by the way in which it happens to fit in with the prevalent ideology of robust conservative individualism"). Thus, I think that Jerome Bickenbach is wrong when he writes, "*Without intending to,* American disability advocates sent messages that clearly resonated with the growth of neoconservatism that went on to dominate the political landscape during the 1980s and 1990s." Bickenbach, *supra* note 81, at 576 (emphasis added). It seems to me the appeal to neoconservatives was quite intentional.

103. *See, e.g.,* Edsall & Edsall, *supra* note 97, at 129–31, 136, 148, 152–53.

104. For a discussion of this episode, see Berkowitz, *supra* note 6, at 124–51; Susan Gluck Mezey, No Longer Disabled: The Federal Courts and the Politics of Social Security Disability 76–87, 121–39, 147–68 (1988).

105. For a description of these events, see Percy, *supra* note 99, at 88–96.

106. *See* Evan J. Kemp Jr., *Aiding the Disabled: No Pity, Please,* N.Y. Times, Sept. 3, 1981, at A19. For a discussion of the attack on the Jerry Lewis telethon, see Shapiro, supra note 6, at 20–24. For further discussion, see the three pieces on the telethon issue in the Ragged Edge collection: Anne Finger, . . . *And the Greatest of These Is Charity,* in The Ragged Edge, *supra* note 51, at 115; Mary Johnson, *A Test of Wills: Jerry Lewis, Jerry's Orphans, and the Telethon,* in The Ragged Edge, *supra* note 51, at 120; Julie Shaw Cole & Mary Johnson, *Time to Grow Up,* in The Ragged Edge, *supra* note 51, at 131.

107. Shapiro, *supra* note 6, at 121. Edward Berkowitz described the events this way: "The handicapped rights movement leader Evan Kemp argued that their goals and those of the Reagan administration were not dissimilar: Both accused big government of stifling initiative; both believed in welfare only for the truly needy; both denounced paternalistic government; and both were 'antibureaucratic.' In short, both believed in independence." Berkowitz, *supra* note 6, at 222.

108. *See* Berkowitz, *supra* note 6, at 222–23; Percy, *supra* note 99, at 95–96; Shapiro, *supra* note 6, at 120–21.

109. On the political and cultural fragmentation of people with disabilities into impairment-specific groups, see Gary L. Albrecht, The Disability Business: Rehabilitation in America 281 (1992) ("[P]ersons with disabilities, their parents, and friends have constituted self-help groups around such conditions as colostomies, multiple sclerosis, AIDS, and diabetes. These diverse groups, while sharing common interests, do not constitute a united lobby. Rather they seek their own objectives, often competing with one another for resources."); Barnartt & Scotch, *supra* note 16, at 66

("Because the self-interests of people with impairments are potentially as different as the impairments themselves, mobilization is difficult, perhaps more so than it was in the women's movement or the civil rights movement."); John B. Christiansen & Sharon N. Barnartt, Deaf President Now! The 1988 Revolution at Gallaudet University 217 (1995) (stating that "[i]n general, the disability rights movement has been somewhat fragmented into groups representing different disabilities" and that "[o]ne of the most glaring instances of this fragmentation is the fact that the movement for deaf rights has not followed the same course as have other parts of the disability rights movement"); Scotch, *supra* note 18, at 31–34 (describing proliferation of impairment-specific disability organizations through the 1960s); Shapiro, supra note 6, at 126 ("The disability rights movement spanned a splintered universe. There are hundreds of different disabilities, and each group tended to see its issues in relation to its specific disability."); Groch, *supra* note 18, at 67 (arguing that this fragmentation has "hampered the development of a broad-based oppositional consciousness among" different "subgroups of the disability community"); Johnson, supra note 17, at 91 (arguing that the separation of people with disabilities into impairment-specific "subcultures" "tended to prevent their wholesale participation in and identification with a general disability movement"); Roberts, *supra* note 7, at 233 ("This [charity-based] approach has also specialized disabilities thereby leading to a fragmentation of the disabled community and its supporters. (The charities devoted to cerebral palsy have little common cause with charities devoted to the hearing impaired, for example.)"); Scotch, *supra* note 18, at 382–85 (describing the fragmentation and dispersion of people with disabilities); Zola, *supra* note 79, at 57 ("While organizing around specific diseases may occasion great success in raising research monies, it has divided our strength and caused one disease group to vie against another. This has led not only to overspecialization of services but also to underdevelopment of our consciousness.").

110. *See, e.g.*, Albrecht, *supra* note 109, at 282 (arguing that the disability "movement will become more powerful if individuals transcend such specific identities as blindness or spinal cord injury and generalize to the shared social position of all people with disabilities"); *see also* Linton, *supra* note 28, at 12 (claiming that the disability movement has sought "to build a coalition of people with significant impairments, people with behavioral or anatomical characteristics marked as deviant, and people who have or are suspected of having conditions, such as AIDS or emotional illness, that make them targets of discrimination").

111. Snow et al., *supra* note 89, at 475. *See also, e.g.*, Alberto Melucci, Nomads of the Present: Social Movements and Individual Needs in Contemporary Society 30–36 (1989); Gamson, *Social Psychology of Collective Action*, *supra* note 89, at 58–61; *see also* Debra Friedman & Doug McAdam, *Collective Identity and Activism: Networks, Choices, and the Life of a Social Movement*, *in* Frontiers in Social Movement Theory, *supra* note 89, at 156 (arguing that collective identity can serve as a form of selective incentive that overcomes barriers to mobilization); Gamson, *Constructing Social Protest*, *supra* note 89, at 100–101; Hunt et al., *supra* note 89, at 185 ("[I]dentity constructions, whether intended or not, are inherent in all social movement framing activities."); Klandermans, *supra* note 89, at 88–89 (arguing that changes in under-

standings of collective identity alter potential movement adherents' perceptions regarding the justice of existing arrangements and hence promote mobilization).

112. Snow and Benford call this "experiential commensurability." Snow & Benford, *Ideology, supra* note 89, at 208–9.

113. *See* Groch, *supra* note 18, at 76–77; see also Robert A. Scott, The Making of Blind Men 108–10 (1969) (describing "the independent blind"); Fred Pelka, The Disability Rights Movement 216–17 (1997). Although the independent living frame surely had appeal for blind activists, it has not been wholly successful in integrating adherents of the National Federation of the Blind into the broader disability movement. *See, e.g.,* Groch, *supra* note 18, at 77 (describing Federationists' opposition to becoming a part of a "pan-disability movement").

114. *See* Shapiro, *supra* note 6, at 184–210.

115. *See* Judy Chamberlin, On Our Own: Patient-Controlled Alternatives to the Mental Health System (1978); see also DeJong, *supra* note 6, at 19 (noting that "[t]he trend to deinstitutionalization is one that cuts across many disabling conditions").

116. On divisions between the culturally Deaf and people with disabilities generally, see Barnartt & Scotch, *supra* note 16, at 49–51; Lane, *supra* note 51, at 154–68.

117. *See* Lane, *supra* note 51, at 164 (arguing that both "culturally Deaf people" and "people with disabilities" seek "to promote their construction of their identity in competition with the interested (and generally better funded) efforts of professionals to promote their construction").

118. *See, e.g.,* Jean Flatley McGuire, *Organizing from Diversity in the Name of Community: Lessons from the Disability Civil Rights Movement,* 22 Pol'y Stud. J. 112, 119 (1994) ("The development of similar ideologies, and especially the evolution of self-empowerment, further linked the various constituencies. People First and other consumer-empowerment efforts organized within virtually every disability. The groups reflected a jointly held commitment to autonomy and self-determination, although the expression of these ideals varied considerably.").

119. *See, e.g.,* Nancy M. Crewe, *Freedom for Disabled People: The Right to Choose, in* Independent Living for Physically Disabled People, *supra* note 6, at 357 (arguing that the "very name of the Independent Living Movement" resonates with a concept of freedom that is "dear to [the] heart and mythology" of our nation); *see also* Vicki Schultz, *Life's Work,* 100 Colum. L. Rev. 1881, 1886–87 (2000) ("Historically and theoretically, what we have called for in citizens is the perceived capacity for 'independence.'").

120. *See, e.g.,* Gamson, *Political Discourse, supra* note 89, at 227 (arguing that social movement "packages" or frames are more potent when they resonate with broader cultural themes); Snow & Benford, *Ideology, supra* note 89, at 210–11 (arguing that the power of a frame to mobilize adherents depends to some extent on "narrative fidelity," i.e., "the degree to which proffered framings resonate with cultural narrations, that is, with the stories, myths, and folk tales that are part and parcel of one's cultural heritage").

121. On the wide penetration of these movements, see Albrecht, *supra* note 109, at 287; DeJong, *supra* note 6, at 13–15.

122. *See* Andrew I. Batavia, *Ideology and Independent Living: Will Conservatism Harm*

People with Disabilities?, 549 Annals Am. Acad. Polit. & Soc. Sci. 10, 11 (1997) (arguing that "[t]he disability community is not the monolith that is often portrayed in policy debates" and supporting that argument with Harris survey data showing "that, while 48 percent of people with disabilities consider themselves Democrats, about as many—44 percent—say that they are not Democrats; 25 percent are Republicans; and 19 are Independents"). *See generally* Charlton, *supra* note 6, at 121–22 (describing diverse political orientations of disability rights activists).

123. *See, e.g.*, Barnartt & Scotch, *supra* note 16, at 43 ("The independent living movement is also making monetary demands. One demand is for federal or state support for personal care attendants, in addition to, or instead of, such support for institutional care."); Shapiro, *supra* note 6, at 251–55 ("Personal assistance services are the new, top-of-the-agenda issue for the disability rights movement.").

124. For discussion of disability rights advocates' increasing engagement with health care issues, see Gerben DeJong & Ian Basnett, *Disability and Health Policy: The Role of Markets in the Delivery of Health Services, in* Handbook of Disability Studies, *supra* note 79, at 610, 614–17. On the importance of guaranteed health care to remove obstacles to employment of people with disabilities, see Robert B. Friedland & Alison Evans, *People with Disabilities: Access to Health Care and Related Benefits, in* Disability, Work, and Cash Benefits (Jerry L. Mashaw et al., eds., 1996).

125. *See* Barnartt & Scotch, *supra* note 16, at 174–78.

126. *Id.* at 74, 150.

CHAPTER 3. DEFINING DISABILITY

1. Rehabilitation Act of 1973, Pub. L. No. 93-112, 87 Stat. 355 (1973) (codified as amended at 29 U.S.C. §§ 701–796 (2000)).
2. 42 U.S.C. § 12102(2).
3. 524 U.S. 624 (1998).
4. *See id.* at 661 (Rehnquist, C.J., dissenting).
5. 527 U.S. 471 (1999).
6. 527 U.S. 516 (1999).
7. 527 U.S. 555 (1999).
8. 534 U.S. 184 (2002).
9. *See, e.g.*, *Sutton*, 527 U.S. at 495 (Ginsburg, J., concurring) (discerning congressional "intent to restrict the ADA's coverage to a confined, and historically disadvantaged, class").
10. *Toyota*, 534 U.S. at 198.
11. *Id.* at 691.
12. *Sutton*, 527 U.S. at 488–89.
13. *See id.* at 481–89.
14. *Id.* at 488–89.
15. *Murphy*, 527 U.S. at 521.
16. *Albertson's*, 527 U.S. at 564.
17. *Id.* at 564–66.

18. *See id.* at 558–60; *Murphy,* 527 U.S. at 518–20; *Sutton,* 527 U.S. at 475–76.

19. See *Sutton,* 527 U.S. at 480 (quoting EEOC and Department of Justice interpretive guidance); *id.* at 499–501 (Stevens, J., dissenting) (quoting the House and Senate committee reports to the bill).

20. *See, e.g.,* Arlene Mayerson & Matthew Diller, *The Supreme Court's Nearsighted View of the ADA, in* Americans with Disabilities: Exploring Implications of the Law for Individuals and Institutions 124 (Leslie Pickering Francis & Anita Silvers eds., 2000); Aviam Soifer, *The Disability Term: Dignity, Default, and Negative Capability,* 47 UCLA L. Rev. 1279, 1299–1307 (2000); Bonnie Poitras Tucker, *The Supreme Court's Definition of Disability Under the ADA: A Return to the Dark Ages,* 52 Ala. L. Rev. 321, 325–26, 372–73 (2000).

21. *See Murphy,* 527 U.S. at 524–25; *Sutton,* 527 U.S. at 491–92.

22. *Sutton,* 527 U.S. at 491.

23. *Id.* at 492.

24. *Id.* at 493.

25. *See* Samuel R. Bagenstos, *Subordination, Stigma, and "Disability,"* 86 Va. L. Rev. 397, 512 (2000).

26. *See Murphy,* 527 U.S. at 524–25.

27. *See, e.g.,* Forrisi v. Bowen, 794 F.2d 931, 934 (4th Cir. 1986). For an argument that the decisions in the *Sutton* trilogy reflect an endorsement of the "truly disabled" cases, see Paula E. Berg, *Ill/Legal: Interrogating the Meaning and Function of the Category of Disability in Antidiscrimination Law,* 18 Yale L. & Pol'y Rev. 1, 3 (1999).

28. Heiko v. Columbia Savings Bank, F.S.B., 434 F.3d 249, 258 (4th Cir. 2006). For other post-*Sutton* examples, see Fraser v. Goodale, 342 F.3d 1032, 1041 (9th Cir. 2003); Parker v. Sony Pictures Entertainment, Inc., 260 F.3d 100, 113 (2d Cir 2001); McGuire v. Dobbs Intern. Servs., Inc., 232 F.3d 895 (9th Cir. 2000). For a review of post-*Sutton* law in the lower courts, see Ruth O'Brien, Crippled Justice: The History of Modern Disability Policy in the Workplace 210–17 (2001). In its principal brief in *Toyota* (written by now Chief Justice John Roberts), the employer argued extensively that the ADA's disability definition should be read as covering only "the truly disabled," and that this limitation is inherent in the Court's decisions in the *Sutton* trilogy. *See* Brief for Petitioner at 3, 10-11, 18, 29–30, Toyota Motor Mfg., Ky. v. Williams, 534 U.S. 184 (2002) (No. 00-1089). Although the Court did not use that precise language, its statement that the ADA must "be interpreted strictly to create a demanding standard for qualifying as disabled," *Toyota,* 534 U.S. at 197, will not dispel the influence of the "truly disabled" idea. For an early criticism of *Toyota,* along the same lines as the academic criticisms of the *Sutton* trilogy, see Ruth O'Brien, *The Supreme Court's Catch-22,* Ragged Edge, Nos. 2 & 3, at 13 (2002).

29. *See* Robert L. Burgdorf Jr., *"Substantially Limited" Protection from Disability Discrimination: The Special Treatment Model and Misconstructions of the Definition of Disability,* 42 Vill. L. Rev. 409, 536–46 (1997); Arlene B. Mayerson, *Restoring Regard for the "Regarded As" Prong: Giving Effect to Congressional Intent,* 47 Vill. L. Rev. 587, 609 & n.99 (1997).

30. Tucker, *supra* note 20, at 370.

31. *Id.* at 373. For an equally harsh criticism of the *Sutton* trilogy, see Soifer, *supra* note 20, at 1299–1312.

32. Tucker, *supra* note 20, at 372; *see also* Mayerson & Diller, *supra* note 20, at 125 ("Imagine this logic in any other area of civil rights and it does not pass even the laugh test. 'No we don't hire women, Jews (fill in the blank) but you can get a job somewhere else, so what's the beef?'").

33. *See, e.g.,* Burgdorf, *supra* note 29, at 568.

34. Matthew Diller, *Judicial Backlash, the ADA, and the Civil Rights Model,* 21 Berkeley J. Emp. & Lab. L. 19, 29 (2000).

35. Linda Hamilton Krieger, *Socio-Legal Backlash,* 21 Berkeley J. Emp. & Lab. L. 476, 516 (2000); *see also* Anita Silvers, *The Unprotected: Constructing Disability in the Context of Antidiscrimination Law, in* Americans with Disabilities, *supra* note 20, at 126, 128 (arguing that the prevalence among people with disabilities of the view that "the ADA was meant to sweep away social practice that arbitrarily relegates people to inferior treatment or outcomes based on their being physically or mentally impaired" has created a "feeling of disorientation" surrounding the *Sutton* trilogy).

36. *See* chapter 2, *supra.*

37. *Sutton,* 527 U.S. at 492.

38. *See id.* at 491 (stating that the ADA definition of disability's "substantially limits" prong is fulfilled if "at a minimum . . . plaintiffs allege they are unable to work in a broad class of jobs").

39. *Id.* at 493.

40. *Id.* at 492.

41. *See* Diller, *supra* note 34, at 48–49; Krieger, *supra* note 35, at 516–17. For excellent discussions of the necessity and moral worth criteria applied to disability benefits programs, see Deborah A. Stone, The Disabled State (1984); Matthew Diller, *Entitlement and Exclusion: The Role of Disability in the Social Welfare System,* 44 UCLA L. Rev. 361 (1996).

42. Diller, *supra* note 34, at 48.

43. Some of the attitude I discuss, however, seems to lurk just below the surface in some lower court cases, which both Diller and I have criticized, that pejoratively characterize accommodation requests by people with relatively minor impairments as requests for a "handout" or an unfair "competitive advantage." *See* Bagenstos, *supra* note 25, at 470 & n.277 (quoting Roth v. Lutheran Gen. Hosp., 57 F.3d 1446, 1460 (7th Cir. 1995) (affirming denial of relief to medical resident who sought to be excused from working long shifts as an accommodation for his strabismus (crossed eyes) and explaining that the court would not "allow[] an individual with marginal impairment to use disability laws as bargaining chips to gain a competitive advantage")); Diller, *supra* note 34, at 48 & n.170 (quoting Hileman v. City of Dallas, 115 F.3d 352, 354 (5th Cir. 1997) ("We refuse to construe the . . . Act as a handout to those who are in fact capable of working in substantially similar jobs.") (alteration in original) (footnote omitted)).

44. *See Toyota,* 534 U.S. at 200 ("Because of the conceptual difficulties inherent in the argument that working could be a major life activity, we have been hesitant to hold as

much, and we need not decide this difficult question today."); *Sutton*, 527 U.S. at 492. The *Sutton* Court reserved the question of whether "working" is a major life activity but noted: "[T]here may be some conceptual difficulty in defining 'major life activities' to include work, for it seems 'to argue in a circle to say that if one is excluded, for instance, by reason of [an impairment, from working with others] . . . then that exclusion constitutes an impairment, when the question you're asking is, whether the exclusion itself is by reason of handicap.'" *Id.* (alterations in original).

45. *See Toyota*, 184 U.S. at 200–201.

46. *Id.*

47. *Id.*

48. *See* chapter 2, *supra*.

49. *Sutton*, 527 U.S. at 494 (Ginsburg, J., concurring).

50. *See Toyota*, 534 U.S. at 202–3.

51. *Sutton*, 527 U.S. at 488.

52. *See id.* at 482 (holding that "both positive and negative" effects of mitigating measures must be considered in the substantial limitation inquiry); *id.* at 484 (arguing that ignoring mitigating measures would "lead to the anomalous result that in determining whether an individual is disabled, courts and employers could not consider any negative side effects" of those measures).

53. *See Bragdon*, 524 U.S. at 641.

54. *Sutton*, 527 U.S. at 484 (citing Curry & Kulling, *Newer Antiepileptic Drugs*, Am. Family Physician, Feb. 1, 1998).

55. *See* Laura Lee Hall, *Making the ADA Work for People with Psychiatric Disabilities, in* Mental Disorder, Work Disability, and the Law 241, 256 (Richard J. Bonnie & John Monahan eds., 1997).

56. In Gilday v. Mecosta County, 124 F.3d 760 (6th Cir. 1997), two of the three judges applied a similar analysis and concluded that, even in its medicated form, the plaintiff's insulin-dependent diabetes might actually impose substantial limitations on his major life activities—in part because of the burdensome nature of the treatment regime. *See id.* at 767–68 (Kennedy, J., concurring in part and dissenting in part); *id.* at 768 (Guy, J., concurring in part and dissenting in part). For a nondiabetes case holding that the mitigating measures may themselves be stigmatizing and thus substantially limiting, see Cehrs v. Northeast Ohio Alzheimer's Research Ctr., 155 F.3d 775, 781 (6th Cir. 1998) (holding that plaintiff presented sufficient evidence to survive summary judgment on the question of whether her intermittently symptomatic psoriasis was a "disability" and noting that plaintiff "receives weekly medication and treatment" that "sometimes causes her to lose her hair and fingernails, and occasionally causes her skin to peel").

57. Joseph P. Shapiro, No Pity: People with Disabilities Forging a New Civil Rights Movement 35 (1993). A more recent television commercial for Nike shoes features a woman with two prosthetic legs running a sprint.

58. *See Sutton*, 527 U.S. at 488 ("[I]ndividuals who use prosthetic limbs or wheelchairs may be mobile and capable of functioning in society but still be disabled because of a substantial limitation on their ability to walk or run."); *see also* Belk v. Southwestern

Bell Tel. Co., 194 F.3d 946, 950 (8th Cir. 1999) (holding post-*Sutton* that a person who experienced residual effects of polio but could "walk and engage in many physical activities with the use of his leg brace" was substantially limited in the major life activity of walking: "The full range of motion in his leg is limited by the brace, and his gait is hampered by a pronounced limp.").

59. Erving Goffman, Stigma: Notes on the Management of Spoiled Identity 43–44 (1963) (describing "stigma symbols" as "signs which are especially effective in drawing attention to a debasing identity discrepancy, breaking up what would otherwise be a coherent overall picture, with a consequent reduction in our valuation of the individual"); *id.* at 92 ("It should be noted that since the physical equipment employed to mitigate the 'primary' impairment of some handicaps understandably becomes a stigma symbol, there will be a desire to reject using it."); *see also id.* at 20 (suggesting the stigma attached to hearing aid use). *See generally* R. C. Smith, A Case about Amy 106–7 (1996) (contrasting the stigma attached to hearing aid use with the lack of stigma attached to wearing eyeglasses). By suggesting that Sutton dictates that a hearing impairment "corrected" through use of a hearing aid might no longer be a disability, the Fifth Circuit disregarded these crucial points in Ivy v. Jones, 192 F.3d 514 (5th Cir. 1999) (remanding the "disability" question for consideration by the district court).

60. 42 U.S.C. § 12102(2)(C).

61. 42 U.S.C. § 12102(2)(B).

62. *See* School Bd. v. Arline, 480 U.S. 273, 281 (1987) (holding such an individual protected under the Rehabilitation Act's "record" prong).

63. *Cf.* EEOC v. R.J. Gallagher Co., 181 F.3d 645, 655–56 (5th Cir. 1999) (finding a jury question as to whether plaintiff whose cancer was in remission, but who had suffered prediagnosis effects, experienced thirty days of hospitalization, and required isolation from other persons after his hospitalization, had a "record" of a disability). *But cf.* Ellison v. Software Spectrum, 85 F.3d 187, 192 (5th Cir. 1996) (holding that a plaintiff who had recovered from breast cancer was not protected under the "record" prong, because nothing in her employment file suggested that her cancer ever substantially limited her in a major life activity, and because she "did not miss a day of work" during a month and a half of radiation therapy).

64. *Cf.* Scheer v. City of Cedar Rapids, 956 F. Supp. 1496, 1502 (N.D. Iowa 1997) (assuming that a plaintiff who was denied a job until he was seizure-free for a certain period of time had a statutory "disability," though finding his requested accommodation unreasonable).

65. *See* chapter 2, *supra.*

66. See S. 2345, 100th Cong. §§ 3(1), 4(a) (1988) (prohibiting discrimination "on the basis of handicap," and defining "on the basis of handicap" to mean "because of a physical or mental impairment, perceived impairment, or record of impairment"); H.R. 4498, 100th Cong. §§ 3(1), 4(a) (1988) (same).

67. *See* National Council on the Handicapped, Toward Independence: An Assessment of Federal Laws and Programs Affecting Persons with Disabilities—With Legislative Recommendations 19, A-22-A-25 (1986). Robert Burgdorf, who worked on Toward

Independence, discusses the National Council's recommendations in detail in Robert L. Burgdorf Jr., *The Americans with Disabilities Act: Analysis and Implications of a Second-Generation Civil Rights Statute*, 26 Harv. C.R.-C.L. L. Rev. 413, 443–45, 448–49 (1991).

68. *See* National Council on Disability, Equality of Opportunity: The Making of the Americans with Disabilities Act 82–83 (1997) [hereinafter National Council on Disability, Equality of Opportunity].

69. See S. 933, 101st Cong. § 3(2) (1989) (defining "disability" in the same terms ultimately enacted); H.R. 2273, 101st Cong. § 3(2) (1989) (same). *See generally* National Council on Disability, Equality of Opportunity, *supra* note 68, at 96–100 (discussing deliberations between disability rights activists and staffers for Senators Harkin and Kennedy, as well as their decision to use the Rehabilitation Act model in the 1989 ADA bill); Chai R. Feldblum, *The (R)evolution of Physical Disability Antidiscrimination Law: 1976–1996*, 20 Mental & Physical Disability L. Rep. 613, 617 (1996) (explaining that many disability rights advocates "did not expect [the National Council's] version of the ADA to move forward, given its significant divergence from several section 504 regulations" and describing the pragmatic decision to "parrot[] the section 504 regulations" in the 1989 bill).

70. *Toyota*, 534 U.S. at 197.

71. Mark Kelman & Gillian Lester, Jumping the Queue: An Inquiry into the Legal Treatment of Students with Learning Disabilities 220 (1997).

72. *Id.*

73. Andrew Weis shows that there is a not insignificant amount of prejudice against people with learning disabilities. *See* Andrew Weis, *Jumping to Conclusions in "Jumping the Queue,"* 51 Stan. L. Rev. 183 (1998).

74. Kelman & Lester, *supra* note 71, at 176–80.

75. *See* chapter 2, *supra.*

76. *Toyota*, 534 U.S. at 200.

77. *Sutton*, 527 U.S. at 492 (quoting Tr. of Oral Arg. 15, *Arline*).

78. *Id.* at 491.

79. *Id.* at 492.

80. *Id.* at 493–94.

81. *Id.* at 490–91.

82. *See, e.g.*, Beatrice A. Wright, Physical Disability—A Psychosocial Approach 32–39 (2d ed. 1983).

83. 42 U.S.C. § 12112(b)(6).

84. *Id.* § 12111(8).

85. Justice Stevens made a very similar point in his *Sutton* dissent, where he argued that the case raised only the question "whether the ADA lets petitioners in the door" to obtain "basic protection from irrational and unjustified discrimination because of a characteristic that is beyond a person's control." *Sutton*, 527 U.S. at 504 (Stevens, J., dissenting).

86. *See* Susan Wendell, *The Rejected Body: Feminist Philosophical Reflections on Disability* 25 (1996).

87. Bagenstos, *supra* note 25.

88. *See, e.g.*, Richard Thompson Ford, Racial Culture: A Critique (2005); Madhavi Sunder, *Cultural Dissent*, 54 Stan. L. Rev. 495 (2001).

89. For a pre-*Sutton* example, see Burgdorf, *supra* note 29.

90. H.R. 3195, 110th Cong., 1st Sess. (2007); S. 1881, 100th Cong., 1st Sess. (2007). The more modest Harkin-Hatch ADA Amendments Act is S. 3406, 110th Cong., 2d Sess. (2008).

91. *See, e.g.*, Runnebaum v. NationsBank of Maryland, N.A., 123 F.3d 156, 169–70 (4th Cir. 1997) (*en banc*).

92. *See Bragdon*, 524 U.S. at 633–37.

93. Disability Discrimination Act, 1992 § 4 (Austl.); *see* Glenn Patmore, *The Disability Discrimination Act (Australia): Time for Change*, 24 Comp. Lab. L. & Pol'y J. 533, 541 (2003).

94. *Compare Bragdon*, 524 U.S. at 637 ("In light of the immediacy with which the [HIV] virus begins to damage the infected person's white blood cells and the severity of the disease, we hold it is an impairment from the moment of infection."), with DDA (Austl.) § 4 (disability includes not only "the presence in the body of organisms causing disease or illness" but also "the presence in the body of organisms capable of causing disease or illness").

95. Melinda Jones & Lee Ann Basser Marks, *A Bright New Era of Equality, Independence and Freedom: Casting an Australian Gaze on the ADA, in* Americans with Disabilities, *supra* note 20, at 371, 374.

96. *Id.* at 375.

97. *Id.*

98. See Australian Gov't Productivity Comm'n, Review of the Disability Discrimination Act 1992 at 367–75 (2004). It should be noted in this regard that under the Australian DDA—unlike under the ADA—complainants who lose may be required to pay their opponents' attorneys' fees. See *id.* at 367.

99. *See* Samuel R. Bagenstos, *Justice Ginsburg and the Judicial Role in Expanding "We the People": The Disability Rights Cases*, 104 Colum. L. Rev. 49 (2004).

CHAPTER 4. THE ROLE OF ACCOMMODATION IN DISABILITY DISCRIMINATION LAW

1. Sherwin Rosen, *Disability Accommodation and the Labor Market, in* Disability and Work: Incentives, Rights, and Opportunities 18, 21 (Carolyn L. Weaver ed., 1991).

2. *See, e.g.*, Samuel Issacharoff & Justin Nelson, *Discrimination with a Difference: Can Employment Discrimination Law Accommodate the Americans with Disabilities Act?*, 79 N.C. L. Rev. 307, 314–15 (2001) (expressing skepticism of the ADA).

3. Carolyn L. Weaver, *Incentives versus Controls in Federal Disability Policy, in* Disability and Work, *supra* note 1, at 3, 5.

4. 42 U.S.C. § 2000e.

5. Pamela S. Karlan & George Rutherglen, *Disabilities, Discrimination, and Reason-*

able Accommodation, 46 Duke L.J. 1, 3 (1996) (supporting the ADA generally as an exciting new innovation in civil rights law).

6. Larry Alexander, *What Makes Wrongful Discrimination Wrong? Biases, Preferences, Stereotypes, and Proxies*, 141 U. Pa. L. Rev. 149, 175 (1992).

7. My argument on this point owes a major debt to David Strauss. *See* David A. Strauss, *The Myth of Colorblindness*, 1986 Sup. Ct. Rev. 99, 120–26.

8. Mark Kelman identifies a number of administrative reasons why antidiscrimination protections might be limited to subordinated group members, even if those laws ultimately seek to enforce a more general principle against animus and irrationality. *See* Mark Kelman, *Market Discrimination and Groups*, 53 Stan. L. Rev. 833, 860–67 (2001). Yet, he concedes that "[t]he [antidiscrimination] norm we recognize is significantly designed as well to protect against the stigma imposed on subordinated group members, and is therefore not purely individualistic as a matter of theory as well as administrative practice." *Id.* at 866.

9. This point is well captured by Alexander Bickel's famous statement that "discrimination on the basis of race is illegal, immoral, unconstitutional, inherently wrong, and destructive of democratic society." Alexander M. Bickel, The Morality of Consent 133 (1975). This statement would lose much of its rhetorical punch if the word "race" were replaced by the phrase "any arbitrary factor."

10. David A. Strauss, *The Law and Economics of Racial Discrimination in Employment: The Case for Numerical Standards*, 79 Geo. L.J. 1619, 1626 (1991).

11. David Charny & G. Mitu Gulati, *Efficiency-Wages, Tournaments, and Discrimination: A Theory of Employment Discrimination Law for "High-Level" Jobs*, 33 Harv. C.R.-C.L. L. Rev. 57, 67 n.42 (1998); *see also* Strauss, *supra* note 10, at 1644 (arguing that forms of rational discrimination are the "most likely to persist in a competitive system").

12. *See, e.g.*, Kenneth J. Arrow, *The Theory of Discrimination, in* Discrimination in Labor Markets 3 (Orley Ashenfelter & Albert Rees eds., 1973); Edmund S. Phelps, *The Statistical Theory of Racism and Sexism*, 62 Am. Econ. Rev. 659 (1972). For a relatively recent overview, see Shelly J. Lundberg & Richard Startz, *Inequality and Race: Models and Policy, in* Meritocracy and Economic Inequality 269, 275–79 (Kenneth Arrow et al. eds., 2000). For a recent argument that rational statistical discrimination is the most significant current race discrimination problem, see Glenn C. Loury, The Anatomy of Racial Inequality (2002). Statistical discrimination is also likely a major form of disability discrimination. *See* William G. Johnson, *The Rehabilitation Act and Discrimination against Handicapped Workers: Does the Cure Fit the Disease?, in* Disability and the Labor Market 242, 246–48 (Monroe Berkowitz & M. Anne Hill eds., 1986).

13. *See* Samuel R. Bagenstos, *"Rational Discrimination," Accommodation, and the Politics of (Disability) Civil Rights*, 89 Va. L. Rev. 825, 843 & n.50 (2003).

14. *See, e.g.*, Cynthia L. Estlund, *Working Together: The Workplace, Civil Society, and the Law*, 89 Geo. L.J. 1, 28 (2000) ("[D]emographic diversity has also been associated with 'lower levels of satisfaction and commitment, lower performance evaluations

for those who are different, and higher levels of absenteeism and turnover.' One comprehensive review of the literature recently concluded that 'the preponderance of
empirical evidence suggests that diversity is most likely to impede group functioning,'
particularly in the implementation as opposed to the decisionmaking phase of group
performance.").

15. *See* Richard A. Epstein, Forbidden Grounds: The Case against Employment Discrimination Laws 69–72 (1992).

16. Linda Hamilton Krieger, *The Content of Our Categories: A Cognitive Bias Approach
to Discrimination and Equal Employment Opportunity*, 47 Stan. L. Rev. 1161, 1165
(1995); *see also* Charles R. Lawrence III, *The Id, the Ego, and Equal Protection: Reck-
oning with Unconscious Racism*, 39 Stan. L. Rev. 317, 329–44 (1987); Amy L. Wax,
Discrimination as Accident, 74 Ind. L.J. 1129, 1135–45 (1999) (discussing unconscious
mental stereotyping and resulting disparate treatment). For my own contribution, see
Samuel R. Bagenstos, *The Structural Turn and the Limits of Antidiscrimination Law*,
94 Cal. L. Rev. 1 (2006).

17. *See generally* Mahzarin R. Banaji et al., *The Social Unconscious, in Blackwell Handbook of Social Psychology: Intraindividual Processes* 134 (Abraham Tesser & Norbert
Schwarz eds., 2001).

18. *See* Michael Selmi, *Response to Professor Wax—Discrimination as Accident: Old
Whine, New Bottle*, 74 Ind. L.J. 1233, 1239 (1999) (discussing institutional efforts by
employers to eliminate unconscious discrimination). *See also* Susan Sturm, *Second
Generation Employment Discrimination: A Structural Approach*, 101 Colum. L. Rev.
458, 465–79 (2001); Tristin K. Green, *Discrimination in Workplace Dynamics:
Toward a Structural Account of Disparate Treatment Theory*, 38 Harv. C.R.-C.L. L.
Rev. 91, 95–108 (2003); Bagenstos, *supra* note 16.

19. 435 U.S. 702, 716–17 (1978).

20. 499 U.S. 187, 210 (1991).

21. For a discussion of Title VII's application to discrimination motivated by a rational
desire to facilitate informal enforcement of workplace norms, see Epstein, *supra* note
15, at 70–71. For a discussion of Title VII's application to discrimination based on
unconscious cognitive bias, which concludes that the more persuasive reading of the
case law is that disparate treatment based on cognitive bias is actionable as intentional discrimination under current Title VII law—though it may be difficult for a
plaintiff to prevail on such a claim given the proof structure created by the Supreme
Court—see Wax, *supra* note 16, at 1146–52. For a discussion of Title VII's application
to statistical discrimination that concludes that "Title VII clearly" prohibits statistical
discrimination against protected workers, see John J. Donohue III, *Employment Discrimination Law in Perspective: Three Concepts of Equality*, 92 Mich. L. Rev. 2583,
2598 (1994).

22. *See Manhart*, 435 U.S. at 708 ("Even a true generalization about the class is an insufficient reason for disqualifying an individual to whom the generalization does not
apply."). *See generally Johnson Controls*, 499 U.S. at 210 ("The extra cost of employing members of one sex, however, does not provide an affirmative Title VII defense
for a discriminatory refusal to hire members of that gender."). A fortiori, antidiscrimi-

nation law also prohibits employers from engaging in discrimination to cater to the preferences of current employees or customers to work with or be served by members of a particular race or sex. *See, e.g.,* Fernandez v. Wynn Oil Co., 653 F.2d 1273, 1276–77 (9th Cir. 1981); Diaz v. Pan Am. World Airways, 442 F.2d 385, 389 (5th Cir. 1971).

23. One might question whether the Supreme Court's recent skeptical attitude toward race-conscious affirmative action calls into doubt the picture of antidiscrimination law I paint in the text. After all, the prohibition on rational discrimination is "fundamental[ly] simila[r]" to affirmative action in that it requires employers to take race into account. Strauss, *supra* note 7, at 130. I agree that there is significant tension between the acceptance of a prohibition on rational discrimination and the skepticism toward affirmative action (a tension that it was Strauss's major purpose to elaborate, *see id.*).

24. *See* Owen M. Fiss, *A Theory of Fair Employment Laws*, 38 U. Chi. L. Rev. 235, 259–60 (1971).

25. Paul Brest, *Foreword: In Defense of the Antidiscrimination Principle*, 90 Harv. L. Rev. 1, 7 (1976).

26. *See id.* at 7–8 (defining "racially selective sympathy and indifference" as "the unconscious failure to extend to a minority the same recognition of humanity, and hence the same sympathy and care, given as a matter of course to one's own group"). In a similar vein, Professor Strauss argues that actions that violate his "reversing the groups" test—viz., would the decisionmaker have done the same thing if the identities of the beneficiary and disadvantaged groups had been flipped?—fit any plausible definition of discriminatory intent even if the decisionmaker is unconscious of the bias. *See* David A. Strauss, *Discriminatory Intent and the Taming of* Brown, 56 U. Chi. L. Rev. 935, 956–65 (1989).

27. Brest, *supra* note 25, at 8.

28. Fiss, *supra* note 24, at 259.

29. *See, e.g.,* Banaji et al., *supra* note 17, at 143 (noting "abundant evidence that stereotypes that operate unconsciously defend their territory fiercely, influencing social interactions even when perceivers are consciously vigilant and motivated to defeat them").

30. For an argument to this effect, see Sujit Choudhry, *Distribution vs. Recognition: The Case of Antidiscrimination Laws*, 9 Geo. Mason L. Rev. 145, 156–157 (2000).

31. *See, e.g.,* Brest, *supra* note 25, at 6 ("Regulations and decisions based on statistical generalizations are commonplace in all developed societies and essential to their functioning. And it is often rational for decisionmakers to rely on weak and even dubious generalizations."); Peter J. Rubin, *Equal Rights, Special Rights, and the Nature of Antidiscrimination Law*, 97 Mich. L. Rev. 564, 572–73 (1998) ("We routinely and necessarily make decisions on the basis of generalizations about various characteristics of the people we meet. Indeed, conducting the interactions that make up our lives would be an overwhelming and unmanageable task without the ability to do exactly this."); Strauss, *supra* note 7, at 114 ("Employers engaged in hiring are not the only ones who generalize. People generalize constantly; that is, they observe that a person has one characteristic, and on that basis they infer that he has another. One

cannot survive in the world without doing this."). This point is a major theme of Professor Glenn Loury's recent work on the persistence of racial inequality. *See generally* Loury, *supra* note 12, at 18–19 ("[W]hether 'race' is a part of the calculation or not, classifying human subjects in this general way is a universal practice, one that lies at the root of all social-cognitive behavior.").

32. *See* Frederick Schauer, Profiles, Probabilities, and Stereotypes (2003).

33. Cass R. Sunstein, *The Anticaste Principle*, 92 Mich. L. Rev. 2410, 2418 (1994); *see also* Owen M. Fiss, *Groups and the Equal Protection Clause*, 5 Phil. & Pub. Aff. 107, 157–58 (1976) (arguing that "'arbitrary discrimination' is the species, not the genus," and that what makes such discrimination wrong is that it "particularly hurt[s] a disadvantaged group"); *cf. id.* at 123 (noting that while the "foundational concept" of an antidiscrimination principle "is individualistic," "elements of groupism appear as one moves up the superstructure" of doctrine that implements such a principle).

34. *See, e.g.,* Brest, *supra* note 25, at 8 ("[B]ecause acts of discrimination tend to occur in pervasive patterns, their victims suffer especially frustrating, cumulative and debilitating injuries."); *id.* at 10 ("The cumulative disadvantage caused by the use of race as a proxy even for legitimate characteristics provides an independent ground for disfavoring nonbenign race-dependent decisions regardless of the integrity of the process by which they were made."); Sunstein, *supra* note 33, at 2430 ("In the areas of race and sex discrimination, a large part of the problem is this sort of systemic disadvantage. A social or biological difference has the effect of systematically subordinating members of the relevant group—not because of nature, but because of social and legal practices."). To similar effect, see Strauss, *supra* note 10, at 1626–30. For an argument to this effect in the disability context, see Samuel R. Bagenstos, *Subordination, Stigma, and "Disability,"* 86 Va. L. Rev. 397, 453–55 (2000).

35. *See* Fiss, *supra* note 24, at 260.

36. *Id.*

37. *Id.* at 261.

38. *See id.* at 313 (concluding that "the antidiscrimination prohibition is a strategy for conferring benefits on a racial class—blacks"); *see also* Fiss, *supra* note 33, at 147 (arguing that interpretation of the Fourteenth Amendment's Equal Protection Clause should be guided by "a theory of primary reference—that blacks were the intended primary beneficiaries, that it was a concern for their welfare that prompted the Clause"); *id.* at 157 (arguing that the basic concern of equal protection analysis "should be with those laws or practices that particularly hurt a disadvantaged group" by "aggravat[ing] (or perpetuat[ing]?) the subordinate position of a specially disadvantaged group").

39. Lucinda M. Finley, *Transcending Equality Theory: A Way out of the Maternity and the Workplace Debate*, 86 Colum. L. Rev. 1118, 1120–21 (1986). For endorsements of this point from those on both sides of the "equal treatment versus special treatment" debate, see Linda J. Krieger & Patricia N. Cooney, *The Miller-Wohl Controversy: Equal Treatment, Positive Action, and the Meaning of Women's Equality*, 13 Golden Gate U. L. Rev. 513, 518–36 (1983), which advocates the "special treatment" position, and Wendy W. Williams, *Equality's Riddle: Pregnancy and the Equal Treatment/Special Treatment Debate*, 13 N.Y.U. Rev. L. & Soc. Change 325, 359–65 (1985), which

advocates the "equal treatment" position; *see also* Mary E. Becker, *Prince Charming: Abstract Equality*, 1987 Sup. Ct. Rev. 201, 244 (arguing that the problem of guaranteeing women equal access to the workplace "can only be solved by changing workplace policies and practices so that it is easier for women to combine wage work and reproduction"); Samuel Issacharoff & Elyse Rosenblum, *Women and the Workplace: Accommodating the Demands of Pregnancy*, 94 Colum. L. Rev. 2154, 2155–56 (1994) ("The first task in the full integration of women in the work force is to define the necessary accommodations for pregnancy leave; these accommodations will play a critical role in allowing women the equal capacity to participate and to achieve in the employment market.").

40. Krieger & Cooney, *supra* note 39, at 533.
41. 479 U.S. 272 (1987).
42. *Id.* at 289. The Court also noted that the state statute did not require employers to limit parental leaves to women; an employer could comply with the statute without any discrimination by providing parental leaves to all of its employees. *See id.* at 290–91. This point was the sole basis for Justice Scalia's concurrence in the judgment. *See id.* at 296 (Scalia, J., concurring).
43. 535 U.S. 391 (2002).
44. *Id.* at 397.
45. 527 US. 581 (1999).
46. *Olmstead*, 527 U.S. at 587.
47. *See id.* at 598.
48. *Id.* at 600.
49. *Id.*
50. *Id.* at 601.
51. *See id.* at 600 (quoting Allen v. Wright, 468 U.S. 737, 755 (1984), to the effect that "'[t]here can be no doubt that [stigmatizing injury often caused by racial discrimination] is one of the most serious consequences of discriminatory government action'") (bracketed phrase inserted by the *Olmstead* Court).
52. *See, e.g.*, Issacharoff & Nelson, *supra* note 2, at 310–11.
53. *See, e.g.*, Louis Michael Seidman & Mark V. Tushnet, Remnants of Belief: Contemporary Constitutional Issues (1996); Cass R. Sunstein, *Lochner's Legacy*, 87 Colum. L. Rev. 873 (1987).
54. *See, e.g.*, Bagenstos, *supra* note 34, at 428–32. For a philosophical argument consistent with (and seeking to justify) that claim, see, for example, Anita Silvers, *Formal Justice, in* Disability, Difference, Discrimination: Perspectives on Justice in Bioethics and Public Policy 13, 129–31 (1998) [hereinafter Silvers, *Formal Justice*], and Anita Silvers, *The Unprotected: Constructing Disability in the Context of Antidiscrimination Law, in* Americans with Disabilities: Exploring Implications of the Law for Individuals and Institutions 126, 139 (Leslie Pickering Francis & Anita Silvers eds., 2000).
55. "Might not" is an important qualification here. Although they capture a common intuition, Professors Pamela Karlan and George Rutherglen go wrong in stating that the ADA gives protected employees the right to "insist upon discrimination in their favor." Karlan & Rutherglen, *supra* note 5, at 3. One view, prominent among disability

rights activists, is that employers accommodate nondisabled employees in various ways all the time, so the ADA's accommodation requirement merely operates as an antidiscrimination requirement. *See, e.g.,* Harlan Hahn, *Accommodations and the ADA: Unreasonable Bias or Biased Reasoning?,* 21 Berkeley J. Emp. & Lab. L. 166, 189–90 (2000). To the extent that this phenomenon occurs (and I am persuaded that it occurs in many, but far from all, of the accommodation cases potentially adjudicated under the ADA), there is really no difference at all between antidiscrimination and accommodation requirements; accommodation requirements simply identify a specific kind of discrimination. But nothing in the ADA requires a showing that an employer's nondisabled employees received accommodations that were denied to employees with disabilities. In that sense, the accommodation requirement is, at least on its face, distinct from an antidiscrimination requirement, and some additional argument is required to demonstrate the equivalence of the two types of provisions.

56. Bonnie Tucker hints at this act/omission distinction by suggesting that the ADA, unlike traditional civil rights laws, requires employers "to act as good Samaritans." Bonnie Poitras Tucker, *The ADA's Revolving Door: Inherent Flaws in the Civil Rights Paradigm,* 62 Ohio St. L.J. 335, 339 (2001).

57. Matt Cavanaugh, Against Equality of Opportunity 171 (2002).

58. *See* Strauss, *supra* note 7, at 100 (arguing that the prohibition against discrimination is "deeply race-conscious; like affirmative action, the prohibition against discrimination reflects a deliberate decision to treat blacks differently from other groups, even at the expense of innocent whites").

59. *See id.* at 111.

60. *Id.*

61. *Id.* at 114. Professor Peter Rubin argues that this is among the reasons many people see antidiscrimination law as providing "special rights" to favored classes. *See* Rubin, *supra* note 31, at 573–74.

62. This is a point that Professor Issacharoff, in particular, has consistently emphasized in his work that has challenged efforts to assimilate pregnancy and disability accommodation to antidiscrimination law. *See* Issacharoff & Nelson, *supra* note 2, at 340–41; Issacharoff & Rosenblum, *supra* note 39, at 2214–20.

63. Bd. of Trs. v. Garrett, 531 U.S. 356, 367–68 (2001).

64. Gary S. Becker, The Economics of Discrimination 16–17 (2d ed. 1971), refers to such motivation as a "taste for discrimination."

65. Christine Jolls, *Antidiscrimination and Accommodation,* 115 Harv. L. Rev. 642, 686 (2001).

66. *See, e.g.,* Robert L. Burgdorf Jr., *"Substantially Limited" Protection from Disability Discrimination: The Special Treatment Model and Misconstructions of the Definition of Disability,* 42 Vill. L. Rev. 409, 530–33 (1997); Hahn, *supra* note 55, at 189–90. "Equal treatment" feminists made a similar point in the pregnancy-in-the-workplace debate—that employers accommodated conditions with efficiency effects similar to pregnancy all the time, so the failure to accommodate pregnancy was simple discrimination. *See, e.g.,* Williams, *supra* note 39, at 355–58.

67. For examples of articles collecting evidence that most disability accommodations im-

pose little if any direct cost on employers, see Peter David Blanck, *Empirical Study of Disability, Employment Policy, and the ADA*, 23 Mental & Physical Disability L. Rep. 275, 276–78 (1999); Peter David Blanck, *The Economics of the Employment Provisions of the Americans with Disabilities Act: Part I—Workplace Accommodations*, 46 DePaul L. Rev. 877, 902–3 (1997); Michael Ashley Stein, *Empirical Implications of Title I*, 85 Iowa L. Rev. 1671, 1674–76 (2000) [hereinafter Stein, *Empirical Implications*]; and Michael Ashley Stein, *Labor Markets, Rationality, and Workers with Disabilities*, 21 Berkeley J. Emp. & Lab. L. 314, 322–23 (2000). For skepticism that these results reflect the full story, see Thomas N. Chirikos, *Will the Costs of Accommodating Workers with Disabilities Remain Low?*, 17 Behav. Sci. & L. 93, 94 (1999), and Stein, *Empirical Implications, supra*, at 1677.

68. *See, e.g.,* Cehrs v. Northeast Ohio Alzheimer's Research Ctr., 155 F.3d 775, 783 (6th Cir. 1998) (holding summary judgment for defendant improper where employer "routinely granted medical leave to employees" but rejected disabled plaintiff's request for leave as accommodation); Criado v. IBM Corp., 145 F.3d 437, 444 (1st Cir. 1998) (holding plaintiff's request for leave to accommodate her disability was reasonable where she "was not asking for more leave than would be granted to a non-disabled, sick employee"); Leslie v. St. Vincent New Hope, Inc., 916 F. Supp. 879, 882–83 (S.D. Ind. 1996) (denying summary judgment to employer where plaintiff requested transfer to open light-duty position as accommodation for her disability and employees frequently shifted among positions).

69. *See, e.g.,* Higgins v. New Balance Athletic Shoe, 194 F.3d 252, 257–58, 264–65 (1st Cir. 1999) (holding summary judgment for defendant inappropriate where employer refused to provide employee with a hearing impairment a fan at his workstation—an amenity provided to certain other employees—when "steam-induced perspiration was ruining his hearing aid").

70. *See* Bagenstos, *supra* note 34, at 439–40; Burgdorf, *supra* note 66, at 530.

71. Rob Imrie vividly describes the way in which architects have almost willfully subordinated concerns with accessibility to their own conception of their professional role of "'architect as artist' and/or rational technicist." Rob Imrie, Disability and the City: International Perspectives 75–79 (1996); *see also* George A. Covington & Bruce Hannah, Access by Design 15 (1997) ("Designers have been very exclusive about who they design for, the statistical 'norm'; Joe & Josephine Smith, both perfect in their entirety. Joe & Josephine never aged, never got fat, never tired, never varied in their daily discipline. In fact, they never missed a beat.").

72. *See* Bagenstos, *supra* note 34, at 441–42.

73. For elaborations of this argument, see Patricia Illingworth & Wendy E. Parmet, *Positively Disabled: The Relationship between the Definition of Disability and Rights under the ADA, in* Americans with Disabilities, *supra* note 54, at 3, 10; and Silvers, *Formal Justice, supra* note 54, at 128–31. The costs of retrofitting in such circumstances can be considerable. To take an extreme example from outside the employment context, the United States Court of Appeals for the Third Circuit held in November 1993 that the City of Philadelphia had violated the ADA by failing to install curb ramps when streets were resurfaced after the statute's January 1992 effective date. See Kinney

v. Yerusalim, 9 F.3d 1067, 1069 (3d Cir. 1993). As one commentator subsequently noted, "Requiring Philadelphia to implement curb cuts at all of its 80,000 intersections resurfaced since the effective date of the ADA would cost the city $140 million, three times the city's budget for all street improvements." Seth J. Elin, Comment, *Curb Cuts under Title II of the Americans with Disabilities Act: Are They Bringing Justice or Bankruptcy to Our Municipalities?*, 28 Urb. Law. 293, 320 (1996). Even in the more paradigmatic context of making buildings accessible, retrofitting to full accessibility can be costly—"an average of 3 percent of a building's value." U.S. Comm'n on Civil Rights, Accommodating the Spectrum of Individual Abilities 81 (1983). The costs of including accessible features in the initial design of a facility, by contrast, are relatively tiny—"an estimated one-tenth to one-half of 1 percent of construction costs." *Id.*

74. For commentators making this point, see, for example, Illingworth & Parmet, *supra* note 73, at 10. A variety of cases might be cited as illustrations. *See, e.g.*, Lyons v. Legal Aid Soc'y, 68 F.3d 1512, 1515 (2d Cir. 1995) (holding that employer-paid parking space might be reasonable accommodation for an employee whose disability made her unable to take public transportation to work, even though the space cost "$300–$520 a month, representing 15–26 percent of her monthly net salary"); Borkowski v. Valley Cent. Sch. Dist., 63 F.3d 131, 140–41 (2d Cir. 1995) (Calabresi, J.) (holding summary judgment for defendant inappropriate where plaintiff teacher sought full-time teacher's aide as accommodation for her disability and defendant school failed to demonstrate that classroom management was an essential function of plaintiff's job that would be eliminated as a result of the proposed accommodation); Nelson v. Thornburgh, 567 F. Supp. 369, 376, 382 (E.D. Pa. 1983) (Pollak, J.) (holding public employer was required, as reasonable accommodation, to provide blind plaintiffs with half-time services of a reader, at the cost of "roughly $6,638 per year for each plaintiff").

75. Fiss, *supra* note 24, at 261.

76. *See, e.g.*, Vande Zande v. Wis. Dep't of Admin., 44 F.3d 538, 542–43 (7th Cir. 1995) (Posner, C.J.) (drawing the parallel between "reasonable accommodation" under the ADA and "reasonable care" in negligence law); David Benjamin Oppenheimer, *Negligent Discrimination*, 141 U. Pa. L. Rev. 899, 943–44 (1993) (offering the ADA's requirement of reasonable accommodation as an example of a legal prohibition on negligent discrimination).

77. *See* Bagenstos, *supra* note 16.

78. 29 C.F.R. pt. 1630 app. § 1630.9. This doctrine draws directly from a statement in the House Education and Labor Committee's report on the proposed ADA. See H.R. Rep. No. 101-485, pt. 2, at 64 (1990).

79. 29 C.F.R pt. 1630 app. § 1630.9.

80. *Id.*

81. See EEOC, A Technical Assistance Manual on the Employment Provisions (Title I) of the Americans with Disabilities Act § 3.4 (1992) ("Equipment or devices that assist a person in daily activities on and off the job are considered personal items that an employer is not required to provide.").

82. See Brookins v. Indianapolis Power & Light Co., 90 F. Supp. 2d 993, 1003–04 (S.D. Ind. 2000); Burnett v. W. Res., Inc., 929 F. Supp. 1349, 1358 (D. Kan. 1996).

83. See Nelson v. Ryan, 860 F. Supp. 76, 82–83 (W.D.N.Y. 1994).

84. See Williams v. United Ins. Co., 253 F.3d 280, 282–83 (7th Cir. 2001).

85. For discussion of the difficulty with using the ADA as a tool to obtain personal assistance services, see Simi Litvak, *Personal Assistance Services, in* Implementing the Americans with Disabilities Act 365, 370–74 (Jane West ed., 1996).

86. *See, e.g.,* 42 U.S.C. § 12111(9)(B) (providing that "reasonable accommodation" includes "provision of qualified readers or interpreters"); *Borkowski,* 63 F.3d at 141–42; *Nelson,* 567 F. Supp. at 382.

87. *See, e.g., Nelson,* 567 F. Supp. at 376 (noting that readers would cost approximately half of plaintiffs' salary, or roughly $6,638 per plaintiff per year in 1983 dollars).

88. *See* Wade v. Gen. Motors Corp., No. 97-3378, 1998 WL 639162, at * 2 (6th Cir. Sept. 10, 1998) (holding employer not required to provide transportation to and from work); Lori A. Bowman et al., Employment Law Yearbook § 9:7.7 (2003) (reporting the EEOC's position that "barriers outside the workplace, such as a difficulty in getting to work, are not 'workplace created barriers'" subject to the accommodation obligation).

89. *See Lyons,* 68 F.3d at 1516–17; Smallwood v. Witco Corp., No. 94 CIV. 7766 (LMM), 1995 WL 716745, at *1 (S.D.N.Y. Dec. 6, 1995) ("There is nothing inherently unreasonable in requiring an employe[r] to furnish an otherwise qualified disabled employee with assistance related to her ability to get to work.").

90. 179 F.3d 557.

91. *Id.* at 562.

92. *See id.* at 559.

93. *See id.* at 560.

94. *Id.*

95. *See* US Airways v. Barnett, 535 U.S. 391, 397 (2002) (employment case) ("The Act requires preferences in the form of 'reasonable accommodations' that are needed for those with disabilities to obtain the same workplace opportunities that those without disabilities automatically enjoy."); PGA Tour v. Martin, 532 U.S. 661, 683 n.37 (2001) (public accommodations case) ("'The statute seeks to assure that a disabled person's disability will not deny him equal access to (among other things) competitive sporting events" (quoting *id.* at 703 (Scalia, J., dissenting))); Olmstead v. L.C. ex rel. Zimring, 527 U.S. 581, 597, 603 n.14 (1999) (public services case) (holding that states might be required to create community placements for individuals with mental disabilities, but rejecting characterization of that holding as requiring states to provide to individuals with disabilities services different from services provided to others, while holding that "States must adhere to the ADA's nondiscrimination requirement with regard to the services they in fact provide"); Alexander v. Choate, 469 U.S. 287, 301, 303 (1985) (public services case) (holding under the Rehabilitation Act—the predecessor to the ADA—that "an otherwise qualified handicapped individual must be provided with meaningful access to the benefit that the grantee offers," but that the statute "does not require the State to alter [its] definition of the benefit being offered simply to meet

the reality that the handicapped have greater medical needs"). The ADA's access/ content distinction finds an imperfect parallel in jurisprudence under the Individuals with Disabilities Education Act (IDEA) and its predecessor statute, the Education for All Handicapped Children Act. The Supreme Court has held that the IDEA imposes a non-cost-qualified requirement that school districts provide services necessary for individuals with disabilities to obtain access to the classroom. *See, e.g.*, Cedar Rapids Cmty. Sch. Dist. v. Garret F. ex rel. Charlene F., 526 U.S. 66, 77–79 (1999). But it has also held that school districts have a much more limited obligation under the statute to alter the content of the instruction provided. See Bd. of Educ. v. Rowley, 458 U.S. 176, 198–204 (1982).

96. Courts have applied this analysis in cases involving both condition-specific and treatment-specific limitations on insurance coverage. For examples of condition-specific limitations, see McNeil v. Time Ins. Co., 205 F.3d 179, 189, 188–89 (5th Cir. 2000) (rejecting challenge to AIDS cap in health insurance policy and stating that, "[b]ecause Title III does not reach so far as to regulate the content of goods and services, and because it is undisputed this limitation for AIDS is part of the content of the good that Time offered, Mr. McNeil's Title III claim must fail"); *Doe*, 179 F.3d at 559–60; Modderno v. King, 82 F.3d 1059, 1062 (D.C. Cir. 1996) (rejecting challenge to insurance plan's $75,000 lifetime cap on mental health benefits—a cap not paralleled by any similar limitation on benefits for physical conditions—essentially on access/content grounds). *But cf.* Carparts Distrib. Ctr. v. Auto. Wholesaler's Ass'n, 37 F.3d 12, 19 (1st Cir. 1994) (stating that "a sharp distinction between" access and content may be "illusory"). For examples of treatment-specific limitations, see Bythway v. Principal Health Care of Del., Nos. CIV. A. 97-435-GMS & CIV. A. 97-600-GMS, 1999 WL 33220042, at *2–3 (D. Del. Sept. 29, 1999) (bone marrow transplant covered for aplastic anemia and acute leukemia but not Hodgkin's disease); Rome v. MTA/N.Y. City Transit, No. 97-CV-2945 (JG), 1997 WL 1048908, at *4 (E.D.N.Y. Nov. 18, 1997) (speech therapy covered for some conditions but not for autism); Hilliard v. BellSouth Med. Assistance Plan, 918 F. Supp. 1016, 1026–27 (S.D. Miss. 1995) (high-dose chemotherapy covered for some cancers but not multiple myeloma); Pokorney v. Miami Valley Career Tech. Ctr. Sch. Dist., No. C-3-94-247, 1995 WL 1671909 (S.D. Ohio July 14, 1995) (Taxol rejected as "experimental" treatment for lung cancer when it was covered for other cancers). *But see* Henderson v. Bodine Aluminum, 70 F.3d 958, 960–61 (8th Cir. 1995) (granting preliminary injunction to woman with breast cancer who challenged insurance policy's refusal to cover high-dose chemotherapy treatment (HDCT) for breast cancer when it covered HDCT for some other cancers). For a general discussion of the case law, see Mary Crossley, *Becoming Visible: The ADA's Impact on Health Care for Persons with Disabilities*, 52 Ala. L. Rev. 51, 80 (2000) ("Although some courts have been willing to scrutinize insurance practices to protect the interests of people with disabilities, the trend of the case law over the past several years has been for courts to take a fairly hands-off approach"). With only a few exceptions, courts have not found it necessary to rely on the safe harbor provision. Although a number of cases discuss that provision, they tend to do so only as additional support for their decisions or to rebut the contention

that the safe harbor provision is itself evidence of Congress's intent that the statute regulate the content of insurance policies. *See* Rogers v. Dep't of Health & Envtl. Control, 174 F.3d 431, 435–37 (4th Cir. 1999); Ford v. Schering-Plough Corp., 145 F.3d 601, 610–12 (3d Cir. 1998); Parker v. Met. Life Ins. Co., 121 F.3d 1006, 1012–13 (6th Cir. 1997); *Modderno*, 82 F.3d at 1063–65. Some courts and judges, to be sure, have relied primarily on the safe harbor provision in such cases, but they are a distinct minority. *See, e.g., Ford*, 145 F.3d at 614–15 (Alito, J., concurring in the judgment); *cf.* Leonard F. v. Isr. Disc. Bank of N.Y., 199 F.3d 99, 106 (2d Cir. 1999) (stating, in challenge to long-term disability policy that capped coverage for mental conditions, that "we agree with the district court that, if MetLife's LTD policy is consistent with state law and was adopted prior to the passage of the ADA, it is exempt from regulation under the Act pursuant to the safe harbor provision," but vacating judgment against the plaintiff (footnote omitted)).

97. This is the core of Kelman's critique of the accommodation requirement. *See* Kelman, *supra* note 8. I tried to challenge that critique in Bagenstos, *supra* note 13, at 870–98.

98. US Airways v. Barnett, 535 U.S. 391, 413 (2002) (Scalia, J., dissenting).

99. *See* Issacharoff & Nelson, *supra* note 2, at 344–45.

100. Justice Scalia has particularly emphasized this point in dissents that accuse the Court of disregarding the limitations that he believes properly apply to the accommodation requirement. *See US Airways*, 535 U.S. at 413–14 (Scalia, J., dissenting) ("When one departs from this understanding [of accommodation as removing a 'disability-related obstacle' to the specific opportunities offered by the defendant], the ADA's accommodation provision becomes a standardless grab bag—leaving it to the courts to decide which workplace preferences (higher salary, longer vacations, reassignment to positions to which others are entitled) can be deemed 'reasonable' to 'make up for' the particular employee's disability."); PGA Tour v. Martin, 532 U.S. 661, 691 (2001) (Scalia, J., dissenting) (criticizing the majority's interpretation of the reasonable accommodation requirement for "exercis[ing] a benevolent compassion that the law does not place it within our power to impose"). As I argue in this subsection, it is not just Justice Scalia who seeks to limit the scope of the accommodation requirement—support for limitations seems to be widespread.

101. Deans Stewart Schwab and Steven Willborn make a similar point in explaining the general rule under the ADA that employers need not accommodate the lesser productivity of a worker with a disability. Although accommodations that remove obstacles to disabled workers who are as productive as nondisabled workers seem "consistent with our meritocratic ideal that jobs should go to the most qualified applicant," they contend, disability advocates may recognize that "[t]he argument that less productive workers with lesser costs are functionally equivalent to more productive, greater cost workers may fail to persuade politically." Stewart J. Schwab & Steven L. Willborn, *Reasonable Accommodation of Workplace Disabilities*, 44 Wm. & Mary L. Rev. 1197, 1233 (2003).

102. *See, e.g.,* Seidman & Tushnet, *supra* note 53, at 110–15; Sunstein, *supra* note 53, at 897–98.

103. Alexander v. Choate, 469 U.S. 287, 299 (1985) (employing the access/content distinction in interpreting the reasonable accommodation requirement imposed by Section 504 of the Rehabilitation Act of 1973).

104. As Michael Waterstone has emphasized, some sympathetic courts have done just that. See Michael Waterstone, *The Untold Story of the Rest of the Americans with Disabilities Act*, 58 Vand. L. Rev. 1807, 1845–48 (2005).

105. *Cf.* Mark Kelman, A Guide to Critical Legal Studies 279–80 (1987) (arguing that our legal culture's focus on individual duties makes it hard to envision rights to societal provision).

106. Karlan & Rutherglen, *supra* note 5, at 41.

107. *See* Bagenstos, *supra* note 34, at 435.

CHAPTER 5. DISABILITY AND SAFETY RISKS

1. *See* Abbott v. Bragdon, 163 F.3d 87, 90 (1st Cir. 1998), *cert. denied*, 526 U.S. 1131 (1999).

2. For examples of cases in which employers refused to hire people with insulin-dependent diabetes for positions that require driving, see Kapche v. City of San Antonio, 176 F.3d 840, 847 (5th Cir. 1999) (noting that time has come for "reevaluation" of the per se rule established in Chandler v. City of Dallas, and directing district court to determine whether there exists "new and improved technology . . . that could now permit insulin-dependent diabetic drivers" to operate vehicles safely); Gonzales v. City of New Braunfels, 176 F.3d 834, 838 (5th Cir. 1999) (affirming grant of summary judgment for defendant City despite acknowledging that "blanket exclusion of insulin-dependent diabetics from positions that require driving may no longer be viable"); Chandler v. City of Dallas, 2 F.3d 1385, 1395 (5th Cir. 1993) (holding as a matter of law in Rehabilitation Act case that driver with insulin-dependent diabetes "presents a genuine substantial risk that he could injure himself and others").

3. *See* Chevron U.S.A., Inc. v. Echazabal, 536 U.S. 73, 76 (2002).

4. *See, e.g.,* Palmer v. Circuit Court, 117 F.3d 351, 351–52 (7th Cir. 1997) (affirming grant of summary judgment on ground that "the Act does not require an employer to retain a potentially violent employee," even if violence "was precipitated by mental illness").

5. *See* Albertson's, Inc. v. Kirkingburg, 527 U.S. 555 (1999) (involving employer's exclusion of commercial truck driver with monocular vision); Murphy v. United Parcel Serv., 527 U.S. 516 (1999) (involving employer's rejection of commercial mechanic with high blood pressure); Sutton v. United Air Lines, 527 U.S. 471 (1999) (involving employer's exclusion of commercial airline pilots with severe myopia); Bragdon v. Abbott, 524 U.S. 624 (1998) (involving dentist's refusal of services to HIV-positive patient); Pa. Dep't of Corr. v. Yeskey, 524 U.S. 206 (1998) (involving state's exclusion of prisoner with hypertension from sentence-reducing boot camp); School Board v. Arline, 480 U.S. 273 (1987) (involving school board's discharge of teacher with tuberculosis); Southeastern Community College v. Davis, 442 U.S. 397 (1979) (involving

nursing program's denial of admission to individual with serious hearing disability on ground that she posed risk to patients).

6. Safety considerations have been invoked in defense of sex discrimination as well, but it is telling that in only one case — involving Alabama's refusal to allow female prison guards to work in male maximum security penitentiaries — has the Supreme Court ever held that such concerns justified intentional discrimination. See Dothard v. Rawlinson, 433 U.S. 321, 334–37 (1977); *cf.* International Union v. Johnson Controls, Inc., 499 U.S. 187 (1991) (fetal protection policy that excluded women of childbearing age from positions in areas with high levels of ambient lead in the air violated Title VII).

7. *See* Stephen Breyer, Breaking the Vicious Circle: Toward Effective Risk Regulation 22–27 (1993); W. Kip Viscusi, Rational Risk Policy 98 (1998) [hereinafter Viscusi, Rational Risk Policy].

8. *See, e.g.,* Breyer, *supra* note 7, at 20–27 (stating that regulations vary widely in costs they impose per life saved, from low of $100,000 to high of $92 billion); *see also* Viscusi, Rational Risk Policy, *supra* note 7, at 98 tbl.6.3 (presenting similar list of regulations and their costs).

9. *See* Breyer, *supra* note 7, at 12–13, 22–23; Viscusi, Rational Risk Policy, *supra* note 7, at 70–77; Jonathan Baert Wiener & John D. Graham, *Resolving Risk Tradeoffs, in* Risk versus Risk: Tradeoffs in Protecting Health and the Environment 226, 241–42 (John D. Graham & Jonathan Baert Wiener eds., 1995).

10. On overestimates of small risks and underestimates of large ones, see Viscusi, Rational Risk Policy, *supra* note 7, at 6. Viscusi has at times suggested that this bias results from a lack of mathematical comprehension: "[I]ndividuals have great difficulty comprehending extremely low-probability events." W. Kip Viscusi, Fatal Tradeoffs: Public and Private Responsibilities for Risk 150 (1992) [hereinafter Viscusi, Fatal Tradeoffs]; *see also* Breyer, *supra* note 12, at 36 (making the same point). But Viscusi has also constructed a model under which such a bias is a rational response to decisionmaking under uncertainty. See Viscusi, Rational Risk Policy, *supra* note 7, at 6–11. Whether or not it is rational for an individual to overestimate small risks and underestimate large risks, Viscusi and Breyer plainly believe that it is not rational to base policy on such misperceptions. On overreaction to prominent or sensational sources of risk, see Breyer, *supra* note 7, at 35–36; Viscusi, Rational Risk Policy, *supra* note 7, at 21–25; Wiener & Graham, *supra* note 9, at 234. On the status quo bias, see Viscusi, Rational Risk Policy, *supra* note 7, at 16–17; on framing effects, see Breyer, *supra* note 7, at 36; on the zero-risk mentality, see Viscusi, Fatal Tradeoffs, supra note 15, at 151; Viscusi, Rational Risk Policy, supra note 12, at 15–16. On excessive response to risks deemed "new," see Peter Huber, *The Old-New Division in Risk Regulation,* 69 Va. L. Rev. 1025, 1028–29 (1983); on the fear of involuntarily imposed risks, see Viscusi, Fatal Tradeoffs, *supra,* at 152.

11. *See* Breyer, *supra* note 7, at 59–79; Viscusi, Fatal Tradeoffs, *supra* note 10, at 249–51.

12. *See, e.g.,* Paul Slovic, *Perception of Risk,* 236 Science 280, 285 (1987) ("[Lay people's] basic conceptualization of risk is much richer than that of experts and reflects legitimate concerns that are typically omitted from expert risk assessments."); *see also, e.g.,*

Clayton P. Gillette & James E. Krier, *Risk, Courts, and Agencies*, 138 U. Pa. L. Rev. 1027, 1075 (1990) ("Disagreements between lay people and expert risk assessors cannot be attributed to simple ignorance or ineptitude on the part of either group. The divide, instead, results from fundamentally different world views."); *cf.* Daniel A. Farber, Eco-pragmatism: Making Sensible Environmental Decisions in an Uncertain World 67 (1999) (observing that pro-environmental, pro-regulatory views are strongest among people with the most education, and arguing that it is therefore hard to write off such views as "based on ill-considered prejudices or bias"). Lisa Heinzerling has argued that the very figures that report high and disparate costs per life saved rest on assumptions that themselves reflect value judgments—often value judgments that directly contradict those made by politically accountable regulatory agencies. *See* Lisa Heinzerling, *Regulatory Costs of Mythic Proportions*, 107 Yale L.J. 1981, 2069–70 (1998). For another critique of those figures, see Thomas O. McGarity, *A Cost-Benefit State*, 50 Admin. L. Rev. 7, 50–54 (1998) (stating that the technocratic vision "tends to exalt expertise over the lay judgment that is critical to a functioning democracy").

13. *See* Gillette & Krier, *supra* note 12, at 1078; Lisa Heinzerling, *Political Science*, 62 U. Chi. L. Rev. 449, 450 (1995); Donald T. Hornstein, *Reclaiming Environmental Law: A Normative Critique of Comparative Risk Analysis*, 92 Colum. L. Rev. 562, 614–15 (1992); McGarity, *supra* note 12, at 59–62.

14. *See* chapter 2, *supra*.

15. On HIV, see Allan M. Brandt, *AIDS: From Social History to Social Policy, in* AIDS: The Burdens of History 147, 153–57 (Elizabeth Fee & Daniel M. Fox eds., 1988). On psychiatric disability, see Jean Campbell, *Unintended Consequences in Public Policy: Persons with Psychiatric Disabilities and the Americans with Disabilities Act*, 22 Pol'y Stud. J. 133, 136, 142 (1994); Caroline L. Kaufmann, *Reasonable Accommodation to Mental Health Disabilities at Work: Legal Constructs and Practical Applications*, 21 J. Psychiatry & L. 153, 168 (1993); John Monahan, *"A Terror to Their Neighbors": Beliefs about Mental Disorder and Violence in Historical and Cultural Perspective*, 20 Bull. Am. Acad. Psychiatry & L. 191, 192 (1992); John Monahan & Jean Arnold, *Violence by People with Mental Illness: A Consensus Statement by Advocates and Researchers*, 19 Psychiatric Rehabilitation J. 67, 69–70 (1996).

16. For the first elaboration of the doctrine, see School Bd. v. Arline, 480 U.S. 273, 287–89 (1987).

17. *See* 42 U.S.C. §§ 12113(b), 12182(b)(3). For the similar codification of the defense in the Rehabilitation Act, see 29 U.S.C. § 705(20)(D); and in the Fair Housing Act, see 42 U.S.C. § 3604(f)(9).

18. There remains some dispute regarding whether the "direct threat" doctrine provides the exclusive means by which an employer can justify safety-based discrimination. One court of appeals has held that an employer may impose "a pre-existing safety-based qualification standard [that] applies across-the-board for the position, such as a requirement that a bus driver meet certain sight requirements," without defending that standard under the "direct threat" test. EEOC v. Exxon Corp., 203 F.3d 871, 874 (5th Cir. 2000). According to the *Exxon* court, such categorical exclusions may be upheld as "qualification standards" if they are "job-related and consistent with business

necessity." *Id.* To the extent that the *Exxon* decision is correct, the discussion in the text must be qualified. Even under the *Exxon* rule, however, a safety-based exclusion may not be based on an entirely categorical judgment, for an employee who is excluded by application of a "qualification standard" must still receive an individualized "reasonable accommodation" where that will enable the employee to perform the job at issue. 42 U.S.C. § 12113(a).

19. For the statement of this principle in the case law, see *Arline*, 480 U.S. at 287 (noting that individualized "inquiry is essential if § 504 [of the Rehabilitation Act] is to achieve its goal of protecting handicapped individuals from deprivations based on prejudice, stereotypes, or unfounded fear"). For the statement of this principle in the regulations implementing the employment provisions of the ADA, see 29 C.F.R. § 1630.2(r) ("The determination that an individual poses a 'direct threat' shall be based on an individualized assessment of the individual's present ability to safely perform the essential functions of the job."); *see also id.* pt. 1630, app. § 1630.2(r) ("Determining whether an individual poses a significant risk of substantial harm to others must be made on a case by case basis. The employer should identify the specific risk posed by the individual."). For the similar statement in the regulations implementing the public accommodations provisions of the ADA, see 28 C.F.R. § 36.208(c); *id.* pt. 36, app. B § 36.208.

20. *See* 42 U.S.C. § 12111(3) (defining "direct threat" as a "significant risk to the health or safety of others"); id. § 12182(b)(3) (same); *Bragdon*, 524 U.S. at 649 ("Because few, if any, activities in life are risk free, *Arline* and the ADA do not ask whether a risk exists, but whether it is significant."); *see also* 29 C.F.R. pt. 1630, app. § 1630.2(r) ("An employer, however, is not permitted to deny an employment opportunity to an individual with a disability merely because of a slightly increased risk. The risk can only be considered when it poses a significant risk, *i.e.*, high probability, of substantial harm; a speculative or remote risk is insufficient.").

21. *See* 42 U.S.C. §§ 12111(3), 12182(b)(3); *Arline*, 480 U.S. at 287 nn.16 & 17, 289 n.19.

22. *See Bragdon*, 524 U.S. at 649–50; 28 C.F.R. § 36.208(c) (providing that public accommodation "must make an individualized assessment, based on reasonable judgment that relies on current medical knowledge or on the best available objective evidence"); 29 C.F.R. § 1630.2(r) ("This assessment shall be based on a reasonable medical judgment that relies on the most current medical knowledge and/or on the best available objective evidence."). The post-ADA case law leaves the burden-of-proof point unclear, but the text of the ADA's employment discrimination title specifically identifies establishment of a "direct threat" as a defense to liability. See 42 U.S.C. § 12113(b) (stating, in statutory provision entitled "Defenses," that "[t]he term 'qualification standards' may include a requirement that an individual shall not pose a direct threat to the health or safety of other individuals in the workplace").

23. *Bragdon*, 524 U.S. at 650.

24. *Arline*, 480 U.S. at 288.

25. *Id.* at 286 n.15.

26. *See Bragdon*, 524 U.S. at 650 ("The views of [public health] organizations are not conclusive, however. A health care professional who disagrees with the prevailing

medical consensus may refute it by citing a credible scientific basis for deviating from the accepted norm."). The First Circuit in *Bragdon* had adopted "a rule which gives prima facie force to the views of public health authorities, but which permits a service provider to challenge those views based on contrary, properly supported opinions voiced by other recognized experts in the field (*e.g.*, research studies published in peer-reviewed journals)." Abbott v. Bragdon, 107 F.3d 934, 945 (1st Cir. 1997). The Supreme Court stated that "[f]or the most part, the Court of Appeals followed the proper standard in evaluating petitioner's position," and its remand included no instructions to alter the degree of deference accorded to public health authorities. *Bragdon*, 524 U.S. at 650, 655.

27. Until enactment of the Civil Rights Act of 1991, 42 U.S.C. § 1981a (1994), Title VII authorized only equitable remedies. *See* 42 U.S.C. § 2000e-5(g); Chauffeurs, Teamsters & Helpers Local 391 v. Terry, 494 U.S. 558, 572 (1990). That limitation prevented defendants from invoking a right to trial by (a potentially prejudiced) jury under the statute. *See* Brian K. Landsberg, Enforcing Civil Rights: Race Discrimination and the Department of Justice 55 (1997) (discussing difficulty, recognized by advocates of the proposed civil rights law, of obtaining findings of discrimination from Southern juries, and noting that "[i]n providing primarily for injunctive relief, the Civil Rights Acts of 1957, 1960, and 1964 avoided the need for jury trials of cases under them").

28. *See* Kathleen M. Sullivan & Martha A. Field, *AIDS and the Coercive Power of the State*, 23 Harv. C.R.-C.L. L. Rev. 139, 179 (1988) (warning that popular anxiety, irrationality, and hysteria about AIDS may lead to vindictive and discriminatory verdicts). The prejudice point is a commonplace in arguments about jury competence. *See, e.g.*, Neil K. Komesar, Imperfect Alternatives: Choosing Institutions in Law, Economics, and Public Policy 141 (1994) ("The majoritarian character of the jury is sometimes unattractive. Consider for example the resolution of legal claims that members of a targeted minority have been discriminated against by the majority. A randomly chosen jury may be a subset of the injuring group."). A similar point is likely to apply to judges, who, after all, come from the same society as juries, though we expect judges' professional culture (and the fact that judges see many cases) to constrain the influence of bias to some extent. *See* Lawrence O. Gostin, *The Americans with Disabilities Act and the Corpus of Antidiscrimination Law: A Force for Change in the Future of Public Health Regulation*, 3 Health Matrix 89, 118 (1993) ("Courts are simply unprepared to respond to th[e] dilemma [posed by low-risk, high-consequence transmission] by the application of a rational set of standards.").

29. Although the risk regulation literature is contentious, all participants appear to agree on one point: society cannot eliminate all risk. *E.g.*, Farber, *supra* note 12, at 84 ("We may want to pretend that th[e] amount [we can spend to reduce risk] is infinite, but the harsh reality is that there are limits to the resources we can or should devote to safety."); Viscusi, Fatal Tradeoffs, *supra* note 10, at 3 ("[W]e cannot eliminate risk from our lives. The difficulty of reaching a zero-risk society is universal."); Gillette & Krier, *supra* note 12, at 1028 ("[T]he objective of risk management must be not the elimination of risk, but rather the minimization of all risk-related costs."). Democrats, as might be expected, disagree with technocrats about the point at which reduction

of risk becomes infeasible. *See, e.g.*, Hornstein, *supra* note 13, at 616–29 (arguing that technocrats' focus on comparing existing risks—and the cost of existing means of eliminating those risks—understates the possibility of fundamental change that would reduce all risks). In *Bragdon*, the Supreme Court recognized this point. *See* 524 U.S. at 649.

30. *See, e.g.*, Reid Hastie & W. Kip Viscusi, *What Juries Can't Do Well: The Jury's Performance as a Risk Manager*, 40 Ariz. L. Rev. 901, 913 (1998) ("[T]he jury tends to take a very narrow view with a focus on the injured person in court, not on the invisible members of the rest of society who will be affected (often positively) by the defendant's response to tort liability outcomes." (paraphrasing Shirley Carroll v. Otis Elevator Co., 896 F.2d 210, 216 (7th Cir. 1990) (Easterbrook, J., concurring))). Although Hastie and Viscusi are discussing the jury's role in tort cases, their basic point—that the individualized nature of adjudication makes it hard for the jury to deal with probabilistic risks—holds here as well. A subsequent paper by Viscusi reports empirical data suggesting that judges are less likely than juries to "fall prey to the zero-risk mentality." W. Kip Viscusi, *Jurors, Judges, and the Mistreatment of Risk by the Courts*, 30 J. Legal Stud. 107, 134 (2001). As the HIV cases indicate, however, judges are not immune from that mentality.

31. Scott Burris, *Public Health, "AIDS Exceptionalism," and the Law*, 27 J. Marshall L. Rev. 251, 268 (1994) (alteration in original) (footnotes omitted) (quoting Doe v. Wash. Univ., 780 F. Supp. 628, 634 (E.D. Mo. 1991), and In re Application of Milton S. Hershey Med. Ctr., 595 A.2d 1290, 1296 (Pa. Super. Ct. 1991)); *see also* Bradley v. Univ. of Tex. M.D. Anderson Cancer Ctr., 3 F.3d 922, 924 (5th Cir. 1993) ("A cognizable risk of permanent duration with lethal consequences suffices to make a surgical technician with Bradley's responsibilities not 'otherwise qualified.'"); Estate of Behringer v. Med. Ctr., 592 A.2d 1251, 1283 (N.J. Super. Ct. Law Div. 1991) ("Where the ultimate harm is death, even the presence of a low risk of transmission justifies the adoption of a policy which precludes invasive procedures when there is 'any' risk of transmission."). For other examples, see Doe v. Univ. of Md. Med. Sys. Corp., 50 F.3d 1261, 1266 (4th Cir. 1995) ("We hold that Dr. Doe does pose a significant risk to the health and safety of his patients that cannot be eliminated by reasonable accommodation. Although there may presently be no documented case of surgeon-to-patient transmission, such transmission clearly is possible."); Leckelt v. Bd. of Comm'rs., 909 F.2d 820, 829 (5th Cir. 1990) (upholding firing of nurse who refused to take an HIV test "[e]ven though the probability that a health care worker will transmit HIV to a patient may be extremely low" because "the potential harm of HIV infection is extremely high"); Mauro v. Borgess Med. Ctr., 886 F. Supp. 1349, 1353 (W.D. Mich. 1995) ("Because there is a real possibility of transmission, however small, and because the consequence of transmission is invariably death, the threat to patient safety posed by plaintiff's presence in the operating room performing the functions of a surgical technician is direct and significant."), *aff'd*, 137 F.3d 398 (6th Cir. 1998). (The Eleventh Circuit's post-*Bragdon* decision in Onishea v. Hopper, 171 F.3d 1289, 1296–99 (11th Cir. 1999), purported to apply a similar analysis, but the result seems to have been driven by the unique imperatives of the prison setting in which that case arose.) As Jeffrey Van Detta notes,

courts have engaged in a similarly exclusionary analysis in cases involving other conditions. Jeffrey A. Van Detta, *"Typhoid Mary" Meets the ADA: A Case Study of the "Direct Threat" Standard Under the Americans with Disabilities Act*, 22 Harv. J.L. & Pub. Pol'y 849, 934–35 (1999) (discussing treatment of epilepsy- and diabetes-based exclusions in the transportation context).

32. Linda Hamilton Krieger, *Socio-Legal Backlash*, 21 Berkeley J. Emp. & Lab. L. 476, 483 (2000).

33. *See, e.g.*, Scott Burris, *Rationality Review and the Politics of Public Health*, 34 Vill. L. Rev. 933, 953–54 (1989) (arguing that the real dispute in *Arline*—a dispute "over the acceptability of whatever level of risk [Arline] was determined to present"—"does not become medical merely because it is placed in medical hands").

34. For extensive and nuanced discussion of the danger faced by civil rights plaintiffs under legal standards that defer to professionals—as well as the opportunities such standards occasionally present for such plaintiffs—see Susan Stefan, *Leaving Civil Rights to the "Experts": From Deference to Abdication under the Professional Judgment Standard*, 102 Yale L.J. 639, 646 (1992).

35. Consider this description by Paul Starr, who seems largely sympathetic to claims for a broader sphere of "public health" activity: "The maintenance of the public's health allows—some would say demands—concern with almost every aspect of life. Breathtaking definitions of public health, offered by some of the field's own leaders, suggest how far claims of its jurisdiction may reach." Paul Starr, The Social Transformation of American Medicine 180 (1982); *see also* Bernard J. Turnock, Public Health: What It Is and How It Works 16 (2d ed. 2001) (discussing the "broad and ever-increasing scope" of public health); Lawrence O. Gostin et al., *The Law and the Public's Health: A Study of Infectious Disease Law in the United States*, 99 Colum. L. Rev. 59, 69 (1999) ("Any activity that aims to encompass environmental protection, medical care, personal behavior, and the 'development of social machinery' for health makes ambitious, if not hubristic, claims of jurisdiction. By this definition, the health department ought to be the biggest agency in state government.").

36. *See* Gostin et al., *supra* note 35, at 113–14.

37. Lawrence O. Gostin, *The Future of Public Health Law*, 12 Am. J.L. & Med. 461, 480 (1986); *see also* Sullivan & Field, *supra* note 28, at 155 ("There is strong evidence to suggest that similar patterns of selective enforcement have marked earlier episodes of quarantine, such as the quarantine of venereal disease toward the beginning of this century.").

38. On racism, see, for example, Jew Ho v. Williamson, 103 F. 10, 23–24 (C.C.N.D. Cal. 1900) (striking down San Francisco Board of Health order that imposed quarantine on the city's Chinatown section to prevent spread of asserted bubonic plague outbreak on ground that quarantine was enforced only against Chinese residents of quarantine area); Wendy E. Parmet, *From Slaughter-House to Lochner: The Rise and Fall of the Constitutionalization of Public Health*, 40 Am. J. Legal Hist. 476, 493 & n.131 (1996) (discussing Louisiana Board of Health's 1898 ban on immigrants into large areas of the state subject to a yellow fever quarantine, a ban that was upheld in Compagnie Française de Navigation à Vapeur v. La. State Bd. of Health, 186 U.S. 380, 385

(1902)); *cf.* Sheila M. Rothman, Living in the Shadow of Death: Tuberculosis and the Social Experience of Illness in American History 184 (1994) ("Explanations [by early twentieth-century public health officials] as to why the immigrant population was most prone to tuberculosis, like the Progressive analyses of poverty itself, focused equally on underlying social conditions and on personal moral failings."). On classism, see, for example, Parmet, *supra*, at 501 (observing that early twentieth-century public health interventions often focused on coercive measures directed at the poor); Sheila M. Rothman, *Seek and Hide: Public Health Departments and Persons with Tuberculosis, 1890–1940*, 21 J.L. Med. & Ethics 289, 290 (1993) (same). On homophobia, see, for example, David Charny, *Economics of Death*, 107 Harv. L. Rev. 2056, 2078 (1994) (book review) (discussing "the clear evidence of dilatoriness and bias in government's initial response to AIDS" as the "public health establishment . . . decid[ed] that the lives of gays were not worth saving"). (As I argue below, however, the overall picture is somewhat more complicated. Although slow to act, public health agencies became a very sympathetic forum for the claims of gay men and other groups most affected by the HIV epidemic.)

39. *See, e.g.,* James Q. Wilson, Bureaucracy: What Government Agencies Do and Why They Do It 59–65, 90–110 (1989) (discussing role of professional norms in the culture of various government agencies).

40. *See, e.g.,* Turnock, *supra* note 35, at 226–38 (describing the many systematic ways in which public health agencies gather timely and comprehensive data); *id.* at 64–69; *see also id.* at 95–96 ("Public health practice . . . seeks to deploy its limited resources to avoid the worst outcomes (at the level of the group). Some level of risk is tolerated at the collective level to prevent an unacceptable level of adverse outcomes from occurring.").

41. *Cf.* Cass R. Sunstein, *Cognition and Cost-Benefit Analysis*, 29 J. Legal Stud. 1059, 1059–60 (2000) (arguing that cost-benefit analysis generally serves such a safeguarding function).

42. *See* Jonathan M. Mann, *Medicine and Public Health, Ethics and Human Rights, in* New Ethics for the Public's Health 83, 89 (Dan E. Beauchamp & Bonnie Steinbock eds., 1999) ("Again in the context of AIDS, public health has learned that discrimination toward HIV-infected people and people with AIDS is counterproductive."); *see generally* Jonathan M. Mann et al., *Introduction, in* Health and Human Rights 1, 1–2 (Jonathan M. Mann et al. eds., 1999) ("Stigmatization and discrimination thwart medical and public health efforts to help people with disease or disability."); Turnock, *supra* note 35, at 14–16 (describing "social justice orientation" of public health); Gostin et al., *supra* note 35, at 92–93 (discussing the important role of the antistigma project in protecting the public health).

43. *See* Gillette & Krier, *supra* note 12, at 1068 ("The diffuseness of public risks, coupled with the fact that materialization of any physical injury will usually be remote in time (latent) and in probability, reduces incentives to contribute much to the common cause. So does the nonexclusive nature of favorable agency action."). For other writers similarly emphasizing the skewed distribution of stakes in affecting regulatory outcomes, see, for example, Komesar, *supra* note 28, at 53–97; James Q. Wilson, *The*

Politics of Regulation, in The Politics of Regulation 357, 369 (James Q. Wilson ed., 1980).

44. There are obviously some exceptions. Some industries may be disproportionately affected by the risks associated with people with particular disabilities. The medical industry, for example, is likely to bear the brunt of any risk of transmission associated with HIV, for medical settings are the ones in which contact between body fluids is particularly likely in the aboveground economy. Similarly, the transportation industry is likely to be disproportionately affected by the safety risks associated with insulin-dependent diabetes, because insulin shock poses a particular risk when it affects a person who is driving or operating heavy machinery. These industries are likely to mobilize to participate in the public health decisionmaking process as well, but — unlike in the regulatory agencies — they are less likely to overwhelm the influence of the disability groups. Where agencies stand between well-matched interest group antagonists, they are often free to pursue the course that is consistent with agency operators' professional norms. *See, e.g.,* Wilson, *supra* note 39, at 81–82 (giving examples of agency behavior when confronted with well-matched interest groups).

45. *See* Ronald Bayer, Private Acts, Social Consequences: AIDS and the Politics of Public Health 134, 174–175, 190–206 (1989).

46. Ronald Bayer & Amy Fairchild-Carrino, *AIDS and the Limits of Control: Public Health Orders, Quarantine, and Recalcitrant Behavior,* 83 Am. J. Pub. Health 1471, 1475 (1993).

47. *Id.*

48. *See* Bayer, *supra* note 45, at 138–42.

49. *See id.* at 69–71, 100, 104–6, 205; *see also, e.g.,* Mary Anne Bobinski, *Risk and Rationality: The Centers for Disease Control and the Regulation of HIV-Infected Health Care Workers,* 36 St. Louis U. L.J. 213, 219 n.20 (1991) (observing that CDC solicited participation from a number of groups — including gay rights groups — when it crafted its guidelines on HIV in the workplace and at school); Michael C. Musheno et al., *Court Management of AIDS Disputes: A Sociolegal Analysis,* 16 Law & Soc. Inquiry 737, 770 (1991) ("[P]ublic health agencies and other state parties, like human rights' [*sic*] commissions, are forming effective alliances with AIDS parties, including gay rights organizations."). *But see* Leonard Robins & Charles Backstrom, *The Role of State Health Departments in Formulating Policy: A Survey on the Case of AIDS,* 84 Am. J. Pub. Health 905, 908 (1994) (reporting results of survey of state public health officials, in which "[a]ffected groups such as persons living with AIDS and organized gays were seen by fewer than 1 in 10 health departments as being very influential.").

50. *See, e.g.,* Chandler Burr, *The AIDS Exception: Privacy vs. Public Health, in* New Ethics for the Public's Health, *supra* note 42, at 211 (providing a classic expression of this view).

51. *See, e.g.,* Bayer, *supra* note 45, at 71 (asserting that public health officials' failure to appreciate the symbolic contribution that closing bathhouses would make to encouraging a public culture of sexual restraint and responsibility "was a profound misjudgment" that was "conditioned by the political forces evoked by the AIDS epidemic"); *id.* at 206 (making similar point about public health officials' rejection of "carefully

defined sanctions" imposed against identified infected individuals who persistently engaged in high-risk conduct).

52. *See* Charny, *supra* note 38, at 2078 ("As is well documented, the public health establishment suppressed knowledge about the disease and stymied research, consciously deciding that the lives of gays were not worth saving. Thousands of gay men died, and continue to die, as a result. Where was the politically powerful gay cabal?" (footnote omitted)).

53. *See* Bayer, *supra* note 45, at 73–89 (describing controversy surrounding Public Health Service recommendations regarding exclusion of blood donations by members of high-risk groups); *id.* at 103–15 (describing controversy surrounding public health officials' advocacy of such widespread HIV testing).

54. *See id.* at 15 ("Rigorous surveillance and attempts at the regulation of the private acts linked to AIDS—were they possible—would not only entail morally repugnant invasions of privacy, evoking images from Orwell, but would be counterproductive as well."); *id.* at 240 (arguing that "public health officials have so universally argued in favor of education as the preeminent line of social defense against the epidemic" because of "the very limited rational role that coercive measures might play in the control of AIDS").

55. 527 U.S. 555, 577–78 (1999).

56. *Id.* at 567–78.

57. See Samuel R. Bagenstos, *The Americans with Disabilities Act as Risk Regulation*, 101 Colum. L. Rev. 1479, 1504–5 n.101 (2001).

58. *Cf.* Turnock, *supra* note 35, at 147 (describing subordination of public health to regulatory goals in shift of environmental health responsibilities from health agencies to environmental regulatory agencies).

59. For example, the Motor Carrier Safety Act of 1984, Pub. L. No. 98-554, tit. II, 98 Stat. 2832 (1984)—under which the FHWA adopted the visual acuity regulations at issue in *Albertson's*—has been read to resolve all uncertainty in favor of the safe operation of motor vehicles; it thus allocates the risk of uncertainty to those, like people with monocular vision, who would seek an exception to an existing safety regulation. *See* Advocates for Highway and Auto Safety v. Federal Highway Admin., 28 F.3d 1288, 1294 (D.C. Cir. 1994) (concluding that the department's statement that it lacked sufficient evidence to enable it to determine riskiness of visual impairments disentitled it to enact waiver program to obtain that evidence because the statute requires that the agency have sufficient evidence to demonstrate safety of its actions before it may go forward). The court concluded: "[W]e are fully aware of the difficulties that the FHWA undoubtedly faces in acquiring the data on which to make an informed judgment as to whether the existing vision standards may safely be relaxed. The requirements of the Motor Carrier Safety Act's waiver provision, however, must be satisfied; and because the FHWA has failed to meet its requirements, we vacate and remand the rule." *Id.*

60. Summarizing her argument, Berg states that OSHA's "failure to identify any goals other than the protection of employee health (such as the protection of the public health generally) and to explicitly value the rights of other parties affected by conta-

gion regulations creates the risk that OSHA will routinely value the rights and interests of employers and employees at the expense of PWIDs [people with infectious
diseases], perceived PWIDs, and the public." Paula E. Berg, *When the Hazard Is
Human: Irrationality, Inequity, and Unintended Consequences in Federal Regulation
of Contagion*, 75 Wash. U. L.Q. 1367, 1389–90 (1997).

61. *See id.* at 1391–92.
62. *Bragdon*, 524 U.S. at 650.
63. 536 U.S. 73 (2002).
64. *Id.* at 76.
65. *Id.* at 76–77.
66. *See id.* at 76.
67. 42 U.S.C. § 12113(b).
68. *Id.* §§ 12111(8), 12112(a).
69. *Id.* § 12113.
70. *Id.* § 12113(a).
71. *Id.* § 12113(b).
72. *Id.* § 12111(3).
73. *Id.* §§ 12111(3), 12113(b).
74. 29 C.F.R. § 1630.15(b)(2) ("The term 'qualification standard' may include a require-
    ment that an individual shall not pose a direct threat to the health or safety of the
    individual or others in the workplace.").
75. *Chevron*, 536 U.S. at 79.
76. *See id.* at 79–80. Those regulations defined "qualified handicapped person"—a term
    that was not defined in the Rehabilitation Act itself—to mean "a handicapped person
    who, with or without reasonable accommodation, can perform the essential functions
    of the position in question without endangering the health and safety of the indi-
    vidual or others." 29 C.F.R. § 1613.702(f) (1990).
77. *See Chevron*, 536 U.S. at 85–86 n.5; *Johnson Controls*, 499 U.S. at 202 ("danger to
    a woman herself does not justify discrimination"); *Dothard*, 433 U.S. at 335 ("In the
    usual case, the argument that a particular job is too dangerous for women may appro-
    priately be met by the rejoinder that it is the purpose of Title VII to allow the indi-
    vidual woman to make that choice for herself.").
78. *See* 42 U.S.C. § 12101(a)(2), (5) (listing "overprotective rules and policies" as among
    the "forms of discrimination" against people with disabilities that "continue to be a
    serious and pervasive social problem"). For just two of the many references to pater-
    nalism in the legislative history, see H.R. Rep. No. 101-485, pt. 2, at 72, 74 (1990)
    (finding it "critical that paternalistic concerns for the disabled person's own safety
    not be used to disqualify an otherwise qualified applicant" because "(p)aternalism
    is perhaps the most pervasive form of discrimination for people with disabilities"),
    and Americans with Disabilities Act: Hearing before the House Comm. on Small
    Business, 101st Cong. 126 (1990) (testimony of Arlene Mayerson) "(L)ike women,
    disabled people have identified 'paternalism' as a major obstacle to economic and
    social advancement."). The writings of disability rights advocates have also frequently
    identified paternalism as a major engine of disability discrimination. *See, e.g.*, James I.

Charlton, Nothing about Us without Us: Disability Oppression and Empowerment 3 (1998) ("Control has universal appeal for DRM (disability rights movement) activists because the needs of people with disabilities and the potential for meeting these needs are everywhere conditioned by a dependency born of powerlessness, poverty, degradation, and institutionalization. This dependency, saturated with paternalism, begins with the onset of disability and continues until death."); Mary Johnson, Make Them Go Away: Clint Eastwood, Christopher Reeve, and the Case Against Disability Rights 187 (2003) (describing "paternalism" as "pity-coated bigotry" whose "role was to insist that there was, in fact, no harm in treating disabled people differently, even as they suffered for it"); *see also* chapter 2, *supra* (discussing antipaternalist strand of the disability rights movement).

79. *Chevron*, 536 U.S. at 80.

80. *Id.*

81. *Id.* at 84–87.

82. The *Chevron* Court acknowledged this point. *Id.* at 80 n.3.

83. 42 U.S.C. § 12101(a)(7).

84. *See Johnson Controls*, 499 U.S. at 202; *Dothard*, 433 U.S. at 335.

85. *Chevron*, 536 U.S. at 82.

86. *Id.* at 83.

87. *Id.* at 82.

88. Robert F. Schopp, Competence, Condemnation, and Commitment: An Integrated Theory of Mental Health Law 18 (2001); *see generally* 1 Michael L. Perlin, Mental Disability Law: Civil and Criminal 44–190 (2d ed. 1998).

89. *See, e.g.,* Stephen J. Morse, *A Preference for Liberty: The Case against Involuntary Commitment of the Mentally Disordered,* 70 Cal. L. Rev. 54 (1982); *Developments in the Law—Civil Commitment of the Mentally Ill,* 87 Harv. L. Rev. 1190, 1223–28 (1974); *see also* 1 Perlin, *supra* note 88, at 159–69 (describing antipaternalist challenges to *parens patriae* civil commitments throughout the 1970s and the resurgence of the *parens patriae* rationale for commitment in the 1980s and 1990s).

90. *See* 29 C.F.R. § 1613.702(f) (1990) (defining "qualified handicapped person" as "a handicapped person who, with or without reasonable accommodation, can perform the essential functions of the position in question without endangering the health or safety of the individual or others"); *see also* 29 U.S.C. § 794(a) (1988) (limiting statutory protection to an "otherwise qualified individual with handicaps").

91. *See* 29 U.S.C. § 706(8)(B), (C) (1988).

92. *Id.* § 706(8)(B).

93. *Id.* § 706(8)(C).

94. *Id.* § 706(8)(B).

95. Congress added the "direct threat" provision relating to drug abusers and alcoholics in 1978, a year after the EEOC promulgated its regulations. *See* Pub. L. No. 95-602, § 122(a)(6), 92 Stat. 2955, 2984 (1978). Congress added the "direct threat" provision relating to contagious diseases in 1988. *See* Civil Rights Restoration Act of 1987, Pub. L. No. 100-259, § 9, 102 Stat. 28, 31–32 (1988). The latter provision was obviously intended to codify the Supreme Court's decision in *Arline*, 480 U.S. at 287 n.16 ("A

person who poses a significant risk of communicating an infectious disease to others in the workplace will not be otherwise qualified for his or her job if reasonable accommodation will not eliminate that risk.").

96. *See* 42 U.S.C. § 12111(8) ("qualified" individual is one who, "with or without reasonable accommodation, can perform the essential functions of the employment position that such individual holds or desires").

97. *See, e.g.,* Thomas O. McGarity & Sidney A. Shapiro, Workers at Risk: The Failed Promise of the Occupational Safety and Health Administration 18–20 (1993).

98. *See* Duncan Kennedy, *Distributive and Paternalist Motives in Contract and Tort Law, with Special Reference to Compulsory Terms and Unequal Bargaining Power,* 41 Md. L. Rev. 563 (1982).

99. Full disclosure: I argued the case in the Supreme Court for Mario Echazabal.

100. Ronald Bayer, *Workers' Liberty, Workers' Welfare: The Supreme Court Speaks on the Rights of Disabled Employees,* 93 Am. J. Pub. Health 540, 541 (2003).

101. *Id.* at 544.

102. *Id.*

103. Norman Daniels, Chevron v. Echazabal: *Protection, Opportunity, and Paternalism,* 93 Am. J. Pub. Health 545, 546 (2003).

104. Pauli Murray & Mary O. Eastwood, *Jane Crow and the Law: Sex Discrimination and Title VII,* 35 Geo. Wash. L. Rev. 232, 248 (1965) (footnotes omitted).

105. 208 U.S. 412 (1908).

106. *Id.* at 421.

107. See, for example, these gems unearthed by Justice Ginsburg in her opinion striking down the Virginia Military Institute's exclusion of women:

> Dr. Edward H. Clarke of Harvard Medical School, whose influential book, *Sex in Education,* went through 17 editions, was perhaps the most well-known speaker from the medical community opposing higher education for women. He maintained that the physiological effects of hard study and academic competition with boys would interfere with the development of girls' reproductive organs. See E. Clarke, Sex in Education 38–39, 62–63 (1873); *id.,* at 127 ("identical education of the two sexes is a crime before God and humanity, that physiology protests against, and that experience weeps over"); see also H. Maudsley, Sex in Mind and in Education 17 (1874) ("It is not that girls have not ambition, nor that they fail generally to run the intellectual race [in coeducational settings], but it is asserted that they do it at a cost to their strength and health which entails life-long suffering, and even incapacitates them for the adequate performance of the natural functions of their sex."); C. Meigs, Females and Their Diseases 350 (1848) (after five or six weeks of "mental and educational discipline," a healthy woman would "lose . . . the habit of menstruation" and suffer numerous ills as a result of depriving her body for the sake of her mind).

108. Murray & Eastwood, *supra* note 104, at 237 (footnotes omitted).

109. *E.g., Johnson Controls, supra.*

110. *Cf.* Bayer, *supra* note 100, at 541, 544.

111. *Cf. id.* at 544.
112. See *id.* at 541–42.
113. *Id.* at 544.
114. *Id.*
115. Echazabal v. Chevron USA, Inc., 336 F.3d 1023, 1029 (9th Cir. 2003).
116. Daniels, *supra* note 103, at 548.

CHAPTER 6. DISABILITY, LIFE, DEATH, AND CHOICE

1. *See, e.g.,* Robert H. Mnookin, *Two Puzzles,* 1984 Ariz. St. L.J. 667, 676 (1984).
2. *See, e.g.,* U.S. Comm'n on Civil Rights, Medical Discrimination against Children with Disabilities passim (1989); Martha Minow, Making All the Difference: Inclusion, Exclusion, and American Law 328–33 (1990); Phoebe Haddon, *Baby Doe Cases: Compromise and Moral Dilemma,* 34 Emory L.J. 545, 573–79 (1985).
3. *See* U.S. Comm'n on Civil Rights, *supra* note 2, at 21–23. Unless otherwise noted, my factual discussion of the "Baby Doe" cases is drawn from these pages of the Civil Rights Commission's report.
4. Mnookin, *supra* note 1, at 676.
5. *See, e.g.,* Drew S. Days III, *Turning Back the Clock: The Reagan Administration and Civil Rights,* 19 Harv. C.R.-C.L. L. Rev. 309 (1984).
6. *See* U.S. Comm'n on Civil Rights, *supra* note 2, at 5–7.
7. United States v. Univ. Hosp., State Univ. of N.Y., 729 F.2d 144, 146 (2d Cir. 1984).
8. *Id.* at 157.
9. *See* Bowen v. Am. Hosp. Ass'n, 476 U.S. 610, 647 (1986).
10. Roe v. Wade, 410 U.S. 113 (1973).
11. *Bowen,* 476 U.S. at 634 (plurality opinion). The *Bowen* plurality was written by Justice Stevens and joined by Justices Marshall, Blackmun, and Powell. Chief Justice Burger concurred in the judgment without opinion.
12. *Id.* at 630 (quoting 29 U.S.C. § 794 (1978)).
13. *See, e.g.,* Joseph P. Shapiro, No Pity: People with Disabilities Forging a New Civil Rights Movement 278–80 (1993).
14. *Killing Babies: Left and Right,* Disability Rag, May 1983, *quoted in* Edward D. Berkowitz, Disabled Policy: America's Programs for the Handicapped 223 (1987).
15. *See* Brief for the Am. Coal. of Citizens with Disabilities et al. as Amici Curiae Supporting Petitioner, Heckler v. Am. Hosp. Ass'n, 476 U.S. 610 (1986) (No. 84-1529), 1985 WL 669107 [hereinafter ACCD Brief]; Brief for the Am. Ass'n on Mental Deficiency et al. as Amici Curiae Supporting Petitioner, *Heckler,* 476 U.S. 610 (No. 84–1529), 1985 WL 669104 [hereinafter AAMD Brief]; Brief for the Ass'n for Retarded Citizens et al. as Amici Curiae Supporting Petitioner, Heckler, 476 U.S. 610 (No. 84–1529), 1985 WL 669102 [hereinafter ARC Brief]; Brief for the Disability Rights Ed. & Defense Fund, Inc. and Women's Legal Defense Fund as Amici Curiae Supporting Petitioner, *Heckler,* 476 U.S. 610 (No. 84-1529), 1985 WL 669109 [hereinafter DREDF Brief].

16. For similar arguments from an academic advocate of disability rights, see Martha A. Field, *Killing "the Handicapped"—Before and after Birth*, 16 Harv. Women's L.J. 79, 87 (1993) ("One problem with the quality-of-life arguments is that very often they are based upon prejudice against the handicapped, and even more often they are based upon ignorance about the handicapped.").

17. ARC Brief, *supra* note 15, at 7; *see also* AAMD Brief, *supra* note 15, at 6 ("Discriminatory withholding of necessary and appropriate medical care and treatment from handicapped infants is primarily based on the assumption that these children's handicaps make their lives less valuable than those of babies who have no detectable disability, and even renders them 'not worth living.'").

18. ACCD Brief, *supra* note 15, at 16.

19. AAMD Brief, *supra* note 15, at 12; *see also* ARC Brief, *supra* note 15, at 12 (arguing that those who would withhold treatment from infants with disabilities "consistently underestimate the developmental potential and employability of handicapped persons and ignore the substantial and valuable personal and economic contributions of handicapped children and adults to their families and communities").

20. *See* ARC Brief, *supra* note 15, at 20 ("The relationship between the physician and the parents, is one which has as its foundation the theory that the former is learned, skilled and experienced in those subjects about which the latter ordinarily know little or nothing. Despite the vital importance of both the life and health of the child to the parent, the parent must necessarily place great reliance, faith, and confidence in the professional word, advice, and acts of the physician or other health care provider.") (footnotes omitted).

21. *See* AAMD Brief, *supra* note 15, at 15 n.29 (noting the "unique vulnerability of parents upon being told that their newborn baby is 'deformed' or 'defective'"); ACCD Brief, *supra* note 15, at 29 ("Doctors know of parents' trust in their expertise and of their vulnerability in the turmoil of the newborn period.") (footnotes omitted); ARC Brief, *supra* note 15, at 23 ("After the birth of a sick and handicapped infant, families are often in 'a severe psychological crisis' in which they are foreclosed, as a result of psychological and emotional trauma that generally surrounds the birth of a handicapped infant, from either assimilating properly the information which is provided about the infant's condition or exercising clear and rational judgment concerning a no-treatment decision presented by a physician."). For an academic expression of the point, see Carl E. Schneider, *Rights Discourse and Neonatal Euthanasia*, 76 Cal. L. Rev. 151, 159–60 (1988) ("In the few traumatic days after the birth of a defective child, the parents cannot be said to know their child well, may not have begun to love (and may even have come to hate) their child, suffer under harsh emotional and social pressures, have many interests which conflict with the child's, are thinking often for the first time about moral issues of the cruelest difficulty, and frequently know little about their child's condition and prognosis.").

22. *See* ARC Brief, *supra* note 15, at 23 ("In addition, time pressures, often artificial and unnecessary, imposed on parents to consent or acquiesce in the physician's recommendation affect both the capacity of the parents for rational judgment and the quality of the information upon which to base a judgment.") (footnotes omitted); *see*

also Field, *supra* note 16, at 91 (noting "problems with requiring a quick decision," including "[t]he shock and surprise of the family and the physical condition of the mother," the fact that "many parents are uninformed about disabilities, retardation, likelihood of harm, facilities available to persons with disabilities, attitudes of parents of children who have disabilities, etc.," and the fact that "no one knows the child's condition in any reliable way in the first few days").

23. AAMD Brief, *supra* note 15, at 15.

24. ACCD Brief, *supra* note 15, at 29.

25. AAMD Brief, *supra* note 15, at 18 n.29 (footnote omitted) (citing Eric J. Cassell, *Nurturing a Defective Newborn: Commentary*, 8 Hastings Center Rep. 13, 14 (1978), and R. S. Duff, *Counseling Families and Deciding Care of Severely Defective Children: A Way of Coping with "Medical Vietnam,"* 67 Pediatrics 315, 317 (1981)); *see also* ARC Brief, *supra* note 15, at 19, 24 (citing Duff, *supra*; Cassell, *supra*).

26. ARC Brief, *supra* note 15, at 25 (quoting Jay Katz, *Informed Consent—A Fairy Tale? Law's Vision*, 39 U. Pitt. L. Rev. 137, 142 (1977)); *see also* ACCD Brief, *supra* note 15, at 29 n.81 ("'At the end, it is usually the doctor who has to decide the issue. It is not only cruel to ask the parents whether they want their child to live or die, it is dishonest, because in the vast majority of cases, the parents are consciously or unconsciously influenced by the doctor's opinion.'") (quoting Anthony Shaw, *Dilemmas of Informed Consent in Children*, 289 New Eng. J. Med. 885, 886 (1973)).

27. *See, e.g.,* Shapiro, *supra* note 13, at 277–78. The earliest cases involved the discontinuance of life-sustaining treatment (as in the Schiavo case, which involved the discontinuance of life-sustaining feeding and hydration). As the text shows, disability rights activists later applied the same critiques to physician-assisted suicide. Accordingly, my discussion makes no difference between the discontinuance of life-sustaining treatment and physician-assisted suicide, despite the distinctions typically drawn between them in moral and legal debates.

28. *See, e.g., id.* at 275–77; Paul Steven Miller, *The Impact of Assisted Suicide on Persons with Disabilities—Is It a Right without Freedom?*, 9 Issues L. & Med. 47, 59–60 (1993).

29. *See* Not Dead Yet, In The Courts, http://www.notdeadyet.org/docs/court.html (listing the group's participation in litigation).

30. For an academic argument expressing strong sympathy for disability rights interests, while maintaining that a pro-choice position on abortion does not entail acceptance of a right to die, see Seth F. Kreimer, *Does Pro-Choice Mean Pro-Kevorkian? An Article on Roe, Casey, and the Right to Die*, 44 Am. U. L. Rev. 803 (1995). Of course, some disability rights advocates oppose both assisted suicide and abortion rights. *See, e.g.,* Stephen L. Mikochik, *Assisted Suicide and Disabled People*, 46 DePaul L. Rev. 987, 1001–2 (1997).

31. *See* Miller, *supra* note 28, at 47–48.

32. *Id.* at 52.

33. *See* Paul K. Longmore, Why I Burned My Book and Other Articles on Disability 167 (2003) ("Reading through the literature of the suicide rights activists, one is struck by their willing acceptance of prejudicial assumptions about persons with disabilities.

Disability renders its 'victims' helpless and dependent. It robs them of the possibility of living meaningfully. It makes them emotionally, physically, and financially burdensome to themselves, their families, and society."); Carol J. Gill, *Health Professionals, Disabilities, and Assisted Suicide: An Examination of Relevant Empirical Evidence and Reply to Batavia*, 6 Psychol., Pub. Pol'y & L. 526, 526 (2000); Miller, *supra* note 28, at 49 (arguing that "the right to die movement is reinforcing stereotypical notions about the 'tragedy' of a disabled person's existence"); *id.* at 55 ("Latent prejudice leads to society's condoning suicide for persons with disabilities as a rational decision, or even a preferable solution.").

34. *See, e.g.*, Nat'l Council on Disability, Assisted Suicide: A Disability Perspective 22–28 (1997); Gill, *supra* note 33.

35. Carol J. Gill, *Suicide Intervention for Persons with Disabilities: A Lesson in Inequality*, 8 Issues L. & Med. 37, 39 (1992).

36. Longmore, *supra* note 33, at 166.

37. Id. For an exploration of this issue in the context of tort-law damages, see Samuel R. Bagenstos & Margo Schlanger, *Hedonic Damages, Hedonic Adaptation, and Disability*, 60 Vand. L. Rev. 745 (2007).

38. Miller, *supra* note 28, at 54.

39. Longmore, *supra* note 33, at 160; *see also* Kreimer, *supra* note 30, at 20–28 (detailing risks of coercion in assisted suicide); Martha Minow, *Which Question? Which Lie? Reflections on the Physician-Assisted Suicide Cases*, 1997 Sup. Ct. Rev. 1, 21 (arguing that the legalization of physician-assisted suicide would "systematically and routinely be used to push dying people into death": "The problem is not merely risks of abuse; the problem arises from the inauguration of a regime in which people would have to justify continuing to live. Rooting the permission in a right or protected interest, based in autonomy or dignity, would not save individuals from pressures to die imposed directly or indirectly by family members, physicians, managed care providers, or the patients' own sense of guilt and burden.").

40. *See, e.g.*, Nat'l Council on Disability, *supra* note 34, at 22–28; Gill, *supra* note 33.

41. *See, e.g.*, Nat'l Council on Disability, *supra* note 34, at 37–40; Miller, *supra* note 28, at 56–57; *see also* Kreimer, *supra* note 30, at 810 ("Legalization of euthanasia and assisted suicide, unlike abortion, raises the specter of an increasingly cost-conscious medical system advertently or unconsciously tracking vulnerable populations away from expensive and personally demanding medical treatment or palliative care toward less expensive and easier medical suicide. Desperately ill citizens may feel themselves forced to justify their decision to remain alive.").

42. Miller, *supra* note 28, at 54; *see also* Mark C. Siegel, *Lethal Pity: The Oregon Death with Dignity Act, Its Implications for the Disabled, and the Struggle for Equality in an Able-Bodied World*, 16 Law & Ineq. 259, 282–83 (1998) (discussing the internalization of disability stigma).

43. *See* Nat'l Council on Disability, *supra* note 34, at 41–47.

44. *See, e.g.*, Minow, *supra* note 39, at 22 ("Apparently, it is actually a rather small class of people who would evade 'abuse' of assisted suicide. It would be a lie, in short, to maintain that any regime permitting physician-assisted suicide would safeguard large

numbers of people against abuse."); *see also* Siegel, *supra* note 42, at 287–88 ("It is difficult to visualize an assisted suicide law which would not pose a threat to the lives of disabled persons, especially the severely disabled. To varying degrees, measures like the [Oregon Death with Dignity Act], coupled with societal views of the quality of life of disabled people, inherently impede the efforts of the disabled to integrate themselves into society.").

45. See Washington v. Glucksberg, 521 U.S. 702, 735 (1997); Vacco v. Quill, 521 U.S. 793, 808–9 (1997); *cf.* Gonzales v. Oregon, 546 U.S. 243, 248 (2006) (holding that the Controlled Substances Act cannot be read to prohibit physician-assisted suicide, and noting the "'earnest and profound debate' across the country" regarding the practice).

46. See Kristin Luker, Abortion and the Politics of Motherhood 62–65 (1984).

47. *See id.* at 80–82.

48. *See* William Saletan, Bearing Right: How Conservatives Won the Abortion War 89–90, 160, 164, 184–85 (2004); *see also* Bonnie Steinbock, *Disability, Prenatal Testing, and Selective Abortion, in* Prenatal Testing and Disability Rights 108, 109 (Erik Parens & Adrienne Asch eds., 2000) (noting that "most people who regard abortion as justifiable" treat "a serious disabling condition" as "one of the strongest reasons for terminating a pregnancy," and that even many of those "who are almost always opposed to abortion" will accept it in cases involving "a severe disability in the fetus"). In the academic world, Ronald Dworkin contends that under a "paradigm liberal view," which "represent[s] the moral convictions of many people," abortion is "morally justified" in cases of "severe fetal abnormality"—and perhaps even "morally required" in cases "when the abnormality is very severe." Ronald Dworkin, Life's Dominion: An Argument about Abortion, Euthanasia, and Individual Freedom 33–34 (1993). For criticism, from a disability rights perspective, of some of the rhetoric of pro-choice advocates, see Shapiro, *supra* note 13, at 278–79 ("Proponents of legalized abortion at times have played shamelessly upon parents' fear of giving birth to a child with birth defects—using exaggerated pity talk of 'defective children,' 'a gruesome demand,' and 'a maimed and distorted human-without-a-future' to defend a woman's option to choose abortion.").

49. *See* Luker, *supra* note 46, at 207–8. Of course, Luker's study was conducted before the recent debate over so-called partial-birth abortion, which may now be considered the "worst" form of abortion for many antiabortion activists. *See, e.g.*, Cathy Cleaver Ruse, *Partial-Birth Abortion on Trial*, Human Life Review 87 (Spring 2005), available at http://www.nrlc.org/abortion/pba/RusePBAonTrial.pdf. The point holds, however, that many opponents of abortion oppose disability-selective abortion especially strongly.

50. *See* Ruse, *supra* note 49, at 88–90 (describing California Governor Ronald Reagan's veto of liberalized abortion law because of its "fetal indications" clause); Laurence H. Tribe, Abortion: The Clash of Absolutes 47 (1990) (describing successful efforts of New York state assemblyman Martin Ginsberg, who had a disability as a result of polio, to oppose a law "that permitted abortion in cases of serious fetal deformity").

51. Shapiro, *supra* note 13, at 280.

52. Erik Parens & Adrienne Asch, *The Disability Rights Critique of Prenatal Genetic Testing: Reflections and Recommendations, in* Prenatal Testing and Disability Rights, *supra* note 48, at 3, 3–4.

53. *Id.* at 4; *see also* Edward J. Larson, *The Meaning of Human Gene Testing for Disability Rights,* 70 U. Cin. L. Rev. 913, 932–33 (2002) ("Human gene therapy raises the prospect of correcting disabling genes within the born or unborn, but such techniques remain futuristic and are unlikely to replace selective reproduction as the most practical means of eliminating disabilities.") (footnotes omitted); Michael Bérubé, Life as We Know It: A Father, a Family, and an Exceptional Child 76 (1996) (stating that 90 percent of couples choose abortion when prenatal testing detects Down syndrome).

54. *See, e.g.,* Steinbock, *supra* note 48, at 117–18 ("One of the most common reasons for screening women over thirty-five in the United States is to detect trisomy 21 (Down syndrome). Down syndrome is not a fatal disease; many people with Down's live into their fifties and sixties. Moreover, it is compatible with a good quality of life, with appropriate medical treatment and educational opportunities."). The reaction to the pregnancy of Los Angeles news anchor Bree Walker Lampley, who has ectrodactyly (a hereditary condition that causes fused fingers and toes), is particularly striking in this regard. Many in the public were outraged that Lampley would continue her pregnancy and thus risk "bringing a disabled child into the world." Shapiro, *supra* note 13, at 38–40.

55. Parens & Asch, *supra* note 52, at 13.

56. Larson, *supra* note 53, at 932.

57. *See, e.g.,* Field, *supra* note 16, at 117: Larson, *supra* note 53, at 936. The Supreme Court has recognized that isolation of people with disabilities from the general community "perpetuates unwarranted assumptions that persons so isolated are incapable or unworthy of participating in community life." Olmstead v. L.C. ex rel. Zimring, 527 U.S. 581, 600 (1999); *see generally* Timothy M. Cook, *The Americans with Disabilities Act: The Move to Integration,* 64 Temp. L. Rev. 393 (1991) (demonstrating the importance to disability rights advocates of the goal of integration into the community).

58. *See* Field, *supra* note 16, at 117–18.

59. Marsha Saxton, *Why Members of the Disability Community Oppose Prenatal Diagnosis and Selective Abortion, in* Prenatal Testing and Disability Rights, *supra* note 48, at 147, 150–51.

60. *See, e.g.,* Parens & Asch, *supra* note 52, at 6–7; Field, *supra* note 16, at 121–22 n.163.

61. Adrienne Asch, *Disability Equality and Prenatal Testing: Contradictory or Compatible?,* 30 Fla. St. U. L. Rev. 315, 334 (2003).

62. *Id.* at 335; *see also* Bérubé, *supra* note 53, at 81 ("There are still plenty of medical practitioners who tell their patients that children with Down syndrome cannot learn; there are plenty of doctors, just as there are plenty of professors, who haven't updated their knowledge of the field in twenty years; and there are plenty of doctors who feel it is their duty, as trained professionals, to tell their patients not only what their condition is but what they'd better do about it.").

63. Parens & Asch, *supra* note 52, at 20. To similar effect, see Saxton, *supra* note 59, at 154.

64. *See* Larson, *supra* note 53, at 933–34; *see also* Bérubé, *supra* note 53, at 47 ("If we had no way of knowing how loving, clever, and 'normal' a child like Jamie can be, we would simply have to rely on the advice of 'experts.' And if those experts told us there was no way to raise such a child, we would probably believe them."); Bruce Jennings, *Technology and the Genetic Imaginary: Prenatal Testing and the Construction of Disability, in* Prenatal Testing and Disability Rights, *supra* note 48, at 124, 135–36 (arguing that "genetic counseling cannot be completely neutral or nondirective," and that it "create[s] a new social and discursive reality, which then becomes the touchstone and the reference point for all the information the parents receive and all the decisions they make from that point forward").

65. Mary B. Mahowald, *Aren't We All Eugenicists? Commentary on Paul Lombardo's "Taking Eugenics Seriously,"* 30 Fla. St. U. L. Rev. 219, 233 (2003).

66. *See* Bérubé, *supra* note 53, at 46 (describing himself as "strongly pro-choice"); Parens & Asch, *supra* note 52, at 12 ("Virtually all the major work in the disability critique of prenatal testing emerges from those who are also committed to a pro-choice, feminist agenda"); Steinbock, *supra* note 48, at 109 ("Some of the most passionate advocates of the disability perspective on abortion are generally pro-choice.").

67. *See* Asch, *supra* note 61, at 334–35; Bérubé, *supra* note 53, at 80–81; Janet Dolgin, *The Ideological Context of the Disability Rights Critique: Where Modernity and Tradition Meet,* 30 Fla. St. U. L. Rev. 343, 358–59 (2003); Field, *supra* note 16, at 119; Parens & Asch, *supra* note 52, at 29.

68. Asch, *supra* note 61, at 317.

69. *Id.* at 341; *see also id.* at 333–34 ("[T]he critique of testing and selective abortion is intended to change professional practice and rhetoric and to give more comprehensive information about disability to prospective parents. Critics have never intended to curtail women's decision-making about their reproductive lives.").

70. Planned Parenthood v. Casey, 505 U.S. 833, 848–53 (1992).

71. I do not mean to deny that there are social forces that pressure women to become mothers, and that those pressures are in many if not in most cases more powerful than the pressures that lead women to have abortions. A quick glance at the literature on "repronormativity," Katherine Franke, *Theorizing Yes: An Article on Feminism, Law, and Desire,* 101 Colum. L. Rev. 181, 183–97 (2001), or "pronatalism," Jean E. Veevers, Childless by Choice 110–16 (1980), should demonstrate that the social pressures to have children are great indeed. Any prescriptive analysis of what constitutes "free choice" in the abortion context would have to take account of the pressures militating against, as well as those militating toward, abortion—not to mention all of the other ways in which women's choices are limited. But my goal here is different. My goal is to show how the disability rights critique lends itself to being used by abortion opponents more generally, and thus to highlight some of the tensions in the thinking of disability rights critics.

72. *See Casey,* 505 U.S. at 846–53.

73. *Id.* at 851; *see also* Pamela S. Karlan & Daniel R. Ortiz, *In a Diffident Voice: Relational Feminism, Abortion Rights, and the Feminist Legal Agenda,* 87 Nw. U. L. Rev. 858, 878 (1993) (stating that *Casey* "illustrates the centrality of autonomy-talk to the standard legal defense of abortion rights").

74. Lawrence v. Texas, 539 U.S. 558, 588 (2003) (Scalia, J., dissenting).

75. *Casey,* 505 U.S. at 851.

76. *Lawrence,* 539 U.S. at 574.

77. For discussions of the Legal Realist attack on freedom of contract, see Morton J. Horwitz, The Transformation of American Law, 1870–1960: The Crisis of Legal Orthodoxy 33–39, 194–98 (1992); Joseph William Singer, *Legal Realism Now,* 76 Cal. L. Rev. 465, 482–95 (1988). Jack Balkin and Frances Olsen have drawn a similar connection between the Legal Realist attack on freedom of contract and recent efforts to justify prohibitions of pornography or hate speech in the name of promoting free speech. *See* J. M. Balkin, *Some Realism about Pluralism: Legal Realist Approaches to the First Amendment,* 1990 Duke L.J. 375, 379–82 (1990); Frances Olsen, *Feminist Theory in Grand Style,* 89 Colum. L. Rev. 1147, 1162 (1989). And of course, feminists have applied the Legal Realist critique of choice more generally. *See, e.g.,* Catharine A. Mackinnon, Toward a Feminist Theory of the State 171–214 (1989); Tracy E. Higgins, *Democracy and Feminism,* 110 Harv. L. Rev. 1657 (1997).

78. *See* Harris v. McRae, 448 U.S. 297 (1980); Maher v. Roe, 432 U.S. 464 (1977).

79. *See, e.g., Maher,* 432 U.S. at 483 (Brennan, J., dissenting) ("Th[e] disparity in funding by the State [i.e., funding childbirth but not abortion] clearly operates to coerce indigent pregnant women to bear children they would not otherwise choose to have, and just as clearly, this coercion can only operate upon the poor, who are uniquely the victims of this form of financial pressure.").

80. *Maher,* 432 U.S. at 473 (quoting Whalen v. Roe, 429 U.S. 589, 599–600 (1977)).

81. *See Harris,* 448 U.S. at 316 ("[A]lthough government may not place obstacles in the path of a woman's exercise of her freedom of choice, it need not remove those not of its own creation. Indigency falls in the latter category."); *Maher,* 432 U.S. at 474 ("The indigency that may make it difficult—and in some cases, perhaps, impossible—for some women to have abortions is neither created nor in any way affected by the Connecticut regulation.").

82. *Harris,* 448 U.S. at 317–18.

83. *Casey,* 505 U.S. at 877.

84. *Id.* at 872–73.

85. *Cf.* Chris Whitman, *Looking Back on Planned Parenthood v. Casey,* 100 Mich. L. Rev. 1980, 1988 (2002) (arguing that *Casey* "turns the 'pro-choice' rhetoric of *Roe* supporters against a sympathetic interpretation of the right recognized in that opinion").

86. *Casey,* 505 U.S. at 881 (opinion of O'Connor, Kennedy, & Souter, JJ.).

87. *Id.* at 917 (Stevens, J., concurring in part and dissenting in part); *see* Karlan & Ortiz, *supra* note 73, at 885 (noting that states that enact notice and informed consent laws in the abortion context "normally implant them within regulatory schemes that are clearly intended to dissuade women from choosing abortion").

88. *See Casey,* 505 U.S. at 885–86.

89. *Id.* at 887 (opinion of O'Connor, Kennedy, & Souter, JJ.).
90. *Id.* at 882.
91. *Id.* at 885.
92. Justices Stevens and Blackmun made this argument in separate opinions dissenting from Casey's judgment upholding the informed consent provisions. *See Casey*, 505 U.S. at 918–19 (Stevens, J., concurring in part and dissenting in part); *id.* at 934–38 (Blackmun, J., concurring in part, concurring in the judgment in part, and dissenting in part).
93. *See, e.g.*, A Woman's Choice—East Side Women's Clinic v. Newman, 305 F.3d 684, 685 (7th Cir. 2002) (upholding Indiana "informed consent" requirements that paralleled those upheld in Casey, notwithstanding the district court's undisturbed finding that the requirements would raise the effective cost of abortion, and that "the higher cost will reduce by 10% to 13% the number of abortions performed in Indiana"), *cert. denied*, 537 U.S. 1192 (2003); Gillian E. Metzger, Note, *Unburdening the Undue Burden Standard: Orienting Casey in Constitutional Jurisprudence*, 94 Colum. L. Rev. 2025, 2082–84 (1994) (detailing burdens imposed by the restrictions upheld in *Casey*); Katherine C. Sheehan, *Toward a Jurisprudence of Doubt*, 7 UCLA Women's L.J. 201, 236–37 (1998) (similar); *see also* Sylvia A. Law, *Abortion Compromise—Inevitable and Impossible*, 1992 U. Ill. L. Rev. 921, 931 (arguing that *Casey's* broadening of permissible regulation of abortion "hits hardest those women who are most vulnerable, *i.e.* the poor, the unsophisticated, the young, and women who live in rural areas").
94. Hill v. Colorado, 530 U.S. 703, 765–92 (2000).
95. 127 S. Ct. 1610 (2007).
96. *Hill*, 530 U.S. at 765 (Kennedy, J., dissenting).
97. *Id.* at 789.
98. *Id.*
99. *Id.* at 790.
100. *Id.*
101. *Id.*
102. *Id.* Writing from an avowedly feminist perspective, Ruth Colker argues that women's abortion decisions are often driven by "what their parents, boyfriend, or social workers told them to do" rather than any meaningful reflection, and that those decisions are therefore "often made under conditions of coercion." Ruth Colker, *Feminism, Theology, and Abortion: Toward Love, Compassion, and Wisdom*, 77 Cal. L. Rev. 1011, 1064, 1066 (1989); *see also* Garance Franke-Ruta, *Multiple Choice*, New Republic, Nov. 28, 2005, at 14 ("[A] lot of women getting abortions are doing so precisely because they don't have control over their destinies, and perhaps never did.").
103. *Carhart*, 127 S. Ct. at 1634.
104. *Id.*
105. *Id.*
106. Again, Ruth Colker makes a similar point from a feminist perspective. She contends that "[s]ince the feminist position is 'pro-choice' rather than 'pro-abortion,' feminists do not purport to know the correct decision for each individual woman facing an

abortion decision," that women making abortion decisions often "face a problem of consciousness" that may limit their insight into what they truly want, and therefore that "[r]ather than simply acquiescing to any abortion decision made by a woman, we might want to consider how to improve her qualitative judgment." Colker, *supra* note 102, at 1063; *cf.* Susan Frelich Appleton, *When Welfare Reforms Promote Abortion: "Personal Responsibility," "Family Values," and the Right to Choose*, 85 Geo. L.J. 155, 186–87 (1996) ("Although the term 'prochoice' has acquired scars from its service as a politically charged slogan, its core meaning continues to express support for reproductive self-determination, according equal respect to whatever option an individual freely selects.") (footnotes omitted).

107. *See* Louis Michael Seidman, *Brown and Miranda*, 80 Cal. L. Rev. 673, 724–27 (1992).

108. See Reva B. Siegel, *The New Politics of Abortion: An Equality Analysis of Woman-Protective Abortion Restrictions*, 2007 U. Ill. L. Rev. 991.

109. Indeed, an early version of the recently enacted South Dakota ban on virtually all abortions relied on "evidence" that "abortions are performed without a truly informed or voluntary consent or knowing waiver of the woman's rights and interests." H.B. 1191, 2004 Leg. Assem., 79th Sess. § 3 (S.D. 2004).

110. *See Casey*, 505 U.S. at 871–78 (opinion of O'Connor, Kennedy, & Souter, JJ.).

111. *See* Roger Rosenblatt, Life Itself: Abortion in the American Mind 138 (1992) ("What most Americans want to do with abortion is to permit it but discourage it also."); *see* Kathleen M. Sullivan, *The Supreme Court, 1991 Term — Foreword: The Justices of Rules and Standards*, 106 Harv. L. Rev. 22, 100 (1992) ("Commentators noted the 'coincidence' that the [*Casey*] joint opinion tracked the public ambivalence about abortion: 'permit but discourage.'").

112. *See supra* text accompanying notes 60–61. For academic statements of that position, see Cass R. Sunstein, One Case at a Time: Judicial Minimalism on the Supreme Court 116 (1999) (arguing that a "state could decide, with sufficient reason, that a ban on physician-assisted suicide actually promotes the autonomy of many or most people" and drawing the "general lesson" that "[i]n some circumstances, a decision to override choice can actually enhance freedom"); Kreimer, *supra* note 30, at 820 ("If the prohibitions are necessary to avoid the death of those who actually have not chosen to die, there is no conflict of principle between the State's justification for the prohibitions and its obligation to respect its citizens' choices.").

113. Washington v. Glucksberg, 521 U.S. 702, 752 (1997) (Souter, J., concurring in the judgment).

114. *Id.* at 782.

115. *Id.*

116. *Id.*

117. *See id.* at 782–87.

118. Brief for Amici Curiae Gay Men's Health Crisis et al., *Glucksberg* (hereinafter Autonomy Br.).

119. Autonomy Br. 6.

120. Andrew I. Batavia, *The Relevance of Data on Physicians and Disability on the Right*

to Assisted Suicide: Can Empirical Studies Resolve the Issue?, 6 Psychol. Pub. Pol'y & L. 546, 546 (2000).

121. *Id.* at 550.

122. *See, e.g.*, Emily Bazelon, *Is There a Post-Abortion Syndrome?*, N.Y. Times Mag., Jan. 21, 2007.

123. Note, for example, the position of Senator Edward Kennedy, a strong supporter of abortion rights, who cosponsored a bill (with Senator Sam Brownback, a strong abortion opponent) that would require health care providers to give patients with positive prenatal tests "[u]p-to-date, scientific, written information concerning the life expectancy, clinical course, and intellectual and functional development and treatment options for a fetus diagnosed with or child born with Down syndrome." S. 609, 109th Cong., 1st Sess. § 3 (2005).

124. Some, most notably Peter Singer, disagree; *see* Helga Kuhse & Peter Singer, Should the Baby Live? The Problem of Handicapped Infants 129–39 (1985); Peter Singer, Practical Ethics 169–74 (2d ed. 1993), but theirs is at best a fringe view in our legal and political culture. For a great account by a lawyer with a disability of her debate with Singer regarding his views on infanticide for disabled newborns, see Harriet Mcbryde Johnson, Too Late to Die Young: Nearly True Tales from a Life 201–28 (2005).

125. Martha Field made this point more than a decade ago, but it bears repeating: "True, the spokespersons for the 'handicap rights position' are often the same right-to-life groups that oppose abortion. Nonetheless, support of a 'right to life' for newborns with handicaps is consistent with belief in a broad right to choose abortion." Field, *supra* note 16, at 79.

126. *Cf.* Schneider, *supra* note 21, at 168.

CHAPTER 7. THE LIMITS OF THE ANTIDISCRIMINATION MODEL

1. Statistics in this and the next paragraph come from the 2004 NOD/Harris Survey of Americans with Disabilities.

2. For a general summary, see Samuel R. Bagenstos, *Has the Americans with Disabilities Act Reduced Employment for People with Disabilities?*, 25 Berkeley J. Emp. & Lab. L. 527, 533–34 (2004).

3. Samuel R. Bagenstos, *The Future of Disability Law*, 114 Yale L.J. 1, 19–20 (2004).

4. *See id.* at 534.

5. *See* Daron Acemoglu & Joshua Angrist, *Consequences of Employment Protection? The Case of the Americans with Disabilities Act*, 109 J. Pol. Econ. 915 (2001); Thomas DeLeire, *The Wage and Employment Effects of the Americans with Disabilities Act*, 35 J. Hum. Res. 693 (2000); Christine M. Jolls & J. J. Prescott, *Disaggregating Employment Protection: The Case of Disability Discrimination* (2004) (unpublished manuscript).

6. *See* Christine M. Jolls, *Accommodation Mandates*, 53 Stan. L. Rev. 223, 273–76 (2000); Bagenstos, *supra* note 2, at 537–38.

7. *See* Douglas Kruse & Lisa Schur, *Employment of People with Disabilities Following the ADA*, 42 Indus. Rel. 31, 50–54 (2003).

8. *See, e.g.*, Peter David Blanck et al., *Calibrating the Impact of the ADA's Employment Provisions*, 14 Stan. L. & Pol'y Rev. 267, 278–279 (2003).

9. *See, e.g.*, David H. Autor & Mark G. Duggan, *The Rise in the Disability Rolls and the Decline in Unemployment*, 118 Q. J. Econ. 157 (2003); John Bound & Timothy Waidmann, *Accounting for Recent Declines in Employment Rates among the Working-Aged Disabled*, 37 J. Hum. Res. 231 (2002).

10. *See* Bagenstos, *supra* note 2, at 545–46.

11. *See id.* at 549–50.

12. *See id.* at 553–55.

13. *See, e.g.*, Bagenstos, *supra* note 3, at 10–18.

14. Ruth Colker, The Disability Pendulum: The First Decade of the Americans with Disabilities Act 69 (2005).

15. *See id.*at 70.

16. Sutton v. United Air Lines, Inc., 527 U.S. 471, 491–92 (1999).

17. *See* Samuel R. Bagenstos, *The Americans with Disabilities Act as Welfare Reform*, 44 Wm. & Mary L. Rev. 921, 1019–20 (2003) (making this argument).

18. *See* Richard A. Epstein, Forbidden Grounds: The Case against Employment Discrimination Laws 493–94 (1992).

19. Jerry L. Mashaw, *Against First Principles*, 31 San Diego L. Rev. 211, 231 (1994). Professor Mashaw argued against "repeal," *id.*, but he argued that the ADA's mandates should be replaced with a system of tradable employment quotas, *see id.* at 232–37.

20. *See* Thomas DeLeire, *The Unintended Consequences of the Americans with Disabilities Act*, Regulation, Vol. 23, No. 1, at 21, 24 (2000).

21. *See* Bagenstos, *supra* note 2, at 555; *see also* Richard V. Burkhauser et al., *Accounting for the Declining Fortunes of Working-Age People with Disabilities* (paper presented at NYU Conference on Empirical Study of the ADA, spring 2006).

22. *See* Jolls & Prescott, *supra* note 5, at 17–18.

23. Acemoglu & Angrist, *supra* note 5, at 940.

24. NOD/Harris survey, *supra* note 1.

25. *See* Bagenstos, *supra* note 2, at 556.

26. *See id.*

27. *See* 2004 NOD/Harris Survey, *supra* note 1 (29 percent of respondents with disabilities reported discriminatory denial of promotion in 1998, compared to 17 percent in 2004; 43 percent reported discriminatorily being given less responsibility in 1998, compared to 14 percent in 2004; 34 percent reported pay discrimination in 1998, compared to 12 percent in 2004).

28. 42 U.S.C. § 12188(a)(1); *see* Colker, *supra* note 14, at 172–74.

29. *See, e.g.*, Colker, *supra* note 14, at 184 ("A restaurant that can serve customers who use wheelchairs will also add to its patronage not only from individuals with disabilities but also from the friends and families of those individuals.").

30. *See* 42 U.S.C. §§ 12181(9), 12182(b)(2)(A)(iv), 12183(a).

31. For a discussion of the lack of information about the costs and benefits of accommodation, see Michael Ashley Stein, *The Law and Economics of Disability Accommodations*, 53 Duke L.J. 79, 124–27 (2003).

32. *See* Samuel R. Bagenstos, *Subordination, Stigma, and "Disability,"* 86 Va. L. Rev. 397, 423–24, 438–42 (2000). On unconscious stereotyping generally, see Samuel R. Bagenstos, *The Structural Turn and the Limits of Antidiscrimination Law*, 94 Cal. L. Rev. 1, 5–8 (2006).

33. As I discuss later, the problem may be one that cannot be solved even by making the premises of every store accessible; without accessible transportation, individuals with disabilities may simply be unable to get to those stores.

34. Adam A. Milani, *Wheelchair Users Who Lack "Standing": Another Procedural Threshold Blocking Enforcement of Titles II and III of the ADA*, 39 Wake Forest L. Rev. 69, 112 (2004).

35. Nat'l Council on Disability, Promises to Keep: A Decade of Federal Enforcement of the Americans with Disabilities Act 38 (2000). If anything, the problem only became worse during the second George W. Bush administration. *See, e.g.*, William R. Yeomans, An Uncivil Division, Legal Aff., Sept./Oct. 2005, available at http://www .legalaffairs.org/issues/September-October-2005/argument_yeomans_ sepocto5.msp.

36. *See* Colker, *supra* note 14, at 192 (finding that the Department of Justice reached 107 public accommodations settlements in ten years — "less than one settlement a month by an agency charged with national enforcement").

37. Stewart J. Schwab & Theodore Eisenberg, *Explaining Constitutional Tort Litigation: The Influence of the Attorney Fees Statute and the Government as Defendant*, 73 Cornell L. Rev. 719, 768 (1988).

38. *See* Herbert M. Kritzer, *Seven Dogged Myths Concerning Contingency Fees*, 80 Wash. U. L.Q. 739, 772 (2002); Herbert M. Kritzer, *The Wages of Risk: The Returns of Contingency Fee Legal Practice*, 47 DePaul L. Rev. 267, 302 (1998).

39. Hensley v. Eckerhart, 461 U.S. 424, 433 (1983).

40. City of Burlington v. Dague, 505 U.S. 557, 562 (1992).

41. Blum v. Stenson, 465 U.S. 886, 894 (1984); *see also* Blanchard v. Bergeron, 489 U.S. 87, 94 (1989) (explaining that lodestar is determined by "prevailing billing rates").

42. *Dague*, 505 U.S. at 562.

43. See Peter H. Huang, *A New Options Theory for Risk Multipliers of Attorney's Fees in Federal Civil Rights Litigation*, 73 N.Y.U. L. Rev. 1943, 1967–71 (1998); Thomas D. Rowe Jr., *The Legal Theory of Attorney Fee Shifting: A Critical Overview*, 1982 Duke L.J. 651, 676; Charles Silver, *Incoherence and Irrationality in the Law of Attorneys' Fees*, 12 Rev. Litig. 301, 332 (1993); *cf.* Scott L. Cummings, *The Politics of Pro Bono*, 52 UCLA L. Rev. 1, 133 (2004) (describing cases that "promis[e] both high damages and the potential for attorney's fees" as "the bread-and-butter of public interest firm practice"); Minna J. Kotkin, *Invisible Settlements, Invisible Discrimination*, 84 N.C. L. Rev. 927, 933 (2006) (discussing incentives for civil rights plaintiffs' lawyers to take contingent-fee damages cases); Michael Selmi, *Public vs. Private Enforcement of Civil Rights: The Case of Housing and Employment*, 45 UCLA L. Rev. 1401, 1452–54

(1998) (discussing the importance of the prospect of a damages recovery in encouraging plaintiffs' lawyers to take civil rights cases because statutory fee shifting provides an "insufficient" incentive).

44. Buckhannon Bd. & Care Home, Inc. v. W. Va. Dep't of Health & Human Res., 532 U.S. 598, 605 (2001).

45. *Buckhannon*, 532 U.S. at 609 (quoting Friends of the Earth, Inc. v. Laidlaw Envtl. Servs. (TOC), Inc., 528 U.S. 167, 189 (2000)).

46. See Doran v. N. State Grocery, Inc., 39 Cal. Rptr. 3d 922, 923 (Cal. Ct. App. 2006) ("During the course of the federal litigation, North State removed the architectural barriers to accessibility that Doran claimed were illegal. Therefore, the federal cause of action became moot, as the only remedy under Title III of the ADA—an injunction—was no longer necessary."); Iverson v. Sports Depot, Inc., No. Civ. A. 00-10794-RWZ, 2002 WL 745824 (D. Mass. Feb. 20, 2002); Disability Law, More Molski, http://disabilitylaw.blogspot.com/2005/01/more-molski.html (Jan. 5, 2005, 09:14 EST) (discussing Molski v. Peach Canyon Cellars, No. 2:03-CV-06266-TJH-PLA (C.D. Cal. Dec. 22, 2004)).

47. *See Buckhannon*, 532 U.S. at 600.

48. *Id.* at 608.

49. *See* Samuel R. Bagenstos, *The Perversity of Limited Civil Rights Remedies: The Case of "Abusive" ADA Litigation*, 54 UCLA L. Rev. 1 (2006).

50. Steven L. Willborn, *The Nonevolution of Enforcement under the ADA: Discharge Cases and the Hiring Problem, in* Employment, Disability, and the Americans with Disabilities Act: Issues in Law, Public Policy, and Research 103, 103 (Peter David Blanck ed., 2000). That ratio is consistent with, though perhaps more pronounced than, the skew of employment discrimination cases more generally in recent years. As Professors Donohue and Siegelman (and then Professors Ayres and Siegelman) have shown, the overwhelming majority of employment discrimination cases now seek to protect incumbent workers from job loss rather than to help workers obtain new jobs. *See* John J. Donohue III & Peter Siegelman, *The Changing Nature of Employment Discrimination Litigation*, 43 Stan. L. Rev. 983, 1015 (1991); Ian Ayres & Peter Siegelman, *The Q-Word as Red Herring: Why Disparate Impact Liability Does Not Induce Hiring Quotas*, 74 Tex. L. Rev. 1487, 1504–7 (1996).

51. *See generally* Samuel R. Bagenstos, *Trapped in the Feedback Loop: A Response to Professor Days*, 49 St. Louis U. L.J. 1007, 1010–11 (2005).

52. *See* Bagenstos, *supra* note 2, at 538; Jolls, *supra* note 6, at 275; Willborn, *supra* note 50, at 108.

53. *See* Willborn, *supra* note 50, at 109.

54. *See* Bagenstos, *Structural Turn, supra* note 32, at 12–15.

55. One should not underestimate the extent to which discrimination itself also operates as a barrier well before an individual with a disability ever puts himself or herself in a position to be discriminated against. A person with a disability, knowing that he or she is likely to experience discrimination in the workplace, may be discouraged from investing in education, training, or other forms of human capital—and may indeed be discouraged from attempting to enter the workforce at all. *See, e.g.,* Bagenstos, *Sub-*

ordination, Stigma, supra note 32, at 464. But even if enforcement of the ADA can eliminate that structural barrier to employment, it leaves many significant structural barriers untouched, as I explain in the text.

56. Stephen Kaye observes that 32 percent of people with disabilities who report that they are unable to work also report that they need personal-assistance services. *See* H. Stephen Kaye, Improved Employment Opportunities for People with Disabilities 32–33 (Disability Statistics Ctr., Disability Statistics Rpt. 17, 2003). Although Kaye's study does not identify how many of these respondents cannot work without personal-assistance services, there is good reason to believe that it is a very large fraction. The services provided by personal assistants are so basic to any participation in society that an individual who needs those services for any purpose very likely needs them to work. For discussions of the importance of personal-assistance services to people with disabilities, see Simi Litvak et al., Attending to America: Personal Assistance for Independent Living: A Report of the National Survey of Attendant Services Programs in the United States 1–17 (1987); Andrew I. Batavia et al., *Toward a National Personal Assistance Program: The Independent Living Model of Long-Term Care for Persons with Disabilities,* 16 J. Health Pol. Pol'y & L. 523 (1991); Gerben DeJong & Teg Wenker, *Attendant Care, in* Independent Living for Physically Disabled People, 157, 157–62 (Nancy M. Crewe & Irving Kenneth Zola eds., 1983); and Margaret A. Nosek & Carol A. Howland, *Personal Assistance Services: The Hub of the Policy Wheel for Community Integration of People with Severe Physical Disabilities,* 21 Pol'y Stud. J. 789, 789–90 (1993).

57. On the importance of assistive technology to the employment prospects of people with disabilities, see Andrew I. Batavia, *Health Care, Personal Assistance and Assistive Technology: Are In-Kind Benefits Key to Independence or Dependence for People with Disabilities?, in* Disability, Work and Cash Benefits 389, 402–5 (Jerry L. Mashaw et al. eds., 1996); John C. DeWitt, *The Role of Technology in Removing Barriers, in* The Americans with Disabilities Act: From Policy to Practice 313 (Jane West ed., 1991); and Katherine D. Seelman, *Assistive Technology Policy: A Road to Independence for Individuals with Disabilities,* 49 J. Soc. Issues 115 (1993).

58. On the lack of accessible transportation as a barrier to employment, see Robert A. Katzmann, *Transportation Policy, in* From Policy to Practice, *supra* note 57, at 214, 216.

59. *See* Nat'l Council on Disability, Removing Barriers to Work: Action Proposals for the 105th Congress and Beyond, at Barrier: Many People Would Be Worse Off Financially if They Worked and Earned to Their Potential Than if They Did Not Work (1997), available at http://www.ncd.gov/newsroom/publications/1997/barriers.htm (stating, as the first barrier to work for people with disabilities, that "[p]eople fear, most of all, losing the medical benefits that can literally spell the difference between life and death"); Nat'l Council on Disability, Sharing the Risk and Ensuring Independence: A Disability Perspective on Access to Health Insurance and Health-Related Services, at Findings on Barriers to Health Insurance and Health-Related Services No. 3 (1993) [hereinafter Nat'l Council on Disability, Sharing the Risk], available at http://www .ncd.gov/newsroom/publications/1993/sharing.htm ("Without adequate insurance

coverage, persons with disabilities are likely to forego [*sic*] employment."); *see also* Jerry L. Mashaw & Virginia P. Reno, *Overview, in* Disability, Work and Cash Benefits, *supra* note 57, at 18.

60. *See* Gerben DeJong & Ian Basnett, *Disability and Health Policy: The Role of Markets in the Delivery of Health Services, in* Handbook of Disability Studies 610, 612–13 (Gary L. Albrecht et al. eds., 2001); Gerben DeJong et al., *America's Neglected Health Minority: Working-Age Persons with Disabilities,* 67 Milbank Q. 311, 320–22 (1989); Robert B. Friedland & Alison Evans, *People with Disabilities: Access to Health Care and Related Benefits, in* Disability, Work and Cash Benefits, *supra* note 57, at 357, 358; Kristina W. Hanson et al., *Uncovering the Health Challenges Facing People with Disabilities: The Role of Health Insurance,* Health Aff., Nov. 19, 2003, at W3-552, W3-555, available at http://content.healthaffairs.org/cgi/reprint/hlthaff.w3.552v1.pdf.

61. A GAO report based on government data from 1997 and 1998 found that only 9 percent of individuals with disabilities reported being uninsured, compared with 15 percent of individuals in the rest of the working-age population. *See* GAO, Medicaid and Ticket to Work: States' Early Efforts to Cover Working Individuals with Disabilities 14–15 (2003); *see also* Inst. of Med., Disability in America: Toward a National Agenda for Prevention 253 (Andrew M. Pope & Alvin R. Tarlov eds., 1991) (reporting 1984 statistics that showed that 10.8 percent of individuals with a major activity limitation were uninsured, compared with 13.4 percent of individuals without such a limitation). A nationwide Harris survey conducted for the National Organization on Disability (NOD) in 2000 reported that 90 percent of respondents with disabilities had health insurance, a number essentially identical to the 89 percent of respondents without disabilities who had health insurance. *See* Nat'l Org. on Disability, 2000 N.O.D./Harris Survey of Americans with Disabilities 54 (2000).

62. *See* Inst. of Med., *supra* note 61, at 252; Nat'l Council on Disability, Sharing the Risk, *supra* note 59, at Findings on Barriers to Health Insurance and Health-Related Services No. 1; Andrew I. Batavia, *Health Care Reform and People with Disabilities,* Health Aff., Spring 1993, at 40, 43.

63. *See* Bagenstos, *supra* note 3, at 32–34.

64. *See* Bagenstos, *Structural Turn, supra* note 32.

CHAPTER 8. FUTURE DIRECTIONS IN DISABILITY LAW

1. I discuss the points in this paragraph in some detail in Samuel R. Bagenstos, *The Perversity of Limited Civil Rights Remedies: The Case of "Abusive" ADA Litigation,* 54 UCLA L. Rev. 1 (2006).

2. *See* Christine M. Jolls, *Accommodation Mandates,* 53 Stan. L. Rev. 223, 281 (2000) (suggesting "preserv[ing] the ADA's accommodation mandate while significantly increasing the damages available for violations of its restrictions on hiring differentials"). Along similar lines, Professors Ayres and Siegelman have suggested "adjusting the lodestar used to calculate attorneys' fees in hiring (but not firing) cases." Ian Ayres

& Peter Siegelman, *The Q-Word as Red Herring: Why Disparate Impact Liability Does Not Induce Hiring Quotas*, 74 Tex. L. Rev. 1487, 1519–20 (1996).

3. *See* 42 U.S.C. § 1981a.

4. 42 U.S.C. § 1981a(a)(3).

5. *Cf.* Michael Selmi, *The Value of the EEOC: Reexamining the Agency's Role in Employment Discrimination Law*, 57 Ohio St. L.J. 1, 4 (1996) (arguing that the EEOC "should either be eliminated or substantially reformed so that it concentrates on cases that private attorneys are unlikely to pursue").

6. *See* Steven L. Willborn, *The Nonevolution of Enforcement Under the ADA: Discharge Cases and the Hiring Problem, in* Employment, Disability, and the Americans with Disabilities Act: Issues in Law, Public Policy, and Research 103, 114 (Peter David Blanck ed., 2000) (making this suggestion); Nat'l Council on Disability, Promises to Keep: A Decade of Federal Enforcement of the Americans with Disabilities Act 241 (2000) (same).

7. *See, e.g.*, U.S. Equal Emp. Opportunity Comm'n, FY2005 Performance and Accountability Report, App. B (2005) (listing two ADA hiring cases: EEOC v. Northwest Airlines, Inc., No. 01-705 MJD/JGL (D. Minn. Jan. 12, 2005) (a "nationwide ADA action alleging that Northwest Airlines excluded applicants with insulin dependent diabetes and with seizure disorders requiring antiseizure medication from equipment service employee (ESE) and aircraft cleaner positions because of their disabilities"); and EEOC v. EchoStar Communications Corp., No. 02-CV-00581 (D. Colo. May 6, 2005) (case alleging that the defendant discriminated against a blind applicant)).

8. *See, e.g.*, U.S. Equal Emp. Opportunity Comm'n, Office of General Counsel FY2004 Annual Report—Summary of Accomplishments (2005) (discussing five individual ADA cases brought on behalf of incumbent employees: EEOC v. Heartway Corp., Inc., d/b/a/ York Manor Nursing Center (E.D. Okla. Aug. 17, 2004); EEOC v. Service Management Systems, Inc. (W.D. Ark. May 13, 2004); EEOC v. Spylen of Denville, Inc., d/b/a/ Wendy's (D. N.J. March 16, 2004); EEOC v. SCI Funeral Services of Florida, Inc. (M.D. Fla. Sept. 30, 2004); EEOC v. Daimler Chrysler Corp. (E.D. Mich. Jan. 12, 2004)); *see generally* Nat'l Council on Disability, *supra* note 6, at 196 (2000) (stating that of the 611 ADA cases in which the EEOC participated, only 127 were hiring cases).

9. Willborn, *supra* note 6, at 108.

10. Samuel R. Bagenstos, *Has the ADA Reduced Employment for People with Disabilities?*, 25 Berkeley J. Emp. & Lab. L. 527, 538 (2004).

11. The kind of outcome test advocated by Ian Ayres—in which we would compare the productivity of the employer's disabled and nondisabled workers, and infer discrimination where the workers with disabilities are more productive, see Ian Ayres, Pervasive Prejudice? Unconventional Evidence of Race and Gender Discrimination 404–14 (2001)—would be difficult to conduct in the disability context for the same reason. If an employer has at most a handful of employees with a given disability, the fact that they are more productive than other employees may be a reflection of the small sample size rather than discrimination.

12. *See* U.S. Equal Emp. Opportunity Comm'n, *supra* note 7.

13. For good overviews of testing as a strategy for research and enforcement of civil rights laws, see Ayres, *supra* note 11, at 397–402; Clear and Convincing Evidence: Measurement of Discrimination in America (Michael Fix & Raymond J. Struyk eds., 1993); Julie Lee & Caitlin Lu, *Measuring Discrimination in the Workplace: Strategies for Lawyers and Policymakers*, 6 U. Chi. L. Sch. Roundtable 195, 212–24 (1999).

14. *See, e.g.,* Michael Selmi, *Public v. Private Enforcement of Civil Rights: The Case of Housing and Employment*, 45 UCLA L. Rev. 1401, 1426 (1998); Leland Ware & Steven W. Pequet, *The Admissibility of Matched-Pair Testing Evidence in Fair Housing Cases under Daubert v. Merrell Dow Pharmaceuticals, Inc.*, 14 J. Affordable Housing & Community Dev. L. 23, 25 (2004).

15. *See* Michael J. Yelnosky, *Filling an Enforcement Void: Using Testers to Uncover and Remedy Discrimination in Hiring for Lower-Skilled, Entry-Level Jobs*, 26 U. Mich. J.L. Reform 423 (1993); Anthony F. Spalvieri, Note, *Employment Testers: Obstacles Standing in the Way of Standing under § 1981 and Title VII*, 52 Case W. Res. L. Rev. 753, 757–58 (2002); *Employment Testing Project Shows Bias against Female Mechanics in San Francisco*, Daily Lab. Rep., June 20, 2000, at A-5.

16. *See, e.g.,* Michael Fix et al., *An Overview of Auditing for Discrimination*, *in* Clear and Convincing Evidence, *supra* note 13, at 1, 43 ("[T]esting in employment may have its greatest power in illuminating that phase of the employment transaction—hiring—about which the least is known, in which employers have the greatest incentive to discriminate, and that may hold the most significant policy implications.").

17. In the fair housing context, testing evidence has often been "the sole or predominant basis" for a judicial finding of liability. Ware & Pequet, *supra* note 14, at 25.

18. *Compare* Yelnosky, *supra* note 15, at 459–69 (arguing that the EEOC lacks authorization to engage in testing before a charge is filed), with Leroy D. Clark, *Employment Discrimination Testing: Theories of Standing and a Reply to Professor Yelnosky*, 38 U. Mich. J. L. Reform 1, 40–46 (1994) (disagreeing with Professor Yelnosky on this point).

19. *See* Clark, *supra* note 18, at 37–40.

20. For a good overview of the administrative steps that enforcement testing requires, see Roderic V. O. Boggs et al., *Use of Testing in Civil Rights Enforcement*, *in* Clear and Convincing Evidence, *supra* note 13, at 349–56.

21. *See, e.g.,* Robert G. Schwemm, The Need for Testing Endures after Two Decades: Comments, *in* Clear and Convincing Evidence, *supra* note 13, at 393, 397–98.

22. *See generally Equal Employment Opportunity Commission: Hearings before the Subcomm. on Employer-Employee Relations of the House Comm. on Educ. & the Workforce*, 105th Cong., 2d Sess. (Mar. 3, 1998).

23. *See* Yelnosky, *supra* note 15.

24. *See* Court Gifford, *$18.5 Million Hike in EEOC Budget Approved by House Appropriations Panel*, Daily Lab. Rep., July 16, 1998; Deborah Billings, *Congressional Appropriators Moving to Bar EEOC Pursuit of Employment Tester Program*, Daily Lab. Rep., July 9, 1998.

25. *See, e.g.,* Bill Lann Lee, *An Issue of Public Importance: The Justice Department's En-*

forcement of the Fair Housing Act, Cityscape, Vol. 4, No. 3, at 35, 38–39 (1999); John Relman, *Federal Fair Housing Enforcement at a Crossroads: The Clinton Legacy and the Challenges Ahead, in* Rights at Risk: Equality in an Age of Terrorism 99, 107 (Dianne M. Piché et al. eds., 2002).

26. *See* Havens Realty Corp. v. Coleman, 455 U.S. 363 (1982).

27. *See, e.g.,* Samuel R. Bagenstos, *Comparative Disability Employment Law from an American Perspective,* 24 Comp. Lab. L. & Pol'y J. 649, 653 (2003); Lisa Waddington & Matthew Diller, *Tensions and Coherence in Disability Policy: The Uneasy Relationship between Social Welfare and Civil Rights Models of Disability in American, European, and International Employment Law, in* Disability Rights Law and Policy: International and National Perspectives 241, 256 (Mary Lou Breslin & Sylvia Yee eds., 2002).

28. *See, e.g.,* Lisa Waddington, *Reassessing the Employment of People with Disabilities in Europe: From Quotas to Anti-Discrimination Laws,* 18 Comp. Lab. L.J. 62 (1996).

29. *See, e.g.,* Samuel Issacharoff & Justin Nelson, *Discrimination with a Difference: Can Employment Discrimination Law Accommodate the Americans with Disabilities Act?,* 79 N.C. L. Rev. 307, 344–54 (2001); Jerry L. Mashaw, *Against First Principles,* 31 San Diego L. Rev. 211, 230–31 (1994); Mark C. Weber, *Beyond the Americans with Disabilities Act: A National Employment Policy for People with Disabilities,* 46 Buff. L. Rev. 123, 135–38 (1998).

30. *See* Bagenstos, *supra* note 27, at 654–55; Waddington, *supra* note 28, at 100.

31. *See* Bagenstos, *supra* note 27, at 655–56.

32. *See* Samuel R. Bagenstos, *The Future of Disability Law,* 114 Yale L.J. 1, 72 n.310 (2004).

33. *See* Bagenstos, *supra* note 10, at 561. For the reasons that follow, I am far less convinced now that employment subsidies would be a good idea.

34. *See* Richard V. Burkhauser & Mary C. Daly, *Employment and Economic Well-Being Following the Onset of a Disability, in* Disability, Work and Cash Benefits 59, 87 (Jerry L. Mashaw et al. eds., 1996); Hilary Williamson Hoynes & Robert Moffitt, *The Effectiveness of Financial Work Incentives in Social Security Disability Insurance and Supplemental Security Income, in* Disability, Work and Cash Benefits, *supra,* at 189, 214; Mark C. Weber, *Disability and the Law of Welfare: A Post-Integrationist Examination,* 2000 U. Ill. L. Rev. 889, 947–50. The Work Opportunity Credit, discussed above, currently serves a similar function, but only some individuals with disabilities are eligible. *See* U.S. Gen. Accounting Off., Business Tax Incentives: Incentives to Employ Workers with Disabilities Receive Limited Use and Have an Uncertain Impact 26 (2002) (reporting view among some advocates that the WOC should be expanded to cover all individuals with disabilities).

35. *See* Weber, *supra* note 29.

36. *See* Mashaw, *supra* note 29, at 232; Julie Roin, *Reconceptualizing Unfunded Mandates and Other Regulations,* 93 Nw. U. L. Rev. 351, 364–65 (1999).

37. *See* Ann L. Alstott, *Work vs. Freedom: A Liberal Challenge to Employment Subsidies,* 108 Yale L.J. 967, 1018–47 (1999).

38. *See, e.g.,* Bagenstos, *supra* note 32, at 10–18.

39. *See* Michael Ashley Stein, *The Law and Economics of Disability Accommodations*, 53 Duke L.J. 79, 177 n.540 (2003).

40. *See* Alstott, *supra* note 37, at 1041.

41. The diversity of disabilities embraced by the ADA's protected-class definition, combined with the individualized nature of the "reasonable accommodation" determination, makes it difficult to bring class action suits under the ADA. *See* Ruth Colker, *ADA Title III: A Fragile Compromise*, 21 Berkeley J. Emp. & Lab. L. 377, 379 n.19 (2000) (noting that "it is difficult to file class action remedies" under the ADA's public accommodations title because "the community of individuals with disabilities is quite diverse"); Pamela S. Karlan & George Rutherglen, *Disabilities, Discrimination, and Reasonable Accommodation*, 46 Duke L.J. 1, 19 (1996) (noting that "[f]ew of the cases brought under the ADA are class actions" because "[l]itigation under the ADA . . . responds to the complexities in the inherently unique circumstances of many disabled individuals"). The point holds particularly true for cases under the employment discrimination title of the ADA, which has been the primary engine of litigation under the statute. Of course, the overwhelming preponderance of individual over class action litigation is not unique to the ADA; to the contrary, as Professors John Donohue and Peter Siegelman showed in their influential article, employment discrimination litigation generally follows a similar pattern. *See* John J. Donohue III & Peter Siegelman, *The Changing Nature of Employment Discrimination Litigation*, 43 Stan. L. Rev. 983, 1019–21 (1991).

42. Gary A. Smith, Human Servs. Research Inst., Status Report: Litigation Concerning Home and Community Services for People with Disabilities 5–31 (2004), available at http://www.hsri.org/docs/litigation041804.pdf, lists Medicaid cases brought by disability rights organizations such as People First, various state chapters of the ARC (formerly the Association of Retarded Citizens), and various state protection and advocacy agencies.

43. *See* Jane Perkins & Manju Kulkarni, Addressing Home and Community-Based Waiver Waiting Lists through the Medicaid Program 1 (2000), available at http://www.healthlaw.org/docs/200005FactSheet_hcbw.pdf; Smith, *supra* note 42.

44. *See, e.g.*, Smith, *supra* note 42, at 5 ("As of February 2004, lawsuits seeking community services for people with developmental disabilities had been filed in twenty-five states."). These lawsuits contend that the waiting lists violate such statutory directives as the statute's "reasonable promptness" provision, 42 U.S.C. § 1396a(a)(8) (2000) (requiring that a state's Medicaid plan "provide that all individuals wishing to make application for medical assistance under the plan shall have opportunity to do so, and that such assistance shall be furnished with reasonable promptness to all eligible individuals"); the statute's "comparability" provision, *id.* § 1396a(a)(10)(B) (requiring that medical assistance provided to any eligible individual "shall not be less in amount, duration, or scope than the medical assistance made available to any other such individual"); the statute's "best interests" provision, *id.* § 1396a(a)(19) (requiring that services be provided "in a manner consistent with simplicity of administration and the best interests of the recipients"); and the statute's "free choice" provision, *id.*

§ 1396n(c)(2)(C) (requiring, under the statute's home-based and community-based waiver provision, that beneficiaries be "informed of the feasible alternatives, if available under the waiver, at the choice of such individuals, to the provision of inpatient hospital services, nursing facility services, or services in an intermediate care facility for the mentally retarded").

45. See Bryson v. Shumway, 308 F.3d 79, 88 (1st Cir. 2002) (stating that failure to fill available home-based and community-based waiver slots can violate "reasonable promptness" provision but remanding for a determination whether the defendants had in fact violated that provision); Lewis v. N.M. Dep't of Health, 275 F. Supp. 2d 1319, 1345 (D.N.M. 2003) (stating that failure to provide home-based and community-based services to individuals eligible for open home- and community-based waiver slots violates "reasonable promptness" provision); Boulet v. Cellucci, 107 F. Supp. 2d 61, 76–80 (D. Mass. 2000) (holding that waiting list for residential placements for individuals receiving services under state's home-based and community-based waiver program violates "reasonable promptness" and "freedom of choice" provisions); Benjamin H. v. Ohl, No. 3:99-0338, 1999 U.S. Dist. LEXIS 22469, at *39–43, *44–45 (S.D. W. Va. July 15, 1999) (granting preliminary injunction on basis of claim that waiting lists violate "reasonable promptness" and "freedom of choice" requirements). For examples of settlements, see Rancourt v. Concannon, No. 01-CV-159 (D. Me. July 9, 2003), available at http://www.drcme.org/rancourt.html (agreement settling litigation challenging Maine's denial of timely Medicaid services to adults with mental retardation); Makin v. Hawaii, No. CV 98-00997 DAE, slip op. at 2 (D. Haw. Apr. 25, 2000) (agreement settling litigation challenging waiting list for home-based and community-based services in Hawaii); and Hawaii Disability Rights Center v. Hawaii, No. 03-00524 HG-KSC (D. Haw. filed Oct. 21, 2003), available at http://www.hawaiidisabilityrights.org/Forms/SMComplaint10.01.03(web).doc (complaint alleging lack of compliance with the Makin settlement and renewing challenge to Hawaii waiting list).

46. See, e.g., Sandra L. Yue, A Return to Institutionalization Despite Olmstead v. L.C.? The Inadequacy of Medicaid Provider Reimbursement in Minnesota and the Failure to Deliver Home- and Community-Based Waiver Services, 19 Law & Ineq. 307, 330–37 (2001).

47. 42 U.S.C. § 1396a(a)(30)(A).

48. See Bagenstos, supra note 32, at 58.

49. For durable medical equipment, see 42 U.S.C. § 1396d(a)(7) (authorizing states to cover home health services); and 42 C.F.R. § 440.70(b)(3) (defining home health services to include the provision of medical equipment). For prosthetics, see 42 U.S.C. § 1396d(a)(12) (authorizing states to cover "prosthetic devices"). See, e.g., Jane Perkins, Medicaid: Past Successes and Future Challenges, 12 Health Matrix 7, 24 (2002) ("Medicaid has provided essential services for people with disabilities that are not generally available through private health insurance coverage. . . . [T]he benefits package offered by Medicaid includes coverage of long-term care services and services which help maximize functioning, such as home health services, durable medi-

cal equipment, prosthetic devices, and personal care attendant services."); Sandra Tanenbaum, *Medicaid and Disability: The Unlikely Entitlement*, 67 Milbank Q. 288, 295–96 (1989).

50. See Letter from Timothy Westmoreland, Dir., Ctr. for Medicaid & State Operations, Health Care Fin. Admin., to State Medicaid Directors attachment 3-g (July 25, 2000), available at http:// www.cms.hhs.gov/states/letters/smd725a0.asp.

51. *See* Bagenstos, *supra* note 32, at 59–60.

52. *See id.* at 61–62.

53. This may be an area where the ADA's accommodation approach can do a great deal of good. The statute's integration mandate, as interpreted in *Olmstead*, might well prevent a state from cutting back on integration-enhancing services that are optional under the Medicaid law. As I noted in chapter 4, however, the access/content distinction significantly limits the usefulness of the ADA in this respect.

54. Pub. L. No. 106-170, 113 Stat. 1860 (codified in scattered sections of 26 and 42 U.S.C.). For discussion of the role of disability rights advocates in drafting and lobbying for TWWIIA, see 145 Cong. Rec. S14,981 (daily ed. Nov. 19, 1999) (statement of Sen. Jeffords) ("In addition to staff, we received countless hours of assistance and advice from the Work Incentives Task Force of the Consortium for Citizens with Disabilities. These individuals worked tirelessly to educate Members of Congress about the need for and the effects of this legislation."); 145 Cong. Rec. S7060-61 (daily ed. June 16, 1999) (statement of Sen. Dodd) ("In support of this important legislation are the Consortium for Citizens with Disabilities, the ARC, Easter Seals, the National Alliance for the Mentally Ill, the Paralyzed Veterans of America, the United Cerebral Palsy Association, and the National Education Association."); Susan Page, *Clinton Aims to Help Disabled Workers*, USA Today, Jan. 13, 1999, at 12A (noting Justin Dart's support of the statute that became TWWIIA); and Joshua Harris Prager, *Back to Work: Loss of Health Benefits No Longer Threatens Disabled Job-Seekers*, Wall St. J., Oct. 22, 1999, at A1 ("In December 1996, several advocacy groups for the disabled convened in Washington, D.C., and Oakland, Calif., to push the idea of Medicaid buy-in programs.").

55. *See* § 202(a) (codified at 42 U.S.C. § 426(b)).

56. *See id.* § 112 (codified at 42 U.S.C. §§ 423(i), 1383(p)).

57. *See id.* § 111(a) (codified at 42 U.S.C. § 421(m)).

58. *See* GAO, Major Management Challenges and Program Risks: Social Security Admin. 10–11 (2003); GAO, Social Security Administration: Status of Achieving Key Outcomes and Addressing Major Management Challenges 19–20 (2001).

59. *See* GAO, Disability Programs Lag in Promoting Return to Work 19 (1997); Burkhauser & Daly, *supra* note 34, at 59, 77–85; Bonnie O'Day & Monroe Berkowitz, *Disability Benefit Programs: Can We Improve the Return-to-Work Record?*, in Handbook of Disability Studies 633, 636–38 (Gary L. Albrecht et al. eds., 2001).

60. *See* Theodore R. Marmor, The Politics of Medicare 153 (2d ed. 2000) ("[T]he structure of the benefits themselves, providing acute hospital care and intermittent physician treatment, was not tightly linked to the special circumstances of the elderly as a group. Left out were provisions that addressed the particular problems of the chroni-

cally sick elderly: medical conditions that would not dramatically improve and the need to maintain independent function rather than triumph over discrete illness and injury.").

61. *See* Bagenstos, *supra* note 32, at 64–66.

62. Section 201 is codified at 42 U.S.C. § 1396a(a)(10)(A)(ii)(XV). Disability rights activists have also been major supporters of the proposed Family Opportunity Act of 2003, S. 622, 108th Cong. (2003), which would authorize states to allow parents of children with disabilities to buy into the Medicaid program, *see* S. Rep. No. 108-157, at 5–7 (2003).

63. *See* Harriet McBryde Johnson & Lesly Bowers, *Civil Rights and Long-Term Care: Advocacy in the Wake of Olmstead v. L.C. ex rel. Zimring*, 10 Elder L.J. 453, 457–58 (2002) ("Passing MiCassa is now the single national goal for American Disabled for Attendant Programs Today (ADAPT), the grassroots organization that effectively applied direct action, including civil disobedience, in its successful, twenty-year fight for accessible public transportation."); ADAPT, A Community-Based Alternative to Nursing Homes and Institutions for People with Disabilities, http://www.adapt .org/casaintr.htm (describing ADAPT's support for MiCASSA); ADAPT, List of Supporters, http://www.adapt.org/casa/supporters.htm (last updated Jan. 13, 2004) (listing organizations that endorsed MiCASSA, including disability rights groups such as ADA Watch, the American Association of People with Disabilities, the Bazelon Center for Mental Health Law, the Disability Rights Center, the Disability Rights Education and Defense Fund, and Justice for All). In September 2003, ADAPT led a fourteen-day march from the Liberty Bell in Philadelphia to the Capitol in Washington, D.C., to draw attention to MiCASSA. At a congressional hearing in March 1998, both ADAPT leader Michael Auberger and Justin Dart, one of the key disability rights advocates in the effort to obtain passage of the ADA, offered strong testimony in support of MiCASSA. *See Community-Based Care for Americans with Disabilities: Hearing before the Subcomm. on Health and the Env't of the House Comm. on Commerce*, 105th Cong. 21–24, 78–87 (1998) [hereinafter Community-Based Care Hearing].

64. See, for example, the MiCASSA issue paper on the Web site of the American Health Care Association, probably the leading nursing home trade association; that paper "strongly calls upon Congress to oppose MiCASSA legislation." Am. Health Care Ass'n, Issue Brief: MiCASSA Legislation 2 (2004), available at http://www.ahca.org/ brief/ib_micassa.pdf.

65. *See, e.g.*, Community-Based Care Hearing, *supra* note 63, at 13 (statement of Rep. Brown); *id.* at 52–57 (statement of Polly Spare).

66. *See, e.g.*, Neil Gilbert, Transformation of the Welfare State: The Silent Surrender of Public Responsibility 135 (2002) ("Since the birth of the welfare state, policymakers have debated the defining principles that guide the allocation of social benefits. The classic line of this debate draws the distinction between universalism and selectivity.").

67. *See* Peter H. Schuck & Richard J. Zeckhauser, Targeting in Social Programs: Avoiding Bad Bets, Removing Bad Apples (2006).

68. The saying is variously credited to Richard Titmuss and to Wilbur Cohen, one of

the founding fathers of Social Security. For examples of commentators noting the political advantages to framing social welfare programs as universal social-insurance entitlements, see Michael J. Graetz & Jerry L. Mashaw, True Security: Rethinking American Social Insurance 288–89 (1999); Theda Skocpol, Social Policy in the United States: Future Possibilities in Historical Perspective 250–72 (1995); and William Julius Wilson, The Truly Disadvantaged: The Inner City, the Underclass, and Public Policy 118 (1987); *see also* Jacob S. Hacker, The Divided Welfare State: The Battle over Public and Private Social Benefits in the United States 40 (2002) (calling this claim "ubiquitous"). There also may be efficiency advantages to universalism, which can circumvent adverse selection and moral hazard problems. *See, e.g.,* Graetz & Mashaw, *supra*, at 38–39.

69. For contrary views, *see* Paul Pierson, Dismantling the Welfare State? Reagan, Thatcher, and the Politics of Retrenchment 103, 101–3, 128 (1994) (explaining that "the biggest programmatic losers in the 1980s were often universal programs" and "the biggest winners were in fact targeted ones"); and Christopher Howard, The Welfare State Nobody Knows, Debunking Myths about U.S. Social Policy 92–108 (2007). Although this is not the place for full engagement with the long-running targeting/universalism debate, I should note that I find Pierson's and Howard's arguments for the political durability of targeting unpersuasive as a critique of the Skocpol argument for "targeting within universalism." What Howard shows, in particular, is that targeted programs have thrived when, because of their low visibility or their political framing, they are not seen as programs for the poor. *See id.* at 103. But that, it seems to me, is fairly consistent with the overall thrust of Skocpol's argument. Moreover, I think Howard undersells the real administrative and political backlash against the Earned Income Tax Credit—which is one of his examples of a targeted program that has expanded over time. On that backlash, see Dorothy Brown, *Race and Class Matters in Tax Policy*, 107 Colum. L. Rev. 790 (2007).

70. *See, e.g.,* Graetz & Mashaw, *supra* note 68, at 285–86; Skocpol, *supra* note 68, at 263–66.

71. Professor Theda Skocpol explicitly draws the comparison between Social Security and welfare in Theda Skocpol, *The Limits of the New Deal System and the Roots of Contemporary Welfare Dilemmas, in* The Politics of Social Policy in the United States 293, 295–98 (Margaret Weir et al. eds., 1988). *See also* Skocpol, *supra* note 68, at 255–59. For good post-1996 treatments of the American politics of welfare, *see generally* R. Kent Weaver, Ending Welfare as We Know It (2000); Harold L. Wilensky, Rich Democracies: Political Economy, Public Policy, and Performance 323–24 (2002); and Hugh Heclo, *The Politics of Welfare Reform, in* The New World of Welfare 169 (Rebecca M. Blank & Ron Haskins eds., 2001).

72. *See, e.g.,* Jonathan Zasloff, *Children, Families, and Bureaucrats: A Prehistory of Welfare Reform*, 14 J.L. & Pol. 225, 308 n.259 (1998) (arguing that the means-tested SSI program has fared well politically, notwithstanding its targeted nature, because the program's beneficiaries—including, inter alia, people with disabilities—have "substantial political support among the general public").

73. This is a classic example of what Professor Martha Minow has labeled the "dilemma

of difference," in which "[t]he stigma of difference may be recreated both by ignoring and by focusing on it." Martha Minow, Making All the Difference: Inclusion, Exclusion, and American Law 20 (1990).

74. Irving Kenneth Zola, *Toward the Necessary Universalizing of a Disability Policy*, 67 Milbank Q. 401, 401 (1989).

75. Sara D. Watson, *An Alliance at Risk: The Disability Movement and Health Care Reform*, Am. Prospect, Winter 1993, at 60, 63, available at http://www.prospect.org/print/V4/12/watson-s.html.

76. *See* Bagenstos, *supra* note 32, at 74.

77. Watson, *supra* note 75, at 63.

78. *See, e.g.*, Gerben DeJong & Teg Wenker, *Attendant Care, in* Independent Living for Physically Disabled People 161–62 (Nancy M. Crewe & Irving Kenneth Zola eds., 1983); Mary Johnson, *The Choice That Nobody's Heard Of*, Ragged Edge, Jan./Feb. 1998, at 22, available at http://www.ragged-edge-mag.com/jan98/choice.htm.

79. *See, e.g.*, Edward D. Berkowitz, Disabled Policy: America's Programs for the Handicapped 201–4 (1987); Andrew I. Batavia et al., *Toward a National Personal Assistance Program: The Independent Living Model of Long-Term Care for Persons with Disabilities*, 16 J. Health Pol. Pol'y & L. 523, 529–30 (1991); Gerben DeJong, *Defining and Implementing the Independent Living Concept, in* Independent Living, *supra* note 78, at 14–20; *see also* Pamela J. Dautel & Lex Frieden, Consumer Choice and Control: Personal Attendant Services and Supports in America (1999) (urging change in Medicaid personal-assistance rules to recognize nonmedical nature of that assistance in recommendation number 5 of blue-ribbon panel on personal-attendant services).

80. For the version of the bill introduced in the 110th Congress, see S. 799, 110th Cong., 1st Sess. (2007).

81. Johnson & Bowers, *supra* note 63, at 458. Toby Olson, then the head of the Washington State Governor's Committee on Disability Issues and Employment, gave a powerful example of the restrictions Nurse Practice Acts place on the services unlicensed attendants can perform:

> Under Washington state's current nurse practice law, "it's illegal to use your own judgment and rent a pair of hands," as Olson put it.
> "If you can tell someone, 'pick up that blue pill—not that light blue one, but the long blue capsule—and put it in my mouth'—if you're competent to do that, but you can't put the pill in your mouth by yourself, then you're not allowed to have just anyone working for you do it." It has to be a nurse.

Mary Johnson, *In Thrall to the Medical Model*, Ragged Edge, Jan./Feb. 1999, at 12, available at http://www.ragged-edge-mag.com/0199/a199ft1.htm.

82. Johnson & Bowers, *supra* note 63, at 458.

83. *See, e.g.*, Valerie J. Bogart, *Consumer Directed Assistance Program Offers Greater Autonomy to Recipients of Home Care*, N.Y. St. Bar Ass'n J., Jan. 2003, at 8, 8–9 (describing amendments to New York's statute); Johnson & Bowers, *supra* note 63, at 458 n.25 (describing recent amendment to South Carolina's statute); *see generally* Johnson, *supra* note 81 (discussing efforts to reform Nurse Practice Acts).

84. See *Consumer Directed Services: Improving Medicaid Beneficiaries' Access to Quality Care: Hearing before the Subcomm. on Health of the House Comm. on Energy and Commerce*, 108th Cong. 1–30 (2003) (discussing experience under the cash-and-counseling demonstration); *"Consumer Direction" Goes Off in a Completely New Direction*, 27 Rep. on Disability Programs, Feb. 19, 2004, at 25, 25–26 (discussing plans for expansion of cash and counseling demonstration); Leslie Foster et al., *Improving the Quality of Medicaid Personal Assistance through Consumer Direction*, Health Aff., Mar. 26, 2003, at W3-162, W3-163 to W3-164, http://content.healthaffairs .org/cgi/reprint/hlthaff.w3.162v1.pdf (discussing results of cash-and-counseling demonstration in Arkansas); *see also* Kaiser Comm'n on Medicaid & the Uninsured, An Overview of the Independence Plus Initiative to Promote Consumer-Direction of Services in Medicaid (2003) (discussing the Bush administration's Independence Plus Initiative, which allows states to adopt a cash-and-counseling approach to, among other things, personal-assistance services through a Medicaid waiver).

85. See Sharon M. Keigher, *Austria's New Attendance Allowance: A Consumer-Choice Model of Care for the Frail and Disabled*, 27 Int'l J. Health Services 753, 755–57 (1997) (describing an Austrian program, established in 1992, that provides fixed cash payments to individuals with disabilities to enable them to purchase attendant services); Joshua M. Wiener et al., *Consumer-Directed Home Care in the Netherlands, England, and Germany* (Oct. 2003) (unpublished manuscript), available at http:// research.aarp.org/health/2003_12_ eu_cd.pdf (discussing voucher- and cash-grant programs in the Netherlands, England, and Germany).

86. See Bob Kafka, *Empowering Service Delivery*, Ragged Edge, Sept./Oct. 1998, at 28, available at http://www.ragged-edge-mag.com/0998/b998ft6.htm ("This traditional independent-living movement approach to how personal attendant services should be delivered may work for some individuals who have the desire and skills to run things on their own. But for the vast numbers of people who have disabilities, it's just not working.").

87. Kaiser Comm'n on Medicaid and the Uninsured, *Olmstead v. L.C.: The Interaction of the Americans with Disabilities Act and Medicaid* 5 (2004).

88. See Kafka, *supra* note 86.

INDEX

Abbott, Sidney, 35

abortion, 4, 95–99, 102–110, 112; counseling, 98–100, 103–104; informed consent, 107–109; partial-birth abortion, 109; and prenatal testing, 96–97, 99, 102–104, 111; restrictions on, 96–97, 104; selective abortion, 96, 103–104, 111–115; woman's choice, 96, 105–110

access/content distinction, 69–74, 218n53

accessibility, 6–7, 18–20, 68, 123–125

accommodation mandates. *See* reasonable accommodation

Acemoglu, Daron, 122

ADAPT. *See* American Disabled for Attendant Programs Today

affirmative action, 21, 28, 175n23, 178n58

age discrimination, 79

AIDS and HIV, 17–19, 35, 41, 42, 52, 71, 74, 76, 78, 80, 82–84, 192n44

Aid to Families with Dependent Children, 143

Albertson's, Inc. v. Kirkingburg, 35–36, 41, 85–86, 193n59

Alexander v. Choate, 73

Alstyne, William van, 21

American Coalition of Citizens with Disabilities, 99

American Council of the Blind, 31

American Disabled for Accessible Public Transportation. *See* American Disabled for Attendant Programs Today

American Disabled for Attendant Programs Today, 16–17, 219n63

Americans with Disabilities Act (1990): and antidiscrimination protection, 2, 5, 8–10, 38–39, 45, 55–56, 74, 128–130, 136–137, 148–149, 178n55; arguments for abandoning, 121–123; and community integration of disabled, 33, 116–117; compared to Disability Discrimination Act, 52–53; congressional support of, 4–5, 125; and damages remedy, 123, 127, 132–133; and direct threat doctrine, 79, 85–90; effect on employment rates, 2, 116–122; enactment of, 1; enforcement of, 123, 125–127, 132–135; public resistance to, 2; safe harbor provision, 71–72, 182n96; and serial litigation, 132; Title I, 70, 87; Title II, 64, 70–71; Title III, 71, 182n96, 210n46; as welfare/redistributive program, 38–40, 56, 64–65, 73–74, 143; as welfare to work program, 2, 5, 10, 26, 32–33, 39–40, 56, 69, 117–120, 122

Americans with Disabilities Act Amendments Act (2008), 2, 51

Americans with Disabilities Act Restoration Act (2007), 51, 53

Angrist, Joshua, 122

antiabortion movement, 95–97, 99–100, 102, 105, 108–109, 115

antidiscrimination, equivalency to accommodation, 56–57, 64–68, 72–75